1993

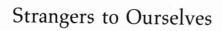

Strangers to Ourselves

Other works by Julia Kristeva
published by Columbia

STRANGERS
TO
OURSELVES

Julia Kristeva

TRANSLATED BY

Leon S. Roudiez

 Columbia University Press
New York

Columbia University Press wishes to express its appreciation of assistance given by the
government of France through Le Ministère de la Culture in the preparation of the
translation.

Columbia University Press
New York   Oxford
Étrangers à nous-mêmes copyright © Librairie Artheme Fayard
Copyright © 1991 Columbia University Press

Library of Congress Cataloging-in-Publication Data

Kristeva, Julia
   [Etrangers à nous-mêmes. English]
   Strangers to ourselves / Julis Kristeva ; translated by Leon
Roudiez.
      p.   cm. — (European perspectives)
   Translation of: Etrangers à nous-mêmes.
   Includes index.
   ISBN 0-231-07156-6
   1. Alienation (Social psychology) in literature.
2. Psychoanalysis and literature.   3. Assimilation (Sociology) in
literature.   4. Alientation (Social psychology)   5. Assimilation
(Sociology)   I. Title.   II. Series.
PN56.A45K7513   1991
809'.93353—dc20   90-22990
                                                        CIP

Casebound editions of Columbia University Press
books are Smyth-sewn and printed on permanent and durable acid-free paper

Printed in the United States of America

c 10 9 8 7 6 5 4 3 2

European Perspectives
A Series in Social Philosophy and Cultural Criticism

Lawrence D. Kritzman and
Richard Wolin, Editors

European Perspectives seeks to make available works
of interdisciplinary interest by leading European
thinkers. By presenting classic texts and outstanding
contemporary works, the series hopes to shape the
major intellectual controversies of our day and
thereby to facilitate the tasks of historical understanding.

Giles Deleuze, *Empiricism and Subjectivity*
Theodor W. Adorno, *Notes to Literature*, vol. 1

Contents

Contents

Hypocrite reader, my alias, my twin . . . —BAUDELAIRE

But one's own must be learned as well
as that which is foreign —HÖLDERLIN

In a strange land within my own country —ARAGON

1 Toccata and Fugue
for the Foreigner

Foreigner: a choked up rage deep down in my throat, a black angel clouding transparency, opaque, unfathomable spur. The image of hatred and of the other, a foreigner is neither the romantic victim of our clannish indolence nor the intruder responsible for all the ills of the polis. Neither the apocalypse on the move nor the instant adversary to be eliminated for the sake of appeasing the group. Strangely, the foreigner lives within us: he is the hidden face of our identity, the space that wrecks our abode, the time in which understanding and affinity founder. By recognizing him within ourselves, we are spared detesting him in himself. A symptom that precisely turns "we" into a problem, perhaps makes it impossible, The foreigner comes in when the consciousness of my difference arises, and he disappears when we all acknowledge ourselves as foreigners, unamenable to bonds and communities.

Can the "foreigner," who was the "enemy" in primitive societies, disappear from modern societies? Let us recall a few moments in Western history when foreigners were conceived, welcomed, or rejected, but when the possibility of a society without foreigners could also have been imagined on the horizon of a religion or an ethics. As a still and perhaps ever utopic matter, the question is again before us today as we confront an economic and political integration on the scale of the planet: shall we be, intimately and subjectively, able to live with the others, to live *as others*, without ostracism but also without leveling? The modification in the status of foreigners that is imperative today leads one to reflect on our ability to accept new modalities of otherness. No "Nationality Code" would be practicable without having that question slowly mature within each of us and for each of us.

While in the most savage human groups the foreigner was an enemy to be destroyed, he has become, within the scope of religious and ethical constructs, a different human being who, provided he espouses them, may be assimilated into the fraternities of the "wise," the "just," or the "native." In Stoicism, Judaism, Christianity, and even in the humanism of the Enlightenment, the patterns of such acceptance varied, but in spite of its limitations and shortcomings, it remained a genuine rampart against xenophobia. The violence of the problem set by the foreigner today is probably due to the crises undergone by religious and ethical constructs. This is especially so as the absorption of otherness proposed by our societies turns out to be inacceptable by the contemporary individual, jealous of his difference—one that is not only national and ethical but essentially subjective, unsurmountable. Stemming from the bourgeois revolution, nationalism has become a symptom—romantic at first, then totalitarian—of the nineteenth and twentieth centuries. Now, while it does go against universalist tendencies (be they religious or rationalist) and tends to isolate or even hunt down the foreigner, nationalism nevertheless ends up, on the other hand, with the particularistic, demanding individualism of contemporary man. But it is perhaps on the basis of that contemporary individualism's subversion, beginning with the moment when the citizen-individual ceases to consider himself as unitary and glorious but discovers his incoherences and abysses, in short his "strangenesses"—that the question arises again: no longer that of welcoming the foreigner within a system that obliterates him but of promoting the togetherness of those foreigners that we all recognize ourselves to be.

Let us not seek to solidify, to turn the otherness of the foreigner into a thing. Let us merely touch it, brush by it, without giving it a permanent structure. Simply sketching out its perpetual motion through some of its variegated aspects spread out before our eyes today, through some of its former, changing representations scattered throughout history. Let us also lighten that otherness by constantly coming back to it—but more and more swiftly. Let us escape its hatred, its burden, fleeing them not through leveling and forgetting, but through the *harmonious* repetition of the differences it implies and spreads. *Toccatas and Fugues:* Bach's compositions evoke to my ears the meaning of an acknowledged and harrowing otherness that I should like to be contemporary, *because* it has been brought up, relieved, disseminated, inscribed in an original play being developed, without goal, without boundary, without end. An otherness barely touched upon and that already moves away.

Scorched Happiness

Are there any happy foreigners?
The foreigner's face burns with happiness.

At first, one is struck by his peculiarity—those eyes, those lips, those cheek bones, that skin unlike others, all that distinguishes him and reminds one that there is *someone* there. The difference in that face reveals in paroxystic fashion what any face should reveal to a careful glance: the nonexistence of banality in human beings. Nevertheless, it is precisely the commonplace that constitutes a commonality for our daily habits. But this grasping the foreigner's features, one that captivates us, beckons and rejects at the same time. "I am at least as remarkable, and therefore I love him," the observer thinks; "now I prefer my own peculiarity, and therefore I kill him," he might conclude. From heart pangs to first jabs, the foreigner's face forces us to display the secret manner in which we face the world, stare into all our faces, even in the most familial, the most tightly knit communities.

Furthermore, the face that is so *other* bears the mark of a crossed threshold that irremediably imprints itself as peacefulness or anxiety. Whether perturbed or joyful, the foreigner's appearance signals that he is "in addition." The presence of such a border, internal to all that is displayed, awakens our most archaic senses through a burning sensation. Vivid concern or delight, set there in these other features, without forgetfulness, without ostentation, like a standing invitation to some inaccessible, irritating journey, whose code the foreigner does not have but whose mute, physical, visible memory he keeps. This does not mean the foreigner necessarily appears absent, absent-minded, or distraught. But the insistent presence of a lining—good or evil, pleasing or death-bearing—disrupts the never regular image of his face and imprints upon it the ambiguous mark of a scar—his very own well-being.

For, curiously, beyond unease, such a doubling imposes upon the other, the observer, the feeling that there is a special, somewhat insolent happiness in the foreigner. Happiness seems to prevail, *in spite of everything*, because something has definitely been exceeded: it is the happiness of tearing away, of racing, the space of a promised infinite. Such happiness is, however, constrained, apprehensively discreet, in spite of its piercing intrusion, since the foreigner keeps feeling threatened by his former territory, caught up in the memory of a happiness or a disaster —both always excessive.

Can one be a foreigner and happy? The foreigner calls forth a new idea of happiness. Between the fugue and the origin: a fragile limit, a temporary homeostasis. Posited, present, sometimes certain, that happiness knows nevertheless that it is passing by, like fire that shines only because it consumes. The strange happiness of the foreigner consists in maintaining that fleeing eternity or that perpetual transience.

The Loss and the Challenge

A secret wound, often unknown to himself, drives the foreigner to wandering. Poorly loved, however, he does not acknowledge it: with him, the challenge silences the complaint. It is a rare person who, like some Greeks (such as Aeschylus' *Suppliants*), the Jews (the faithful at the wall of lamentations), or psychoanalysts, leads the foreigner to avow a humbled entreaty. He is dauntless: "You have caused me no harm," he disclaims, fiercely, "It is I who chose to leave"; always further along, always inaccessible to all. As far back as his memory can reach, it is delightfully bruised: misunderstood by a loved and yet absent-minded, discreet, or worried mother, the exile is a stranger to his mother. He does not call her, he asks nothing of her. Arrogant, he proudly holds on to what he lacks, to absence, to some symbol or other. The foreigner would be the son of a father whose existence is subject to no doubt whatsoever, but whose presence does not detain him. Rejection on the one hand, inaccessibility on the other: if one has the strength not to give in, there remains a path to be discovered. Riveted to an elsewhere as certain as it is inaccessible, the foreigner is ready to flee. No obstacle stops him, and all suffering, all insults, all rejections are indifferent to him as he seeks that invisible and promised territory, that country that does not exist but that he bears in his dreams, and that must indeed be called a beyond.

The foreigner, thus, has lost his mother. Camus understood it well: his Stranger reveals himself at the time of his mother's death. One has not much noticed that this cold orphan, whose indifference can become criminal, is a fanatic of absence. He is a devotee of solitude, even in the midst of a crowd, because he is faithful to a shadow: bewitching secret, paternal ideal, inaccessible ambition. Meursault is dead unto himself but keyed up with an insipid intoxication that takes the place of passion. Likewise, his father, who started vomiting while watching an execution, understood that being sentenced to death is the only thing a man might truly consider worth bothering with.

Suffering, Ebullience, and Mask

The difficulties the foreigner will necessarily encounter—one mouth too many, incomprehensible speech, inappropriate behavior—wound him severely, but by flashes. They make him turn gray, imperceptibly, he becomes smooth and hard as a pebble, always ready to resume his infinite journey, farther, elsewhere. The (professional, intellectual, affective) aim that some set for themselves in such an unrestrained fugue is already a betrayal of strangeness, for as he chooses a program he allows himself a respite or a residence. On the contrary, according to the utmost logic of exile, all aims should waste away and self-destruct in the wanderer's insane stride toward an elsewhere that is always pushed back, unfulfilled, out of reach. The pleasure of suffering is a necessary lot in such a demented whirl, and amateur *proxeni* know it unconsciously as they choose foreign partners on whom to inflict the torture of their own contempt, their condescension, or, more deceitfully, their heavy-handed charity.

The foreigner is hypersensitive beneath his armor as activist or tireless "immigrant worker." He bleeds body and soul, humiliated in a position where, even with the better couples, he or she assumes the part of a domestic, of the one who is a bother when he or she becomes ill, who embodies the enemy, the traitor, the victim. Masochistic pleasure accounts for his or her submissiveness only in part. The latter, in fact, strengthens the foreigner's mask—a second, impassive personality, an anesthetized skin he wraps himself in, providing a hiding place where he enjoys scorning his tyrant's hysterical weaknesses. Is this the dialectic of master and slave?

The animosity, or at least the annoyance aroused by the foreigner ("What are you doing here, Mac, this is not where you belong!"), hardly surprises him. He readily bears a kind of admiration for those who have welcomed him, for he rates them more often than not above himself, be it financially, politically, or socially. At the same time he is quite ready to consider them somewhat narrow-minded, blind. For his scornful hosts lack the *perspective* he himself has in order to see himself and to see them. The foreigner feels strengthened by the distance that detaches him from the others as it does from himself and gives him the lofty sense not so much of holding the truth but of making it and himself relative while others fall victim to the ruts of monovalency. For they are perhaps owners of things, but the foreigner tends to think he is the only one to have a biography, that is, a life made up of ordeals—neither catastrophes nor adventures (although these might equally happen), but simply a life in which acts constitute events because they imply choice, surprises, breaks, adaptations, or cunning, but neither routine nor rest. In the eyes of the foreigner those who are not foreign have no life at all: barely do they exist, haughty or mediocre, but out of the running and thus almost already cadaverized.

Aloofness

Indifference is the foreigner's shield. Insensitive, aloof, he seems, deep down, beyond the reach of attacks and rejections that he nevertheless experiences with the vulnerability of a medusa. This is because his being kept apart corresponds to his remaining aloof, as he pulls back into the painless core of what is called a soul the humbleness that, when all is said and done, amounts to plain brutality. There, soured of mawkishness, but of sensitivity as well, he takes pride in holding a truth that is perhaps simply a certainty—the ability to reveal the crudest aspects of human relationships when seduction fades out and proprieties give way before the results of confrontations: a clash of bodies and tempers. For the foreigner, from the height of an autonomy that he is the only one to have chosen when the others prudently remain "between themselves," paradoxically confronts everyone with an asymbolia that rejects civility and returns to a violence laid bare. The brutes' encounter.

Not belonging to any place, any time, any love. A lost origin, the impossibility to take root, a rummaging memory, the present in abeyance. The space of the foreigner is a moving train, a plane

in flight, the very transition that precludes stopping. As to land-
marks, there are none. His time? The time of a resurrection that
remembers death and what happened before, but misses the glory
of being beyond: merely the feeling of a reprieve, of having
gotten away.

Confidence

There remains, however, the self-confidence of being, of being
able to settle within the self with a smooth, opaque certainty—
an oyster shut under the flooding tide or the expressionless joy
of warm stones. Between the two pathetic shores of courage and
humiliation, against which he is tossed by the clashes of others,
the foreigner persists, anchored in himself, strengthened by such
a secret working-out, his neutral wisdom, a pleasure that has
been numbed by an unattainable solitude.

Deep-seated narcissism? Blank psychosis beneath the swirl of
existential conflicts? In crossing a border (. . . or two) the foreigner has changed his discomforts into a base of resistance, a
citadel of life. Moreover, had he stayed home, he might perhaps
have become a dropout, an invalid, an outlaw . . . Without a
home, he disseminates on the contrary the actor's paradox: mul-
tiplying masks and "false selves" he is never completely true nor
completely false, as he is able to tune in to loves and aversions
the superficial antennae of a basaltic heart. A headstrong will, but
unaware of itself, unconscious, distraught. The breed of the tough
guys who know how to be weak.

This means that, settled within himself, the foreigner has no
self. Barely an empty confidence, valueless, which focuses his
possibilities of being constantly other, according to others' wishes
and to circumstances. I do what *they* want *me* to, but it is not
"me"—"me" is elsewhere, "me" belongs to no one, "me" does
not belong to "me," . . . does "me" exist?

Parceling

Nevertheless, such hardness in a state of weightlessness is an absolute that does not last. The traitor betrays himself. Whether a Maghrebian street sweeper riveted to his broom or an Asiatic princess writing her memoirs in a borrowed tongue, as soon as foreigners have an action or a passion, they take root. Temporarily, to be sure, but intensely. For the foreigner's aloofness is only the resistance with which he succeeds in fighting his matricidal anguish. His hardness appears as the metamorphosis of an archaic or potential parceling that runs the risk of bringing his thought and speech down to chaos. Thus does he value that aloofness, his hardness—let us leave it alone.

The flame that betrays his latent fanaticism shows only when he becomes attached—to a cause, to a job, to a person. What he finds there is more than a country; it is a fusion, in which there are not two beings, there is but a single one who is consumed, complete, annihilated.

Social standing or personal talent obviously stamps such a vocation with appreciable variations. Whatever their differences, however, all foreigners who have made a *choice* add to their passion for indifference a fervent extremism that reveals the origin of their exile. For it is on account of having *no one* at home against whom to vent their fury, their conflagration of love and hatred, and of finding the strength not to give in to it, that they wander about the world, neutral but solaced for having developed an interior distance from the fire and ice that had seared them in the past.

A Melancholia

Hard-hearted indifference is perhaps no more than the respectable aspect of nostalgia. We all know the foreigner who survives with a tearful face turned toward the lost homeland. Melancholy lover of a vanished space, he cannot, in fact, get over his having abandoned a period of time. The lost paradise is a mirage of the past that he will never be able to recover. He knows it with a distressed knowledge that turns his rage involving others (for there is always an other, miserable cause of my exile) against himself: "How could I have abandoned them?—I have abandoned myself." And even he who, seemingly, flees the slimy poison of depression, does not hold back, as he lies in bed, during those glaucus moments between waking and sleeping. For in the intervening period of nostalgia, saturated with fragrances and sounds to which he no longer belongs and which, because of that, wound him less than those of the here and now, the foreigner is a dreamer making love with absence, one exquisitely depressed. Happy?

Ironists and Believers

Yet, he is never simply torn between here and elsewhere, now and before. Those who believe they are crucified in such a fashion forget that nothing ties them there anymore, and, so far, nothing binds them here. Always elsewhere, the foreigner belongs nowhere. But let there be no mistake about it: there are, in the way one lives this attachment to a lost space, two kinds of foreigners, and this separates uprooted people of all countries, occupations, social standing, sexes . . . into two irreconcilable categories. On the one hand, there are those who waste away in an agonizing struggle between what no longer is and what will never be—the followers of neutrality, the advocates of emptiness; they are not necessarily defeatists, they often become the best of ironists. On the other hand, there are those who transcend: living neither before nor now but beyond, they are bent with a passion that, although tenacious, will remain forever unsatisfied. It is a passion for another land, always a promised one, that of an occupation, a love, a child, a glory. They are believers, and they sometimes ripen into skeptics.

Meeting

Meeting balances wandering. A crossroad of two othernesses, it welcomes the foreigner without tying him down, opening the host to his visitor without committing him. A mutual recognition, the meeting owes its success to its temporary nature, and it would be torn by conflicts if it were to be extended. The foreign believer is incorrigibly curious, eager for meetings: he is nourished by them, makes his way through them, forever unsatisfied, forever the party-goer, too. Always going toward others, always going farther. Invited, he is able to invite himself, and his life is a succession of desired parties, but short-lived, the brilliance of which he learns to tarnish immediately, for he knows that they are of no consequence. "They welcome me, but that does not matter . . . Next . . . It was only an expenditure that guarantees a clear conscience . . ." A clear conscience for the host as well as the foreigner. The cynic is even more suited for a meeting: he does not even seek it, he expects nothing from it, but he slips in nevertheless, convinced that even though everything melts away, it is better to be with "it." He does not long for meetings, they draw him in. He experiences them as in a fit of dizziness when, distraught, he no longer knows whom he has seen nor who he is.

The meeting often begins with a food fest: bread, salt, and wine. A meal, a nutritive communion. The one confesses he is a famished baby, the other welcomes the greedy child; for an instant, they merge within the hospitality ritual. But this table corner, where they gulp with such pleasure, is covered with the paths of memory: one remembers, makes plans, recites, sings. The nourishing and initially somewhat animal banquet rises to the vaporous levels of dreams and ideas: the hospitality merrymakers also become united for a while through the spirit. A miracle of flesh and thought, the banquet of hospitality is the foreigners' utopia—the cosmopolitanism of a moment, the brotherhood of guests who soothe and forget their differences, the banquet is outside of time. It imagines itself eternal in the intoxication of those who are nevertheless aware of its temporary frailty.

Sole Liberty

Free of ties with his own people, the foreigner feels "completely free." Nevertheless, the consummate name of such a freedom is solitude. Useless or limitless, it amounts to boredom or supreme availability. Deprived of others, free solitude, like the astronauts' weightless state, dilapidates muscles, bones, and blood. Available, freed of everything, the foreigner has nothing, he is nothing. But he is ready for the absolute, if an absolute could choose him. "Solitude" is perhaps the only word that has no meaning. Without other, without guidepost, it cannot bear the difference that, alone, discriminates and makes sense. No one better than the foreigner knows the passion for solitude. He believes he has chosen it for its enjoyment, or been subjected to it to suffer on account of it, and there he is languishing in a passion for indifference that, although occasionally intoxicating, is irreparably without an accomplice. The paradox is that the foreigner wishes to be alone but with partners, and yet none is willing to join him in the torrid space of his uniqueness. The only possible companions would be the members of an affiliation whose uniformity and readiness discourage him, whereas, on the contrary, the lack of accordance on the part of distinguished persons helplessly sends him back to his own distress. Accordance is the foreigner's mirage. More grueling when lacking, it is his only connection—utopic or abortive as it may be. If it appears under the self-satisfying guise of charity or any other right-thinking humanism, he accepts it of course, but in a hard-hearted, unbelieving, indifferent manner. The foreigner longs for affiliation, the better to experience, through a refusal, its untouchability.

A Hatred

"Experiencing hatred": that is the way the foreigner often expresses his life, but the double meaning of the phrase escapes him. Constantly feeling the hatred of others, knowing no other environment than that hatred. Like a woman who, accommodating and conniving, abides by her husband's rebuff as soon as she makes the merest suggestion of a word, gesture, or intention. Like a child that hides, fearful and guilty, convinced beforehand that it deserves its parents' anger. In the world of dodges and shams that make up his pseudo-relationships with pseudo-others, hatred provides the foreigner with consistency. Against that wall, painful but certain, and in that sense familiar, he knocks himself in order to assert, to others and to himself, that he is here. Hatred makes him real, authentic so to speak, solid, or simply existing. Even more so, it causes to resound on the *outside* that other hatred, secret and shameful, apologetic to the point of abating, that the foreigner bears *within himself* against everyone, against no one, and which, in the case of flooding, would cause a serious depression. But there, on the border between himself and others, hatred does not threaten him. He lies in wait, reassured each time to discover that it never misses an appointment, bruised on account of always missing love, but almost pleased with the persistence—real or imaginary?—of detestation.

Living with the other, with the foreigner, confronts us with the possibility or not of *being an other*. It is not simply—humanistically—a matter of our being able to accept the other, but of *being in his place*, and this means to imagine and make oneself other for oneself. Rimbaud's *Je est un autre* ["I is an other"] was not only the acknowledgment of the psychotic ghost that haunts poetry. The word foreshadowed the exile, the possibility or necessity to be foreign and to live in a foreign country, thus heralding the art of living of a modern era, the cosmopolitanism of those who have been flayed. Being alienated from myself, as painful as that may be, provides me with that exquisite distance within which perverse pleasure begins, as well as the possibility of my imagining and thinking, the impetus of my culture. Split identity, kaleidoscope of identities: can we be a saga for ourselves without being considered mad or fake? Without dying of the foreigner's hatred or of hatred for the foreigner?

Detestation tells you that you are an intruder, that you are irritating, and that this will be shown to you frankly and without caution. No one in this country can either defend or avenge you. You do not count for anyone, you should be grateful for being tolerated among us. Civilized people need not be gentle with foreigners. "That's it, and if you don't like it why don't you go back where you came from!" The humiliation that disparages the foreigner endows his master with who knows what petty grandeur. I wonder if Wanda's husband would have dared to act as brazenly like a Don Juan, to discover libertine bents in himself, to flaunt the girlfriends she, alas, did not have the sense of humor to appreciate—if his wife had not come from Poland, that is from nowhere, without the family or friends that constitute, in spite of what people say, a shelter against narcissism and a rampart against paranoid persecutions. I wonder if his in-laws would have so brutally taken his child away from Kwang, at the time of his separation from Jacqueline, if he did not have such an incomprehensible way of pronouncing words and forgetting verbs, what was called an obsequious way of conducting himself and which was just his own way of being polite, and that inability to strike up a friendship with colleagues at a bar, on the occasion of a fishing trip . . . But perhaps Wanda and Kwang are suffering from something more than being foreign, and Marie or Paul might have the same problems if they were a bit different, a bit special, if they did not play the game, if they were like foreigners from within. Or should one recognize that one becomes a foreigner in another country because one is already a foreigner from within?

The Silence of Polyglots

Not speaking one's mother tongue. Living with resonances and reasoning that are cut off from the body's nocturnal memory, from the bittersweet slumber of childhood. Bearing within oneself like a secret vault, or like a handicapped child—cherished and useless—that language of the past that withers without ever leaving you. You improve your ability with another instrument, as one expresses oneself with algebra or the violin. You can become a virtuoso with this new device that moreover gives you a new body, just as artificial and sublimated—some say sublime. You have a feeling that the new language is a resurrection: new skin, new sex. But the illusion bursts when you hear, upon listening to a recording, for instance, that the melody of your voice comes back to you as a peculiar sound, out of nowhere, closer to the old spluttering than to today's code. Your awkwardness has its charm, they say, it is even erotic, according to womanizers, not to be outdone. No one points out your mistakes, so as not to hurt your feelings, and then there are so many, and after all they don't give a damn. One nevertheless lets you know that it is irritating just the same. Occasionally, raising the eyebrows or saying "I beg your pardon?" in quick succession lead you to understand that you will "never be a part of it", that it "is not worth it," that there, at least, one is "not taken in." Being fooled is not what happens to you either. At the most, you are willing to go along, ready for all apprenticeships, at all ages, in order to reach—within that speech of others, imagined as being perfectly assimilated, *some day*—who knows what ideal, beyond the implicit acknowledgment of a disappointment caused by the origin that did not keep its promise.

Thus, between two languages, your realm is silence. By dint of saying things in various ways, one just as trite as the other, just as approximate, one ends up no longer saying them. An internationally known scholar was ironical about his famous polyglotism, saying that he spoke Russian in fifteen languages. As for me I had the feeling that he rejected speech and his slack silence led him, at times, to sing and give rhythm to chanted poems, just in order to say something.

When Hölderlin became absorbed by Greek (before going back to the sources of German), he dramatically expressed the anesthesia of the person that is snatched up by a foreign language: "A sign, such are we, and of no meaning / Dead to all suffering, and we have almost / Lost our language in a foreign land" (*Mnemosyne*).

Stuck within that polymorphic mutism, the foreigner can, instead of saying, attempt doing—house-cleaning, playing tennis, soccer, sailing, sewing, horseback riding, jogging, getting pregnant, what have you. It remains an expenditure, it expends, and it propagates silence even more. Who listens to you? At the most, you are being tolerated. Anyway, do you really want to speak?

Why then did you cut off the maternal source of words? What did you dream up concerning those new people you spoke to in an artificial language, a prosthesis? From your standpoint, were they idealized or scorned? Come, now! Silence has not only been forced upon you, it is within you: a refusal to speak, a fitful sleep riven to an anguish that wants to remain mute, the private property of your proud and mortified discretion, that silence is a harsh light. Nothing to say, nothingness, no one on the horizon. An impervious fullness: cold diamond, secret treasury, carefully protected, out of reach. Saying nothing, nothing needs to be said, nothing can be said. At first, it was a cold war with those of the new idiom, desired and rejecting; then the new language covered you as might a slow tide, a neap tide. It is not the silence of anger that jostles words at the edge of the idea and the mouth; rather, it is the silence that empties the mind and fills the brain with despondency, like the gaze of sorrowful women coiled up in some nonexistant eternity.

"The Former Separations From the Body" (Mallarmé, "Cantique de Saint Jean")

To disagree. Constantly, about nothing, with no one. Coping with that with astonishment and curiosity, like an explorer, an ethnologist. Becoming weary of it and walled up in one's tarnished, neutralized disagreement, through lack of having the right to state it. No longer knowing what one truly thinks, except that "this is not it": that the words, the smiles, the manias, the judgments, the tastes of the native are excessive, faltering, or simply unjust and false, and he cannot imagine—proud as he is of being on his own ground—that one might speak, think, or act differently. In that case, why not tell him so, "argue"? But what right do we have? Perhaps we should ourselves assume that right, challenging the natives' assurance?

No. Those who have never lost the slightest root seem to you unable to understand any word liable to temper their point of view. So, when one is oneself uprooted, what is the point of talking to those who think they have their own feet on their own soil? The ear is receptive to conflicts only if the body looses its footing. A certain imbalance is necessary, a swaying over some abyss, for a conflict to be heard. Yet when the foreigner—the speech-denying strategist—does not utter his conflict, he in turn takes root in his own world of a rejected person whom no one is supposed to hear. The rooted one who is deaf to the conflict and the wanderer walled in by his conflict thus stand firmly, facing each other. It is a seemingly peaceful coexistence that hides the abyss: an abysmal world, the end of the world.

Immigrants, Hence Workers

The foreigner is the one who works. While natives of the civilized world, of developed countries, think that work is vulgar and display the aristocratic manners of offhandedness and whim (when they can . . .), you will recognize the foreigner in that he *still* considers work as a value. A vital necessity, to be sure, his sole means of survival, on which he does not necessarily place a halo of glory but simply claims as a primary right, the zero degree of dignity. Even though some, once their minimal needs are satisfied, also experience an acute pleasure in asserting themselves in and through work: as if *it* were the chosen soil, the only source of possible success, and above all the personal, steadfast, nontransferable quality, but fit to be moved beyond borders and properties. That the foreigner is a worker would seem like a cheap paradox, inferred from the quite controversial existence of "immigrant workers." I have nevertheless come across, in a French village, ambitious farmers who had come from a different region, more hard-working than others and wanting to "make a niche" for themselves by the sweat of their brows, hated as much for being intruders as for being relentless, and who (the worst of insults during demonstrations) heard themselves called Portuguese and Spaniards. Indeed, as they confided, the others (in this case they meant the Frenchmen who were sure of themselves) are never as persistent in their work; you really have to be without anything and thus, basically, to come from somewhere else, to be attached to it to that extent. Now, were they doing the unpleasant work in that village? No, they were simply always doing something, those "foreigners" who had come from another province.

With the second generation, it is true, it happens that these demons for work slacken. As a defiance of industrious parents, or an inevitably excessive aping of native behavior, the children of foreigners are often and from the very start within the code of *dolce vita*, slovenliness, and even delinquency. Many "reasons" are given for that, of course.

But as far as the immigrant is concerned, he has not come here just to waste his time away. Possessed with driving ambition, a pusher, or merely crafty, he takes on all jobs and tries to be tops in those that are scarcest. In those that nobody wants but also in those that nobody has thought of. Man or woman for odd jobs, but also a pioneer in the most up-to-date disciplines, off-the-cuff specialist in unusual or leading occupations, the foreigner devotes himself and exerts himself. If it be true that, in the process, like everyone else he aims at profits and savings for later and for his family, his planning supposes (in order to achieve that aim, and more than with others) an extravagant expenditure of energy and means. Since he has nothing, since he is nothing, he can sacrifice everything. And sacrifice begins with work: the only property that can be exported duty free, a universally tried and tested stock for the wanderer's use. What bitterness then, what disaster it is when one does not obtain one's green card.

Slaves and Masters

Dialectics of master and slave? The amount of strength changes the very balance of power. The weight of foreigners is measured not only in terms of greater numbers—from that standpoint did not slaves always constitute an overwhelming majority?—but is also determined by the consciousness of being somewhat foreign as well. On the one hand, because everyone is, in a world that is more open than ever, liable to become a foreigner for a while as tourist or employee of a multinational concern. On the other hand, because the once solid barrier between "master" and "slave" has today been abolished, if not in people's unconscious at least in our ideologies and aspirations. Every native feels himself to be more or less a "foreigner" in his "own and proper" place, and that metaphorical value of the word "foreigner" first leads the citizen to a feeling of discomfort as to his sexual, national, political, professional identity. Next it impels him to identify—sporadically, to be sure, but nonetheless intensely— with the other. Within this motion guilt obviously has its part but it also fades away to the advantage of a kind of underhanded glory of being a little like those other "gooks" [*métèques*], concerning which we now know that, disadvantaged as they may be, they are running before the wind. A wind that jostles and ruffles but bears us toward our own unknown and who knows what future. There is thus set up between the new "masters" and the new "slaves" a secret collusion, which does not necessarily entail practical consequences in politics or the courts (even if they, too, feel its effects progressively, slowly) but, especially with the native, arouses a feeling of suspicion: am I really at home? am I myself? are *they* not masters of the "future"?

Such a habit for suspicion prompts some to reflect, rarely causes humbleness, and even more rarely generosity. But it also provokes regressive and protectionist rage in others: must we not stick together, remain among ourselves, expel the intruder, or at least, keep him in "his" place? The "master" then changes into a slave hounding his conqueror. For the foreigner perceived as an invader reveals a buried passion within those who are entrenched: the passion to kill the *other*, who had first been feared or despised, then promoted from the ranks of dregs to the status of powerful persecutor against whom a "we" solidifies in order to take revenge.

Void or Baroque Speech

To be of no account to others. No one listens to you, you never have the floor, or else, when you have the courage to seize it, your speech is quickly erased by the more garrulous and fully relaxed talk of the community. Your speech has no past and will have no power over the future of the group: why should one listen to it? You do not have enough status—"no social standing" —to make your speech useful. It may be desirable, to be sure, surprising, too, bizarre or attractive, if you wish. But such lures are of little consequence when set against the *interest*—which is precisely lacking—of those you are speaking to. Interest is self-seeking, it wants to be able to use your words, counting on your influence, which, like any influence, is anchored in social connections. Now, to be precise, you have none. Your speech, fascinating as it might be on account of its very strangeness, will be of no consequence, will have no effect, will cause no improvement in the image or reputation of those you are conversing with. One will listen to you only in absent-minded, amused fashion, and one will forget you in order to go on with serious matters. The foreigner's speech can bank only on its bare rhetorical strength, and the inherent desires he or she has invested in it. But it is deprived of any support in outside reality, since the foreigner is precisely kept out of it. Under such conditions, if it does not founder into silence, it becomes absolute in its formalism, excessive in its sophistication—rhetoric is dominant, the foreigner is a baroque person. Baltasar Graciàn and James Joyce had to be foreigners.

Orphans

To be deprived of parents—is that where freedom starts? Certainly foreigners become intoxicated with that independence, and undoubtedly their very exile is at first no more than a challenge to parental overbearance. Those who have not experienced the near-hallucinatory daring of imagining themselves without parents—free of debt and duties—cannot understand the foreigners' folly, what it provides in the way of pleasure ("I am my sole master"), what it comprises in the way of angry homicide ("Neither father nor mother, neither God nor master . . .").

Eventually, though, the time of orphanhood comes about. Like any bitter consciousness, this one has its source in others. When others convey to you that you are of no account because your parents are of no account, that, as they are invisible, they do not exist, you are suddenly aware thet you are an orphan, and, sometimes, accountable for being so. A strange light then shines on that obscurity that was in you, both joyful and guilty, the darkness of the original dependency, and transforms it into a solidarity with close relatives of earlier days, henceforth forfeited. How could it possibly not have been understood that you were always with them, dependent on a past that only parents know, on the precious, exquisite pain that you will share with no one else? How is it that they, the others, do not know that your

parents are still at your side, unseen witnesses to your problems
with the natives? Well, no! They do not, they do not want to
know it. They thus reveal your own rejection far from those you
have abandoned without really doing so—"I know, but just the
same . . .". They thus also reveal your own underhanded perversion. You then experience as murderous those natives who
never speak of your close relatives—sure, they were close in the
past and elsewhere, unmentionable, buried in another language.
Or else they allude to them in such absent-minded way, with
such offhanded scorn that you end up wondering if those parents
truly exist, and in what ghostly world of an underground hell.
The pain you feel facing those empty eyes that have never seen
them. Loss of self in the presence of those distant mouths that do
not weigh the artifice of the speech that evokes *them.*

But, by the way, who is the murderer? The one who does not
know my relatives, or myself, as I erect my new life like a fragile
mausoleum where their shadowy figure is integrated, like a corpse,
at the source of my wandering? The indifference of others with
respect to my kin makes them at once mine again. The community of my own—translucent, slackened by thousands of kilo-
meters and a near-permanent daytime forgetfulness—is thus
created by the scornful absent-mindedness of others. In the face
of that injustice of which I am both source and victim, a "we"
emerges. Certainly not, I do not idealize them! I do not use the
indifference of others in order to enhance their merit. I know
only too well their insignificancy, and my own . . . And yet
there is a fondness that binds to the grave what is beyond the
grave, the survivor that I am to my forebears. I hear the sound
of bells, a fragrance of warm milk fills my throat: they, the
parents from abroad, are those who come to life again in my
senses, under the blind stare of scornful paternalism.

And nevertheless, no, I have nothing to say to them, to my
parents. Nothing. Nothing and everything, as always. If I tried
—out of boldness, through luck, or in distress—to share with
them some of the violence that causes me to be so totally on my

own, they would not know where I am, who I am, what it is, in others, that rubs me the wrong way. I am henceforth foreign to them. They are my children who do not follow me, sometimes admiring, sometimes fearful, but already bruised, reconciled to being alone in their turn, and doomed not to understand. I must come to terms with it and, with that unassuaged sense of hunger in the body, after having spoken to them, must accept the idea that our "we" is a stirring mirage to be maintained at the heart of disarray, although illusive and lacking real strength. Unless it be precisely the strength of illusion that, perhaps, all communities depend on, and of which the foreigner constantly experiences the necessary, aberrant unreality.

Do You Have Any Friends?

The foreigner's friends, aside from bleeding hearts who feel obliged to do good, could only be those who feel foreign to themselves. Other than that, there are of course paternalists, paranoid and perverse people, who each have the foreigner of their choice, to the extent that they would invent him if he did not exist.

Paternalists: how they understand us, how they commiserate, how they appreciate our talents, provided they can show that they have "more"—more pain, more knowledge, more power, including that of helping us to survive . . .

Paranoid persons: no one is more excluded than they are and, in order to demonstrate that fact, they choose as backdrop to their delirium a basic outcast, the ordinary foreigner, who will be the chosen confidant of the persecutions they themselves suffer even more than he does—until they "discover" in this foreigner in the proper sense of the term a usurper and one of the causes of their misfortune, for if the world does not understand them it is precisely because "foreigners now monopolize public opinion's concern" . . .

Perverse people: their jouissance is secret and shameful and, hidden in their shell, they would gladly put up a foreigner within it, who presumably would be happy thus to have a home, even though it might be at the cost of sexual or moral slavery, which is proffered lecherously, innocently . . .

In that case, all that would be left for foreigners would be to join together? Foreigners of the world, unite? Things are not so simple. For one must take into consideration the domination/exclusion fantasy characteristic of everyone: just because one is a foreigner does not mean one is without one's own foreigner, and the faith that abated at the source is suddenly rekindled at the journey's end in order to make up from whole cloth an identity the more exclusive as it had once been lost. In France, Italians call the Spaniards foreigners, the Spaniards take it out on the Portuguese, the Portuguese on the Arabs or the Jews, the Arabs on the blacks, and so forth and vice versa . . . And even if there are links between one another (are they not on the same side as opposed to the natives?), these unfailingly snap when fanatical bonds fuse together again communities cemented by pure, hard fantasies. Here, on foreign soil, the religion of the abandoned forebears is set up in its essential purity and one imagines that one preserves it better than do the parents who have stayed "back home." As enclave of the other within the other, otherness becomes crystallized as pure ostracism: the foreigner excludes before being excluded, even more than he is being excluded. Fundamentalists are more fundamental when they have lost all material ties, inventing for themselves a "we" that is purely symbolic; lacking a soil it becomes rooted in ritual until it reaches its essence, which is sacrifice.

The "Meursault Case" or, "We are all like Meursault"

How strange is Camus' Meursault (*The Stranger*, 1942), so anesthetized, lacking emotions, all passion having been eradicated, and not a scratch to show for it. One could easily take him for a borderline case, or a false self, in short for a quasi-psychotic, rather than for a prototype of the foreigner.

Meursault is indeed a "case," not at all a "typical Frenchman" among Arabs. Obviously, one might think that it is his mother's death that has torn him away from the community of people, as grief often does. And yet, Meursault seems to shoulder an endemic mourning. For how long indeed has he displayed this detachment affecting his bonds, presumably the closest, with his mother precisely, to whom he knows he has nothing to say? For a long time? Forever? His mourning is without melancholia, clear and sharp like the light in Oran, barren, hot, and inescapable. Passion at the highest point of a burn, perhaps, which, for the psyche, amounts to the low point of freezing: white, empty. As far as sex goes, yes: his embraces of Marie are intense and eager, the tang of their mouths in the sea arouses pleasure in the most distant, the most alert reader. A love? Or rather a feeling brought down to a sensation. A peculiar state, at any rate, in which sensation does not dare reflect upon itself. Fear or else lack of time, it is filtered through iridescent skin, overly keen glances, refined nostrils . . . And into words, brief ones, dense, accurate. They capture an experience that claims to enter into speech without passing through the psyche. Until the final bedazzlement: no maliciousness whatsoever, no anger against the Arabs, no trace of sticky fondness for their opponent, Raymond—the stranger has no soul—nothing more than a loss of consciousness, the effect of the heat and of depersonalization under the sweat, and the gun goes off.

One realizes then that Meursault has always lived as though he were in a state of lost consciousness, of transconsciousness as it were, and the dazzled vertigo, which, at the end, changes him into a murderer, was always there, more deceitful and more indistinct, but permanent. He therefore is not surprised by his blackout, it does not shock him—nothing does. He cannot explain what others experience as a shock. Shocks are only for the conscience. His is indifferent. Why? We shall never know.

Probably a disappointment, Camus implies: the young man early lost his faith in humanity, in everything. There is also his father whose only passion, experienced through vomiting, was to attend an execution that outraged him. Therefore, would murderous humanity deserve only indifference? The commonplace would be too clear, too heavy for the colorless light constituted by Meursault's soul. He has no principles, he has no innerness, he slides along and records sensations. Meursault is Bettelheim's "empty fortress" who has turned into . . . a writer. Who, actually, tells this story of a stranger? Camus? Meursault? Unless the two merge into one . . .

The father-confessor alone, who believes that everyone believes, is able to have the narrator fly off the handle. The man without values, the "stranger," would in short hold as his only value, a negative one, his rage against religion. *Ligare*, to bind. A rage against relationships and the servants of relationships. In that sense, he is a typical stranger [foreigner]: without bond and blasphemer of the paroxystic bond constituted by the sacred.

The strangeness of the European begins with his inner exile. Meursault is just as, if not more, distant from his conationals as he is from the Arabs. At whom does he shoot during the imporous hallucination that overcomes him? At shadows, whether French or Maghrebian, it matters little—they displace a condensed and mute anguish in front of him, and it grips him inside. The sexual passion of his friend Raymond, changed into a homosexual quarrel between hostile brothers, jealous of the same woman, serves as the trigger that will lead to the murderous act; this is what Meursault experiences as indifference toward others. The other, stifled within myself, causes me to be a stranger to others and indifferent to everything: Meursault's neutralism is the opposite of the uncanny [*inquiétante étrangeté*], its negative. While the feeling of the uncanny that I experience when facing the other kills me by inches, on the other hand the anesthetized indifference of the stranger explodes in the murder of an other. Indeed, before being staged on the beach, the murder was there already, silent and invisible, filling with an empty presence the stranger's senses and thoughts, sharpening them, endowing them with a shrill precision, at once cold in their bent and withered tenderness. Senses and thoughts that are like objects, or even weapons. He uses them, heedless and effective, without allowing images, hesitations, remorse, or worry to interfere. Object-words on the level with objects, harrowing only because they are too *clean:*

> *Today mother died, or perhaps it was yesterday. I don't know.*
> *I got a telegram from the home: "Mother passed away. Funeral*
> *tomorrow. Sincerely." It doesn't mean anything. Perhaps it was*
> *yesterday. [. . .] But after a little while I felt my mouth burning*
> *with the salt's bitterness. Marie then caught up with me and*
> *pressed her body against mine in the water. She put her mouth*
> *against mine. Her tongue cooled my lips and we rolled about in*
> *the waves for a moment. [. . .] She then wanted to know if I loved*
> *her. I answered as I had already done once that it didn't mean*
> *anything but I probably didn't love her. "Why marry me in that*
> *case?" she said. I explained that it didn't matter and, if she so*
> *wished, we could get married [. . .] But the heat was such that it*
> *was also painful to remain without moving under the blinding*
> *light that rained down from the sky. To stay here or to leave, it*
> *was the same thing. After a moment I went back toward the*
> *beach and I started to walk. [. . .] The Arab pulled out his knife,*
> *which he displayed for me in the sun. The light splashed against*
> *the steel and it was like a long flashing blade that struck me in*
> *the forehead. [. . .] That burning sword was consuming my eye-*
> *lids and scouring my aching eyes. That is when everything reeled.*
> *The sea heaved a thick, fiery blast. [. . .] The trigger gave way.*

Metallic in their accuracy, those words are not catching, they do not disturb. They dissociate, they dissolve the possible community of readers. They give us back—with respect to objects and states—that "separate" lucidity the community's function is to erase. Meursault's words bear witness to an interior distance: "I am never *at one* with men, nor with things," is what he seems to say. "No one is akin to me, each word is less the sign of a thing than that of my distrust for them. And if I speak, I do not speak to someone, I speak to *myself* about things, or even about people as things, being at the same time inside and outside, but for the most part outside. I do not really have an inside. I am the splitting, the tension put into words that defers all action: I do nothing, and if at times I happen to do something, it is as if I had done nothing, for it is outside myself, myself is outside myself. Speaking or doing, it makes no difference, until death inclusively."

Moreover, if the stranger's words describe actions or are themselves actions, it is because they are barely symbols: as they are insignificant, they can be done or spoken only for the purpose of precisely doing or saying nothing . . . They are neutral:

> Salamo's dog was as good as his wife. The small robot woman was as guilty as the Parisian woman Masson had married or Marie who wanted me to marry her. What did it matter if Raymond was my pal as much as Céleste who was his better? What did it matter if Marie offered her lips to a new Meursault?

Murder appears as the ultimate carrying out of that tension without decision, neither choice nor value, that words kept brushing against without managing to eject it. Putting to death instead of putting a mere nothing into words, an other walled in within myself like a mere nothing. Murder, like words, will then be indifferent and, more than words, insignificant.

As in psychotherapy, his anger at the father-confessor alone reveals to Meursault what he finally accepts as his psychic identity: "For the first time I opened up my being to the world's tender indifference. Experiencing it to be so much like myself, in short so brotherly, I felt that I had been happy, and that I still was." The priest has become a psychotherapist in spite of himself on account of the liberating anger he causes in the stranger. Other than that, Meursault remains outside conversation, outside communication, outside action, outside passion. Condemned, he hardly feels the sentence. Does he die? The reader assumes he does, but does not really believe it, so much the Stranger's indifference seems to place him out of death's reach. Because he has rediscovered hatred, however, Meursault begins to desire: he offers himself in imagination as object of the hateful howls of the spectators at his execution, and the sight of the others' hatred makes him happy, at last. Not without a grating irony: "so that I might feel less alone."

The oddness of this Stranger's condition, which attracted the interest of psychiatrists and esthetes more than that of politicians and lawyers, is nevertheless not foreign to ordinary foreigners. Meursault carries to an extreme the separateness of the uprooted person: his painless grief, his walled in violence against others, his agnosticism, sometimes soothed, sometimes bent on revenge. That strange Stranger further indicates that such strangers, because of the bruised and irreconcilable peculiarity that dwells in them, could not possibly start a new world. They do not constitute a "universe." Brownian motion of microscopic specks, acceleration chambers for atomic particles—one can vary the metaphors: the images must in all instances indicate a split-up group, a fragmentation bomb, the calm, icy distrust of the protagonists for one another creating the only link within this conglomerate of condemned people.

Dark Origins

"And what about your origins? Tell us about them, it must be fascinating!" Blundering fools never fail to ask the question. Their surface kindness hides the sticky clumsiness that so exasperates the foreigner. The foreigner, precisely—like a philosopher at work—does not give the same weight to "origins" as common sense does. He has fled from that origin—family, blood, soil—and, even though it keeps pestering, enriching, hindering, exciting him, or giving him pain, and often all of it at once, the foreigner is its courageous and melancholy betrayer. His origin certainly haunts him, for better and for worse, but it is indeed *elsewhere* that he has set his hopes, that his struggles take place, that his life holds together today. *Elsewhere* versus the origin, and even *nowhere* versus the roots: the motto for daredevils breeds sterile repressions as well as bold undertakings. How does one distinguish censorship from innovative performance? As long as his eyes remain riveted to the origin, the absconder is an orphan consumed by his love for a lost mother. Does he succeed in transferring the universal need for a shoring-up or support on an elsewhere that, henceforth, would no longer be experienced as hostile or domesticated but as the simple axis of a mobility, like the violin clef or the bass clef in a musical score? He is a foreigner: he is from nowhere, from everywhere, citizen of the world, cosmopolitan. Do not send him back to his origins. If you are dying to ask the question, go put it to your own mother . . .

Explosion: Sex or Disease

Eventually, the shattering of repression is what leads one to cross a border and find oneself in a foreign country. Tearing oneself away from family, language, and country in order to settle down elsewhere is a daring action accompanied by sexual frenzy: no more prohibition, everything is possible. It matters little whether the crossing of the border is followed by debauchery or, on the contrary, by fearful withdrawal. Exile always involves a shattering of the former body. Today, sexual permissiveness favors erotic experiences and, even with the fear of AIDS, foreigners continue to be those for whom sexual taboos are most easily disregarded, along with linguistic and familial shackles. The eighteenth-century cosmopolitan was a libertine— and today still the foreigner, although without the ostentation, affluence, or luxury of the Enlightenment, remains that insolent person who, secretly or openly, first challenges the morality of his own country and then causes scandalous excesses in the host country. Witness the erotic outburst of Spanish or Moslem women once they have settled in France: the "French model" might have something to do with it, but how easy it is for the Christian facade and even the tyranny of Islam to be swept away by these new perverts who are willing to stop at nothing, admittedly in order to succeed, but above all in order to joy in their bodies, unto death!

When such an economy of expenditure to the limit cannot be set up (intensive repression, parental prohibitions strongly internalized, and so forth) or else fails, the botched pleasure turns into disease. Nowhere does one find better somatization than among foreigners, so much can linguistic and passional expression find itself inhibited. The disease is all the more serious as sexual liberation was easy but has been suddenly interrupted (abandonment by the partner, separation, unfaithfulness, and so forth). The unbridled drive no longer encounters the check of prohibitions or earlier sublimations but fiercely attacks the body's cells. Eros crosses the threshold of Thanatos. I have known a foreign student, who was a virgin and a strait-laced person when she arrived in Paris, and then threw herself headlong into the "group sex" of the late sixties, impressing her lover with her daring. Now a few months later, after they had broken off, I met up with her again; she was in a welfare institution, suffering from lung disease. Repression hellishly well knows how to fool us! One thinks to have out-smarted it while it is moving around perfidiously, on a lower level, on the borders between soma and psyche, where the sluice gates of jouissance become snagged and unleashed eroticism is obliged to resort to new limits, those of organs, which then falter. The foreigner who imagines himself to be free of borders, by the same token challenges any sexual limit. Often, but not entirely. For a narcissistic wound—insult, betrayal—can disturb his economy of boundless expenditure, which he had thought for a moment to be unshakeable, and invert it into a destruction of psychic and corporeal identity.

But, to begin with, what an incongruous liberation of language! Lacking the reins of the maternal tongue, the foreigner who learns a new language is capable of the most unforeseen audacities when using it—intellectual daring and obscenities as well. Such and such a person who hardly dared to speak in public and made awkward remarks in his native language, discovers himself to be a dauntless speaker in the other one. Initiation into new abstract fields takes place with unprecedented ease; erotic words, on which familial prohibition weighed heavily, are no longer feared. Nevertheless, the foreign language remains an artificial one—like algebra or musical notations—and it requires the mastery of a genius or an artist to create within it something other than artificial redundancies. For often the loquacious and "liberated" foreigner (in spite of his accent and grammatical lapses that he does not hear) stocks a ghostly world with this second and secondary discourse. As in hallucination, his verbal constructs—learned or shocking—are centered in a void, dissociated from both body and passions, left hostage to the maternal tongue. In that sense, the foreigner does not know what he is saying. His unconscious does not dwell in his thought, consequently he is satisfied brilliantly to reproduce *everything* there is to learn, seldom *innovating*. His language does not bother him, because he keeps silent on his drives: the foreigner can utter all sorts of indecencies without being shaken by any repugnance or even excitement, since his unconscious shelters itself on the other side of the border. Analytic therapy or, more exceptionally, an intense solitary exploration through memory and body, might, however, bring forth the miracle of meditation that welds the original and the acquired into one of those mobile and innovative syntheses that great immigrant scholars or artists are capable of. For since he belongs to nothing the foreigner can feel as appertaining to everything, to the entire tradition, and that weightlessness in the infinity of cultures and legacies gives him the extravagant ease to innovate. De Kooning does not say anything else: "After all, I am a foreigner, I am different because I am interested in art in its totality. I have a greater feeling of belonging to a tradition" (1936).

An Ironic Wandering or the Polymorphous Memory of Sebastian Knight

If wandering feeds even the quest for remembrance, then remembrance is exiled from itself and the polymorphous memory
that is freed of it, far from being simply painful, takes on a
diaphanous irony. The most pleasant, the most refined category
of foreigners enjoys the privilege of experiencing its strangeness
as a . . . *Funny Mountain*—a title Nabokov gives to one of the
books of his character, the novelist Sebastian Knight.

The Real Life of Sebastian Knight (written in 1938) is probably
nothing else than its very scription. Consequently, no one could
turn it into a "biography"—not even his half brother—without
mutilating or betraying it by projecting oneself into the place of
the writer, as is expected from the fierce fondness of all interpret-
ers and readers. In his detective and metaphysical, tragical and
comic novel on the elusiveness of the writer, Vladimir Nabokov
goes further, and in a more savory fashion, than the "new nov-
elists," by revealing the essential polymorphism of writing itself.
If the Russian half brother of the great English writer Sebastian
Knight is not able (or willing?) to reconstitute his biography, it is
because the "detective" and the "hero" are (perhaps?) only two
facets of the same process: "Thus—I am Sebastian Knight. I feel
as if I were impersonating him on a lighted stage," is what the
half brother, a failed biographer, concludes at the end of the
book. For the polyphonic mastery of writing consists in ceaselessly doing and undoing a jigsaw puzzle piece by piece—not the
puzzle of a "world" considered by this or that metaphysical artist
to be inaccessible, as a result of one knows not what misdeed, but
that of an *essential enigma*. "And as the meaning of all things
shone through their shapes, many ideas and events which had
seemed of the utmost importance dwindled not to insignificance,
for nothing could be insignificant now, but to the same size which
other ideas and events, once denied any importance, now at-
tained." There is no "final solution" any more than a "final

word": "The asphodel on the other shore remains as obscure as ever," because the scription of the wandering Knight places forms side by side and balances them, and such virtuosity worthy of Cervantes is henceforth carried out with ironic detachment (Knight is the author of *The Prismatic Bezel*—an iridescent mirror?— and, to repeat, *The Funny Mountain*, before being that of *The Doubtful Asphodel*). Like a casual absolute, like an absolute off-handedness.

It is not my intention here to investigate Nabokov's esthetics, his debt toward Russian literature, which is polyphonic to begin with because it is conscious of coming "afterwards," or his modernity, which embodies in an already mediatizing imagination Flaubert's or Joyce's infinite formal concern. I merely wish to emphasize one of the strands of that implacable relativism: the cosmopolitanism, the shuttling back and forth of two idioms (Russian and English), set, in the case of Knight, at the heart of something indiscernible that unbalances a man and replaces him with a language mispronounced into style. One recalls the words the novel ascribes to an old critic on the occasion of Sebastian Knight's premature death: "Poor Knight! He really had two periods, the first—a dull man writing broken English, the second —a broken man writing dull English." Needless to say, the small amount of biography reconstituted by his brother does not at all confirm that sally, in which, nevertheless, many foreigners might recognize themselves.

A foreigner: there is no doubt that Sebastian is one, on account of that fragmented memory—is it his own or his brother's?— which does not succeed in reconstructing a continuous, compact past, for exile has shattered all sense of belonging. "Sebastian's image [. . .] comes to me in a few bright patches, as if he were not a constant member of our family, but some erratic visitor passing across a lighted room and then for a long interval fading into the night." He is nocturnal, this Knight who has eluded the family of observers and leaves others and himself with only tattered memories. A disseminated "oneself."

A foreigner who is nevertheless distanced from his strangeness, he carries it as with pincers and, without ignoring it, mellows it with a soft irony that shares in the coldness of the verb "to be ironical" only if one includes in it a sense of propriety: "No sentimental wanderer will ever be allowed to land on the rock of my unfriendly prose," the novelist writes, as quoted by his brother.

He is a foreigner who is anguished for being confined to his original abode. To his old Cambridge tutor who insists on speaking Russian with him Sebastian asserts that he was born in Sofia, and when the old man intrepidly starts speaking Bulgarian Knight invents a new idiom on the spur of the moment, claiming that this was indeed his "maternal" and "Bulgarian" tongue . . .

He is a foreigner who for a long time had difficulties with English and persisted in keeping his accent ("His 'r's, when beginning a word, rolled and rasped, he made queer mistakes, saying, for instance, 'I have seized a cold' or 'that fellow is sympathetic'—merely meaning that he was a nice chap. He misplaced the accent in such words as 'interesting' or 'laboratory' "), and he is above all a solitary being: "He was aware of his inability to fit into the picture—into any kind of picture. When at last he thoroughly understood this and grimly started to cultivate self-consciousness as if it had been some rare talent or passion, only then did Sebastian derive satisfaction from its rich and monstrous growth, ceasing to worry about his awkward uncongeniality . . ."

From that moment the writer reached a solitude that was accountable only to his borderless culture. Thus is the foreigners' temper achieved, which Knight imposes by disseminating Joyce's exiled smile through a more ordinary and less arid imagination, without the Irishman's austere consecration. Neither rebellious nor provocative, neither nostalgic nor gloomy, neither painful nor anaesthetized, the wandering Knight managed to display that "bright boyish mood" which, even later, "remained as a rainbow across the stormy gloom of his darkest tales." The "dreary tussle

with a foreign idiom," which the critic perhaps rightly imputes
to him, is what the biographer brother experiences and confesses.
In a final burst of masochism or nostalgia, Sebastian's alter ego,
that clear side of his night, even plans to translate into Russian
the writer's final masterpiece. The brother's psychology tends
toward romanticizing, and he is just a little bit Freudian. Does he
not dream, in premonitory fashion, the night before the writer's
death, of waiting for Sebastian in a large dim room, "and the
whole atmosphere of his arrival seemed so uncanny"!?

What about Sebastian? He does not stop wandering, and the
heart disease that gives a Gogolian touch to the latter part of his
life does not shelter him from boyish errors or roamings; they
are like rainbows, which his brother, just as Gogolian in his way,
reflects in the errors and blunders of his own investigation.

The height of that boyishness with its nevertheless gothic hues
is concentrated in what has to do with women. After living with
the soothing Clara, with whom the writer thought for a while he
had found a haven, Knight suffers from a real regression as he
falls for a Russian *femme fatale*. Who is she? There are divergent
and muddled trails. There is a fickle woman, who disappears on
the Mediterranean coast; a Frenchified Russian who conceals her
love affair or else shields a friend . . . The narrator is all confused
and so is the reader. Did the resurgence of the dead mother, with
which S. K. is overcome at the end of his life, actually take place?
Had he been in love? Or was it imagination? The letters written
in Russian that he asked to have burned after his death . . . was
this a machination? Why does he himself write his last letter to
his brother in Russian? The tragedy of nostalgia suddenly comes
close to being a most comical subterfuge. But who is laughing?
Certainly not the foreigner. The writer perhaps.

The lost woman—lost land, lost language—cannot be found.
Far from being solely tragical, this cruel condition lends itself,
toward the end of the book, to insolence directed at the writer
himself. After having forgotten the address of his dying brother,
as he hurries, anxiously, to his bedside, the biographer half-

brother is led to the wrong corpse and, instead of watching over S.K.'s body, he witnesses another's agony. Sebastian thus left no defined memory and, worse yet, his very body evades familial inquiries. Nevertheless, let us remember: when the young Sebastian was looking for the tomb of his own mother, an English woman who died in France, he believed he was meditating in her memory in the garden of her last residence, known as "Les Violettes," in Roquebrune, near Monte-Carlo. A few months later, in London, he learned that his mother died in a town also called Roquebrune, located some distance to the west. And the writer cast that irony of origin and death in his novel *Lost Property* as the premonitory inscription of his own undiscoverable death . . . Like a boomerang, deceit, which had truly speaking uprooted the maternal bond, pulling it up from all soil in order to shelter it only in scription's fleeting memory, affects in the end the image and the body of the writer himself. One will not honor S.K.'s memory, any more than he himself honored his mother's. No, no one blasphemes, neither the son nor the reader. It is simply that, when the mother is disseminated into remembrances and words, when the women that were loved are forgotten-deserted-invented, the very memory that guarantees our identity is shown to be an ongoing metamorphosis, a polymorphy. Let me suggest here, to those who are fond of syntheses, a possible link between Sebastian Knight and Lolita—might it not be the same polymorphism, mnemic on the one hand, sexual on the other?

In contrast to what happened to Camus' Stranger, the casual cosmopolitan Sebastian Knight lost his mother early, did not attend her funeral, links her tomb to no specific place. But, Russian through his father, he assumed her name, that of the English woman. He gave himself a new tongue in choosing English, which, although it was not his maternal language for he did not speak it as a child, was nevertheless that of his nearly unknown mother, the dead language of a dead mother to be brought back to life. He then attempted the return trip toward the language of his Russian childhood, that of the second mother. And he became lost in the kaleidoscope of his multiple identities and untenable memories, leaving of his accumulated exiles merely a track of words.

One who is happy being a cosmopolitan shelters a shattered origin in the night of his wandering. It irradiates his memories that are made up of ambivalences and divided values. That whirlwind translates into shrill laughter. It dries up at once the tears of exile and, exile following exile, without any stability, transmutes into games what for some is a misfortune and for others an untouchable void. Such a strangeness is undoubtedly an art of living for the happy few or for artists. And for others? I am thinking of the moment when we succeed in viewing ourselves as unessential, simple passers by, retaining of the past only the game . . . A strange way of being happy, or feeling imponderable, ethereal, so light in weight that it would take so little to make us fly away . . .

Enchantment for some other time? Or never?

Why France?

Nowhere is one *more* a foreigner than in France. Having neither the tolerance of Anglo-American Protestants, nor the absorbant ease of Latin Americans, nor the rejecting as well as assimilating curiosity of the Germans or Slavs, the French set a compact social texture and an unbeatable national pride against foreigners. Whatever the efforts—both considerable and effective—made by the state and by various organizations in order to welcome foreigners, the latter, in France more than elsewhere, run up against a barrier. What is involved is the very fabric of civilization, faithful to values that have been elaborated while sheltered from great invasions and intermixing of populations and reinforced by monarchistic absolutism, Gallican autonomy, and republican centralism. Even when they are legally and administratively accepted, they are not for all that received into families. Their awkward use of the French language discredits them utterly—consciously or not—in the eyes of the natives, who identify more than in other countries with their beloved, polished speech. His eating or dressing habits are at once seen as an unforgiveable breach of universal, that is French, good taste.

Such a state of affairs can give rise to two opposite attitudes on the part of the foreigner. Either he attempts at all costs to merge into that homogeneous texture that knows no other, to identify with it, to vanish into it, to become assimilated; the process is flattering, for the exile valorizes as much as—if not more than —the French themselves the blessings of the civilization where he seeks shelter. Or else he withdraws into his isolation, humiliated and offended, conscious of the handicap of never being able to become a Frenchman.

And yet, one is nowhere *better* as a foreigner than in France. Since you remain uncurably different and unacceptable, you are an object of fascination: one notices you, one talks about you, one hates you or admires you, or both at the same time. But you are not an ordinary, negligible presence, you are not a Mr. or Mrs. Nobody. You are a problem, a desire—positive or negative, never neutral. As a matter of fact, in all the countries of the world, foreigners give rise to economic or political difficulties that are settled administratively as often uncontrollable explosions follow one upon the other. But "SOS-Racisme" exists only in France, as well as an entire national thought configuration, more or less dispassionate, on the "Code of Nationality."

This does not mean that France is more racist, but in France the discussion being immediately ideological and inspired by passion, it reaches the principles of civilization and the borders of the individual psyche. "What is my relation to the other?" "What are the limits and the rights of a group?" "Why should not every man have the rights of a citizen?" In France, pragmatic matters immediately become ethical. The "completely political" aspires to become the "completely human" within that spirit of lay universalism that was necessarily to confront the Nation, which is universal because it is proud of having invented the "rights of man," with the *very legitimacy of the concept of "foreigner"*. The issue of foreigners comes up for a people when, having gone through the spirit of religion, it again encounters an ethical concern . . . in order not to die of cynicism or of stock market deals. The image of the foreigner comes in the place and stead of the death of God and, with those who are believers, the foreigner is there to bring him back to life.

Finally, when your otherness becomes a cultural exception— if, for instance, you are recognized as a great scientist or a great artist—the entire nation will appropriate your performance, will assimilate it along with its own better accomplishments, and give you recognition better than elsewhere. This will not happen without a twinkling of the eye directed at your oddity, so un-French, but it will all be carried off with great panache and splendor. Such is the case with Ionesco, Cioran, Beckett . . . And even the Spaniard Picasso, who, with Rodin, is the only artist privileged to have a monographic museum in Paris, while the very French Matisse is not. To each his foreigners . . .

2 The Greeks Among Barbarians, Suppliants, and Metics

How can one possibly be a foreigner?

We seldom think of asking such a question, we are so convinced of being naturally citizens, necessary products of the nation-state. Or else, when we allow the topic to cross our minds, we immediately find a niche among those entitled to a nationality and cast out into an unreasonable alienage those who belong to an elsewhere they have been unable to preserve, one that no longer belongs to them, who have expropriated themselves of their identity as citizens. Today the notion of *foreigner* is indeed endowed with a legal meaning: it refers to a person who is not a citizen of the country in which he resides [in the United States, an alien]. Indeed, such a framework is soothing, it allows one to settle by means of laws the prickly passions aroused by the intrusion of the *other* in the homogeneity of a family or a group. It also ignores, without in any way resolving them, the discontents of that singular condition that amounts to claiming a difference at the heart of a set that, by definition, comes into being by excluding the dissimilar. Whether a constraint or a choice, a psychological evolution or a political fate, this position as a *different being* might appear to be the goal of human autonomy (are we not speaking beings only if we distinguish ourselves from others in order to impart to them our personal meaning on the basis of such a perceived and assumed difference?), and thus as a major illustration of the most intrinsic, most essential part of civilization. Moreover, by explicitly, obviously, ostensibly occupying the place of the difference, the foreigner challenges both the identity of the group and his own—a challenge that few among us are apt to take up. A drastic challenge: "I am not like you." An intrusion: "Behave with me as you would among yourselves." A call for love: "Recognize me." In all that there is a mixture of humility and arrogance, suffering and domination, a feeling of having been wounded and being all-powerful. In short, a rage, an extreme state that Greek myths have related and Aeschylus transmitted, as he reaped the memories of an archaic period, in *The Suppliants*,[1] before philosophers and jurists rationalized them by proposing statutes for foreigners. Let us then for a moment forget the laws and examine the foreigners of ancient tragedy.

The First Foreigners: Foreign Women (From Io to the Danaïdes)

It is noteworthy that the first foreigners to emerge at the dawn of our civilization are foreign women—the Danaïdes. Those Egyptian natives, who nevertheless claimed a noble although dramatic Greek descent, arrived in Argos. Aeschylus found his inspiration in a primitive legend developed as an epic, *The Danaïd*, which probably dates back to the first half of the sixth century and brings together and organizes the scared narratives *(hiēroi logoi)* involving the Argos shrine. According to legend, the Danaïdes can be traced back to a prestigious ancestor—Iō, the priestess of Hēra in Argos. Beloved by Zeus, she was metamorphosed by his jealous wife, Hēra, into a heifer. This did not discourage Zeus who, changed into a bull, continued to love her. Hēra nevertheless went on with her vengeance by sending a gadfly that drove Iō into a state of frenzy. Iō wandered from Europe to Asia, finally reaching Egypt. That heifer maddened by a gadfly is quite a disturbing image: like an incestuous daughter punished by her mother's wrath, she saw no solution but to flee continuously, banished from her native home, condemned to wander as if, as the mother's rival, no land could be her own. Her illegitimate passion for Zeus is thus madness. A madness of which the gadfly properly represents animal and (why not?) sexual stimulation. A madness that leads a woman not on a journey back to the self, as with Ulysses (who, in spite of meanderings, came back to his homeland), but toward a land of exile, accursed from the start. It was, however, only outside maternal soil, in Egypt then, that Zeus, who was indeed at the erotic source of her journey, allowed himself to "touch" Iō on the forehead in order to soothe her, give her back a feminine appearance, and permit her to give birth to a son, Epaphus (the "touch" of Zeus).

Would Iō's roaming frenzy be the feminine version of Oedipus' drama? The incestuous man was able to solve the Sphinx's riddles even if he was unaware of his amorous passion for his mother and his murderous rage against his father. Oedipus wanted to know, even though it would cost him plenty, including his eyes. On the other hand the daughter in love with her father was from the very beginning in breach of maternal authority, which was held by Hēra the Argive, goddess of matrimonial rights. Such a conflict triggered her psychosis—the sting of the gadfly, the agent of maternal vengeance, kept driving her wild. And even if Zeus ended up freeing her of her frenzied metamorphosis— but on foreign soil—the mark of violence and anguish would be felt by her descendants.

The son, Epaphus, born of the touched heifer, was to be the ancestor of the Egyptian kings. But Hēra's curse was seemingly visited upon the subsequent generations. The great-grandsons of Epaphus, Danaüs and Aegyptus—who had, respectively, fifty daughters and fifty sons—took up arms against each other, for the sons of Aegyptus wanted to marry forcibly the daughters of Danaüs in order to gain royal rights over Libya. In an attempt to escape the brutality of Aegyptus' fifty sons the Danaïdes fled to

Argos, thus beginning their exile. In what we would today call an unconscious but also inverted memory of their ancestor Iō, the Danaïdes fled their native land; at the same time, however, they were fleeing sexual intercourse. Warlike, cruel virgins, they retained only a cold passion from Iō, which drew them in a different but symmetrical fashion, outside wedlock and outside the law. Unless one deciphers in their very virginity a remainder of the incestuous fate of Iō's stock. Is it not true that virgins,[2] in their father's pantheon, are the daughters that remain faithful and refuse to give him descendants, precisely to preserve the symbolic power of the sole father, to the exclusion of any other man?

Consequently the Danaïdes were foreigners for two reasons: they came from Egypt and were refractory to marriage. Remaining outside the community of the citizens of Argos, they also refused the basic community constituted by the family. That exclusionary process reached its climax when, according to one version of the legend, the Danaïdes murdered the sons of Aegyptus on their own initiative, or, according to another version, in obedience to their father's will. Only two of the fifty sisters did not share in the crime. Let us pause to examine the story of those two exceptional sisters; they open the question of the Danaïdes' ambivalence, murderous to be sure, but also seekers of water, primordial worship officiants (according to Hesiodus and Pausanias), founders of alliances.

An amazon like her sisters, Amymone, in hot pursuit of a doe, missed her target and aroused a half-horse demon, a satyr about to rape her. She was saved by Poseidon, god of deep waters, who spoke to her in soothing rather than desiring terms and proposed marriage: "Your fate is to be wed, and mine to be your husband." Amymone then became hydrophoran and presided over water liturgy as well as wedding rites, under Hēra's supervision. A rebellious Danaïde was thus changed into an accomplice of Hēra's, hence of the social contract based on marriage.

Likewise Hypermnestra refused to strangle her husband, Lynceus, and the wedding—between blood relations who ceased being enemies—gave rise to the royal dynasty from which Heracles, the most celebrated Dorian hero, was issued. Before the court that was to decide whether or not she was right in renouncing vengeance, Hypermnestra was helped by Aphrodite and Hermes who whispered seductive words to her. Found not guilty, she became the first priestess of Hēra.

We now turn to the forty-eight Danaïdes who strangled their husbands during their wedding night. This was the height of criminal outrageousness. Foreignness is carried to forbidden revolt, a hubris giving rise to abjection. Such outrageousness was punished (according to one variant of the legend) by having the Danaïdes and their father put to death, or in more temperate fashion (as Pindar suggests) by having these refractory women renounce their claim to exception—they must marry in their proper order the winners of a race, but without having those weddings give rise to a prestigious lineage. Those who claimed to be beyond the law must submit to the banality of common, uniform regulations. The Greek mind condemned foreignness only when the latter tended to defy the common mean. Amazons and murderous women were disposed of, while foreignness— dissociated from moral outrageousness after having been involved with it—was amenable to the rites and laws of the polis.

The fact remains nonetheless that the Danaïdes pose a problem that is more complex and archaic than that involving the rights of the foreigner. Their story points to an age-old time when an endogamous society became exogamous. Not marrying a blood relation was the first condition, which the Danaïdes, it is true, fulfill brutally by killing their cousins, in order to become wedded to someone foreign to the clan. Such violence against one's kin (brothers and cousins), laden with incestuous passions, must no doubt be undergone if the new alliance is to be founded—the marriage between persons "equal by rights," just as Hēra wished to be Zeus' equal *(isotĕlĕs)* as well as his concubine.[3] She remained, however, below the surface of the matrimonial institution, representing its secret aspect. Such is the dark passion between husband and wife who are, after all, strangers to each other, a passion displayed during initiatory rites related to Demētēr's cult and that of her sacred Thesmophoria, supposedly brought to Greece by the Danaïdes. There, women, separated from the polis at its very core, constituted a fearsome gynecocracy that was entitled to spill blood in addition to pouring water into the bottomless cistern they were condemned to fill. By assuming roles as contradictory as that, the Danaïdes appear precisely as the link between "the legal limits of Hēra's domain" and "Demeter's kingdom."[4] As if the legend of the Danaïdes, through the very ambivalence it ascribes to those foreigners, recognized the necessity for the violence of passion (or, on the social plane, the validity of extirpation, or wrenching away, of foreignness itself) as foundation for the basal family alliance.

Strangeness (or foreignness)—the political facet of violence— would underlie elementary civilization, be its necessary lining, perhaps even its font, which no household cistern—not even, to start with, that of the Danaïdes—could permanently harness. Even more so, the foreign aspect of the Danaïdes also raises the problem of antagonism between the sexes themselves in their extramarital alliance, in the amatory and sexual "relation." In short, what is the "relation" between the "population" or "race" of *men* and the "population" or "race" of *women?* The sexual difference, which has been in the course of time either erased or overemphasized in turn, is certainly not destined to be frozen into antagonism. The fact remains that in Greece the bride was thought of as a foreigner, a suppliant. Did that mean a Danaïde? The wedding ritual stipulated that the bride was to be treated neither as a prey nor as a slave but as a "suppliant, placed under protection of the hearth, and taken by the hand to her new abode."[5] A suppliant? What is that exactly?

Suppliants and Proxeni

Aeschylus' restraint, as he did not condemn the Danaïdes, for he clearly believed their outrageous actions to have been in large part a reaction to the brutality of their Egyptian cousins, indeed matches the historical chance that has left us with only that part of the tragedy dealing with the *political acceptance* of the Danaïdes by the Argives. With such a presentation, the foreigners' drama loses some of its passion and presents itself in such a way as to throw light on the ancient Greeks' political, legal, and religious notions concerning foreigners.

According to the text, foreigners were accepted if they were suppliants, if, as symbols of their land, they laid wreaths before the altar of the gods (*The Suppliants*, 506). Danaüs advises his daughters as follows: "Here it is best to act the suppliant, / This rock, this altar of assembled gods, / Stronger than ramparts, a shield impenetrable. / Now quickly prepare white suppliant wreaths, sign of Zeus sacred, held in the left hand; / Mournful, respectful, answer needfully / The strangers; tell distinctly of an exile / Unstained by murder. Let no boldness / Come from respectful eye and modest features. / Not talkative nor a laggard be in speech: / Either would offend them. Remember to yield: / You are an exile, a needy stranger, / And rashness never suits the weaker" (188–203).

The shelter of Zeus' temple, father of the sun, who is also the pure "Apollo, the god, who from heaven once fled" (214), along with ritual gestures and modest behavior will guarantee foreigners a proper welcome. Thus a religious space, before and perhaps in spite of political considerations, secured for the foreigner a place where he was untouchable. For the Argives strongly resented the Danaïdes' foreignness, to which their king's words bore witness: "Whence come these barbarians? / What shall we call you? So outlandishly / Arrayed in the barbaric luxury / Of robes and crowns, and not in Argive fashion / Nor in Greek? But at this I wonder how / Without a herald, without a guide, without patron, / You have yet dared to come" (234–242).

The suppliant wreaths laid at the feet of the gods were apparently not enough. This is where the role of the *proxenus* enters the picture; the institution was perhaps not widespread at the time of Aeschylus, but it was already a custom. Someone took a community under his aegis, made sure that it was represented in the polis, and defended its members. It was a collective, impersonal patronage, very different from the man to man bonds of clientage with Roman patrician families. Such was the role of the proxenus who, for the Danaïdes, was the king himself. He must maintain a proper balance between the respect foreigners are entitled to and the safeguarding of his own people's interests: "I said before that never would I act / Alone, apart from the people, though I am ruler; / So never may people say, if evil comes, / 'Respecting aliens the city you destroyed' " (398–401). Nevertheless, the plea of the suppliants must be respected above all: "If I leave / This debt unpaid, you've warned of pollution / That shall strike unerringly; [. . .] / But yet the wrath of Zeus the Suppliant—/ The height of mortal fear—must be respected" (471–479). The Danaïdes were thus to be protected from the "male outrageousness" of their cousins, and the proxenus-king will present them, along with their father, as suppliants before his people. He did it successfully, as Danaüs explained: " 'Free we are to settle here [mètoikein], subject / Neither to seizure nor reprisal, claimed / neither by citizen nor foreigner. / But if they turn to force, whoever rich / In lands refuses succor, shall be stripped / Of offices and banished publicly. / The king persuaded, prophesying Zeus / The Suppliant would fatten rich his wrath / To feed insatiate suffering, / And show itself as twin defilements, / In and outside the city" (609–621). In Argos, the Danaïdes were to be citizens and foreigners at the same time.

The polis accepted the Danaïdes' plea, surrounded Danaüs with armed attendants, and granted his family a home at no cost to them. Grateful for such greeting, Danaüs remained conscious just the same of his daughters' status; they were far from being considered as integrated in the polis: "Time becomes the touchstone of the alien, / Who bears the brunt of every evil tongue, / The easy target of calumny" (992–994). He consequently advised them, "Honor modesty more than your life" (1112).

The Status of Foreigners in Homeric Times

As early as the Homeric period, the host as well as the suppliant were protected by Zeus Xenios and Athena Xenia, and the *Iliad* proclaims that it is a religious offence to mistreat a host.

Proxeny, which was to be institutionalized during the classical period, was already a widespread custom. Under the aegis of Hermes, the "Shrewd Inventor," the proxenus is "the one who seeks" and actually is the *middleman* between the polis and those belonging to a foreign community, providing a remedy to their statutory incapacity. Proxeny was always the office of a person chosen by a foreign community, sometimes because of his particular qualities, as was the case with Pindar who became proxenus for Athens at the same time as he was rewarded for his dithyramb in honor of the city.

That ancient world remained closed upon itself. Voyages inspired fear and, if we are to believe Homer, appealed more to people on the fringe of society (illegitimate sons, for instance, see *The Odyssey* 14.199–286). Patrilineal descent itself had locked the polis, the father's Greek citizenship being sufficient to transmit Greek identity; prejudices against those foreign to the group were strongly marked.

Within that framework of "peer" citizens whose ideal, realized in Sparta, was "parity" *(homoioi)*, foreigners passing by were greeted with suspicion, if not hostility: might those migrating birds not be birds of prey? On the other hand, those foreigners who chose to settle down and whose craft or business were deemed useful to the polis belonged to the category of *metics*, domiciled residents, the word indicating, with Aeschylus, a change of domicile (cf. *mētoikein*). A residency tax was levied on metics, but in Athens they sometimes enjoyed tax exemption, probably in order to attract their presence, valuable to the polis. In the first half of the fifth century, Athens gave foreigners legal protection, administered by a politician who became their patron, the *prostates*. *Proxeny* and *prostasia* were thus two different forms of *civic* protection, both already mentioned in *The Suppliants*. But the rights of property ownership were seldom granted to foreigners: the Danaïdes are renters. As Marie-Françoise Baslez noted in her very fine study, "It was indeed out of the question, at that time, to integrate non Greeks into the civic framework."[6] The Danaïdes were in a way exceptionally well incorporated, and that only because of their double nature, *astoxenoi*, at the same time citizens because of their Argive descent *and* foreigners because they came from Egypt (as they are bestial *and* feminine—in the likeness of Iō—initiated into the cult of Demeter *and* servants of Hēra, criminal killers of men *and* brokers of the marriage contract).

Barbarians and Metics During the Classical Age

Bringing the Greek city-states into conflict with Persia between 490 and 478, the Median wars changed the relationships between the polis and foreigners. The notion of "Barbarian" became crystallized, whereas during the Peloponnesian War, in which city-states grouped around Athens fought those that were allied with Sparta, attention was called to the Greek foreigner, the one who came from another city-state. Athens developed the notion of civic coherence—*koinonia*[7]—by conceiving the community of citizens as based on their participation in political life, not on the basis of racial or social criteria. There was a law, however, that consolidated the monogeneous ethnic leaven of the *koinonia*: Pericles' law of 451, which demanded that any citizen must prove a *dual Athenian descent* both paternal and material: "And the third year following, under the rule of Antidotos, because of the increasing number of citizens and following Pericles' proposition, it was decided not to allow anyone to enjoy political rights who was not born of two citizens."[8] One who does not satisfy that condition is put in the category of illegitimate persons. "I should intrude / There marked by two defects, a stranger's son, / Myself a bastard."[9]

The word "barbarian" then becomes frequently used to refer to non-Greeks. Homer applied the word "barbarophone" to the natives of Asia Minor who fought alongside the Greeks,[10] and seems to have coined the term on the basis of such onomatopeia as *bla-bla, bara-bara,* inarticulate or incomprehensible mumblings. As late as the fifth century, the term is applied to *both Greeks and non-Greeks* having a slow, thick, or improper speech: "The barbarians are all those whose pronunciation is clumsy and coarse."[11] It was possible, however, in ancient Greece, to speak in tongues in sanctuaries, and the barbarians' prayers were heeded. The Median wars intensified the rejection of the barbarian, but this can also be understood as a counterpart to the remarkable development of Greek philosophy, founded on the *logos* seen both as the Greeks' idiom and as the intelligible principle in the order of things. The barbarians are outside this universe on account of their outlandish speech and dress, their political and social peculiarities. Among the three writers of tragedies, Sophocles, Aeschylus, and Euripides, who systematically use the term *barbaros,* Euripides differed from his predecessors by a more frequent use of the word in a more pejorative sense. This would indicate that foreignness was personally more intolerable to him, and, generally speaking, more disturbing as time goes by. For all three dramatists "barbarian" meant "incomprehensible," "non-Greek," and finally "eccentric" or "inferior." The meaning, "cruel,'" that we ascribe to it would have to wait until the barbarian invasions of Rome before showing up. Nevertheless, already with Euripides, "barbarian" points toward an area of inferiority that includes moral inferiority; the word no longer refers to a foreign nationality but exclusively to evil, cruelty, and

savageness.[12] When Andromache addressed the Greeks by saying, "Greeks! Your Greek cleverness is simple barbarity. / Why
kill this child, [. . .]" (The Trojan Women, 764–765), the word
"barbarity" could also have been translated "savageness."[13] The
term was applicable to the Greeks as well as to the Trojans. Far
from suggesting any acceptance of foreigners, such internalization of barbarity indicates the durability of hostile feelings toward
them, as well as the importance of that feeling in assessing others
within the supposedly homogeneous group. With Aeschylus, on
the other hand, the word was applied to the strange behavior
toward the Greeks on the part of the Egyptian herald who accompanied the Danaïdes (825–902); its main value was one of contrast with the blessings of Greek democratic civilization. Indeed,
when Aeschylus put forward the concept of "democracy" ("The
citizens speak") in Agamemnon (456) the reader imagines that
the dramatist who wrote The Persians was sensitive to the difference between his own civilization and that of Persia's Great King
Darius. By means of a contrast with the foreigner, in short,
consciousness of Greek freedom emerged, and henceforth the
barbarian was to be identified as the enemy of democracy.

And yet the barbarians were fascinating and, as if echoing the
Sophists, writers would distinguish good barbarians from the bad,
the best obviously being those who were perfectible—those who
could be assimilated into Greek culture. For Socrates, the name
"Greek" did not apply to a race but "it is that of a culture, and
one calls Greek those who have the same education as we have
rather than those who have the same origin."[14] That foretaste of
cosmopolitanism was to remain strictly intellectual, for the
"isonomy" of citizens (they have an equal role in politics because
they are identical among themselves) drove back into eccentricity,
irrationality, or—more simply but more basically—into incomprehensible speech that other who would always be a Barbarian.

The foreigner who had a domicile in Greece would stand out.
The distinction between established foreigners and transient ones
already existed at the beginning of the second millenium, in

Mesopotamia, in Hammurabi's empire. The social class of *mu-skenu* (cf. the French word *mesquin*), was made up of foreigners who were more or less settled in the country and had certain rights, while passing foreigners were deprived of them.

The Greek's *metic* had contractual dealings with the polis—but in what fashion? Marie-Françoise Baslez rightly calls him the *homo economicus* of the Greek city-state. In contrast with the citizen who was a political and military entity, and without being what today we call an immigrant worker, the metic was "the one who lives with," "who has changed residence."[15] He paid a monthly residence tax that was equivalent to a day's wages. Inferior to the citizen he was nevertheless not a slave, as was suggested by aristocratic minds like Plato or the pseudo-Xenophon. Often artisans but farmers, too, metics were also bankers, owners of personal property, and shippers. In Athens, some become true capitalists (Lampis of Aegina) or renowned intellectuals (Lysias, Isaeus, and the most famous, Aristotle). As in the case of barbarians, some were singled out as good (Cephalus, for instance, father of the orator Lysias, who "provided democratic resistance with shields," and in whose house Plato set his dialogue *The Republic*) who in some circumstances could achieve fiscal equality with citizens but never enjoy ownership of goods; others were viewed as bad (like Athenogenes, a swindler, a coward, and a traitor, in the pay of women and tyrants). Athens increasingly specified the financial responsibilities of metics: as early as 378 a special allotment tax burdened them with one sixth of their residence cost; they shared, but in discriminate fashion, in the heavy honorary expenses of religious rites. On the other hand, metics could only exceptionally take part in competitions, choruses, or national defense (when a war drags on and the "safety of the people and all those who live in the state" is at stake). In case they illegally assumed the privileges of a citizen, metics were degraded to the condition of slaves. Plato (*Laws*, 915b) advocated that metics be expelled from the polis when their capital became equal to that of farmers who own their land.

Nevertheless, not so much out of gratitude than in order to show themselves faithful to the Greek's lavish spirit, those resident foreigners often made a name for themselves as generous bene-factors of the polis. Without being liberal partisans of Athenian democracy, as some foreigners believed on the basis of other instances, metics would infiltrate—without becoming integrated —all the city-states that needed their economic assistance. Alone Sparta's xenelasia constituted an exception to the rule and re-jected any foreign participation. When all is said and done, it would appear as though the establishment of a metic class was conceived as a moderate political and demographic device, avoid-ing *cosmopolitanism* as well as *xenophobia.*

Observing the present-day reactions toward foreigners who have settled in Western nations, one might well wonder if our mentality has not remained similar to that of the Greeks. Indeed, spontaneous reactions are less weighted toward the rights of man for all—including foreigners—than toward balancing the status of these "metics" on the basis of the dominant criterion, that of their economic usefulness to the community. Economic necessity remains a gangplank—or a screen—between xenophobia and cosmopolitanism.

When business is booming and merchants sweep into ports, when tourism develops and people travel out of intellectual curi-osity, at the same time as professors infiltrate among amateurs of culture, one feels the need to confine foreigners. Beginning with the fifth century, passing foreigners seldom go beyond the limits of ports. Although not a true ghetto, the *emporion,* a port au-thority, was a commercial (stores, markets, wharfs) and sexual (brothels) area that was distinguished from the *agora,* the center of political and military life. Aristotle even suggested that the *agora* be split in two: a "free" zone (for civic and political activity) and a "shopping" zone (grouping imported products and importers!).

Passing foreigners, clearly distinguished from citizens, thus did not share the privileges of metics.

At the same time, individual and spontaneous proxeny became a public office: the proxenus who protected the foreigner was henceforth to be chosen by "a decree of the polis whose interests he shall defend."[16] His "evergetism"[17] turns into a real diplomatic responsibility. What is remarkable is that proxeny remains open to citizens and non-citizens, Greeks and barbarians—and that is an additional sign, if one were needed, of a relaxing of internal relations among the city-states and of external ones with the non-Greek world. With a concern not for integrating foreigners but for favoring exchanges among foreigners to the polis' benefit, Plato brilliantly expresses this wholly pragmatic tolerance of foreigners, which, while keeping them apart from public life, consists in using them with a benevolence that is not exempt of cynicism: "The intercourse of cities with one another is apt to create a confusion of manners; strangers are always suggesting novelties to strangers. When states are well governed by good laws the mixture causes the greatest possible injury; but seeing that most cities are the reverse of well-ordered, the confusion which arises in them from the reception of strangers, and from the citizens themselves rushing off into other cities, when any one either young or old desires to travel anywhere abroad at whatever time, is of no consequence. On the other hand, the refusal of states to receive others, and for their own citizens never to go to other places, is an utter impossibility, and to the rest of the world is likely to appear ruthless and uncivilized; it is a practice adopted by people who use harsh words, such as xenelesia or banishment of strangers, and who have harsh and morose ways, as men think" (*Laws*, 12:950). Such a tolerance would endow the host nation with a good reputation among other nations; it should, however, be practiced only with cautious discrimination, taking into account the *various types of foreigners*, which Plato distinguishes as follows. There are the *summer visitors*, who are "like birds of passage, taking wing in pursuit of commerce; they are received in public buildings outside the city by magistrates who supervise their activities but they "are not allowed to make any innovation." Then there are the *spectators* who come "to see with their eyes and hear with their ears the festivals of the Muses"; priests and ministers of the temples must take them in hand, but if they have committed misdeeds their case must be heard by the warden of the agora. Next there are the various *dignitaries* from foreign lands. Finally, there are the foreigners "who come from another land to look at ours," and "such visits will be rare"; they come either to see something that is far superior to what exists elsewhere or to tell about something similar elsewhere. The case of the foreigner who has something to teach the native is considered exceptional; in addition, Plato wishes that, once he has accomplished what he came for, the foreigner "shall depart, as a friend taking leave of friends, and be honored by them with gifts and suitable tributes of respect" (12:952–953). Political pragmatism, as can be seen, never ceases to guide a morality that saw itself as most enlightened with respect to foreigners.

Hellenistic Cosmopolitanism

A number of Panhellenic ideas, previously inconceivable, were beginning to appear. Intellectuals such as Herodotus of Halicarnassus, the historian, or Hippodamus of Miletus, the architect, both refugees, willingly take part in Pericles' project involving a colony "established by representatives of the whole of Greece."[18] The change, noticeable since the fourth century, became more pronounced thanks to the intermixing of people following progress made in navigational and travel techniques, which shortened geographic distances. Hellenism proved to be more curious than reluctant where foreigners were concerned. For instance, the following statements could be noted: "The only homeland, foreigner, is the world we live in; a single Chaos has given birth to all mortals" (Meleager of Gadara, first century B.C.); or, according to Terence's Latin translation, Menander's famous saying, "I am a man, and nothing human is foreign to me."[19] We owe the first political cosmopolitanism to the Stoics and their ethics, which was based on individual judgment. That the city-state might embrace the far limits of the world—such was the ideal of those logicians, physicists, doctors, seers, and above all moralists, an ideal that nevertheless found no actual political implementation. "A multitude of men, living together, and governed by one law," was what Cleanthes announced.[20] His project called for a religious community, a mystical coming together of fraternizing foreigners, much more than a political dominion always concerned with the economic interests of the polis.

Stoic Conciliation: Universalism . . .

The ancient Stoics, already it would seem at the time of their founder, Zeno of Citium (c.335–264 B.C.), but very explicitly with Chrysippus (c.281–c.205 B.C.), considered that every living being was supported by the principle called *oikeiosis*, a complex notion that might be translated as "conciliation." Moreover, *oikeiosis* referred to the permanent taking hold of oneself, a kind of "inner touch," of vital dynamic that puts the subject in agreement with himself. That is what the Roman Stoics translated as *conciliatio* and *commendatio* (Cicero) or *committo* (Seneca)—"I am committed to myself." Hence such notions as *amor nostri* and *caritas*, seen as the basis of conscious life by the Stoics. Furthermore, that original concilation binds us not only to ourselves but also to the concentric spheres that would represent the arrangement of our fellow men—starting with close relatives and ending up with the whole of mankind, according to Hierocles' theory; in reverse, by tightening the circles, we succeed in absorbing all men, of whatever race or blood, into ourselves. That human universality, which is asserted in such manner for the first time, was founded on the community of reason. Because they are reasonable, men apply *amor nostri* and *caritas* to all of mankind: *caritas generis humani*.[21] This Stoic ethics found its perfect expression in Terence's famous text. To Menedemus who asks, "Chremes, does your own business leave you so much spare time that you also busy yourself with that of others, which in no

way concern you?" Chremes answers, "I am a man: I consider
that nothing human is foreign to me."[22] Cicero, who comments
on the phrase, thinks regretfully that "as we have stronger feelings for the luck and unluck that befalls us than for that which
befalls others, and we see things as if there were a wide space
between others and ourselves, we judge them very differently
from the way we judge ourselves."[23] At the same time he came
closer to the biblical and Christian precept commanding that we
love our neighbor as we do ourselves.

Thus founded on *oikeiosis*, on conciliation, that universalist
ethics leads one, on the political plane, to challenge separate city-
states and substitute a tolerant cosmopolitanism. *Megapolis*, the
large polis, is an ideal often brought out during the imperial era,
and it includes the entire universe, from citizens to the stars.
Eratosthenes already advised Alexander the Great to deal with
Barbarians as with Greeks, and Chrysippus saw no difference
between slaves and other servants. One is a slave, according to
the ancient stoics, neither by nature nor by conquest. With them,
distinctions fade between Greeks and barbarians, free men and
slaves, but also between men and women, since all are endowed
with a longing for the same virtue. Inhabitants of a common
abode, all men are "a part of God, and the Whole that contains
us is also God: we are his associates *(socii)* and his members."[24]

And yet, such a cosmopolitan universalism was to remain
utopic, even as, along with Stoicism, big Hellenistic monarchies
took over from the former city-states.[25] One of the reasons it was
impossible to carry out the Stoic doctrine was that, under the
cover of its egalitarian aspect, an elitism of the reasonable wise
man was unfurled; that wise man was separated from the rest of
mankind, which, no matter what didactic efforts were considered,
could not have access to virtue. The pride of the wise Stoic
actually produced, under the guise of a reason apparently acknowledged in all, a new class of foreigners: those who did not
attain virtue, did not live according to the law, or talked non-
sense.[26]

In that perspective, the notion of foreigner changed meaning. A foreigner was one who showed himself unable to interpret the laws of Providence ("If to be foreign to the world is to be unaware of the beings that are within it, one is not less so when unaware of what happens in it. He who exiles himself from the rules of the City is an exile. He who closes the eyes of his mind is blind"),[27] or who excluded himself from the common solidarity that is based on reason ("Finally he who draws his soul apart from that of other citizens, which ought to constitute a single, identical soul with his, he is, I say, like a useless limb in that city, and he breaks all bonds of society").[28]

It would seem eventually that Stoicism was less a thought of the other that would integrate the foreigner's difference than an *autarchy* that assimilates the other and erases him under the common denominator of reason, the one not amenable to it falling into the category of the insane. "One must not esteem those one loves but love those one holds in esteem!" Theophrastus asserted.[29] Nevertheless, it is also true that some of those who did not deserve it were honored by Cicero's friendship, when he demanded justice for enemies and ranked clemency above warlike virtues.[30]

In fact, beginning with Panaetius of Rhodes who introduced ancient Stoicism in Rome, moral sternness became more flexible, the abyss separating the wise from the insane seemed blurred, and one conceived human nature as diverse. Just the same, while Stoicism foreshadowed some aspects of Christianism, the two are not identical, *oikeiosis* is not *agape*;[31] rather, it is individualism enlightened by reason. The distinction of the *other* is immediately outweighed by the apology of the *self* within an ethics that caught a glimpse of otherness only to deny it: "Friends, brothers, close relatives, relatives by marriage, fellow citizens, and everyone, in short, since we wish the society of men to be one, deserves to be sought after for himself *(propter se)*: each one is an end in himself."[32]

. . . and Perversion

There is, moreover, in the Greek Stoics' cosmopolitanism a *cynical stamp* that undoubtedly can be traced back to their predecessors (such as Antisthenes and especially Crates, and others) but foreshadows the libertarian cosmopolitism of the eighteenth century.[33] Thus Zeno's *Republic*, in a controversy with Plato's *Republic*, rejects the constraining usage invented by men to the benefit of a "pure *logos*," with no regard for propriety or restraint, returning to the universal naturalness of men. Whether a youthful indiscretion or an outrageous piece of writing, this lost text by Zeno has made commentators ill at ease; a few accounts are left, however, which enable one to glimpse the cosmopolitan ideal of Stoicism's founder. No more distinct States nor peoples, but a single law ruling the human flock, happy in its pasture. Love prevails over men and women who freely belong to one another, dressed in the same manner, having abolished marriage, schools, courts, money, and even temples—only the inner god of the Spirit was revered. Cannibalism, incest, prostitution, pederasty, and of course the destruction of the family are also accepted among the features of that ideal State. One feels that cosmopolitanism emerges from the core of a global movement that makes a clean sweep of laws, differences, and prohibitions; and that by defying the polis and its jurisdiction one implicitly challenges the founding prohibitions of established society and perhaps of sociality itself; that by abolishing state-controlled borders one assumes, logically and beforehand, an overstepping of the prohibitions that guarantee sexual, individual, and familial identity. A challenge to the very principle of *human association* is what is involved in cosmopolitan utopia: the rules governing exchanges with the other having been abolished (no more State, no more family, no sexual difference), is it possible to live without constraints—without limits, without borders—other than individual demands? Two possibilities are then open: either absolute cynicism based on individual pleasure, or the elitism of lucid, self-controlled beings, of wise men who manage to be reconciled with the insane.

The Stoics rationally opted for the second possibility, as did later on the philosophers of the Enlightenment and the founders of the rights of man based on reason, or more recently the cosmopolitans of the Marxist International who decreed the constraints of the "proletariat's interest" above national customs. The essential differences between those three doctrines, which emerged at key moments of Western history, should not hide what unites them. Cosmopolitan conciliation, universalism, represent its pure, utopic facet, whose repressed, corrosive aspect is revealed by Zeno's cynicism and *Rameau's Nephew*, an aspect that, if not spoken and expended, might well become a leaven of arbitrariness, terror, and totalitarianism. In other words, cosmopolitanism will be either libertarian or totalitarian — or else it will not be.

Stoic cosmopolitanism adumbrates a new religion in which Greek individualism, the introspection of Egyptian piety, the banquets of Syrian communities, and Jewish morality merge together . . . From that moment the question arises as to whether cosmopolitanism is anything but a religious reality, without ever being capable of becoming a political reality. The question is still valid today. The flaw lies perhaps in the very project: "cosmopolitanism" means that the ideal of the *polis*, of the political city-state with its rights and its isonomy, is preserved but extended on a world scale, that the entire world finds its place in it. Now, it is possible that the erasing of differences can be effected only in the order of piety. On the other hand, the political order, which governs needs, can only protect its own, entrench disparities, separate disagreements, and, at best, administer the procedures intended to preserve differences.

In contrast with classical and Homeric times, Hellenistic Greece, however, carried out a cosmopolitan policy. In what way? While always distinguishing those who are *foreigners to the polis* (that is, Greeks from another political unit) from those who are *foreigners to the Greek world* (that is, persons differing in race or culture), Greeks of the Hellenistic era acknowledged the community of the former through the birth of international law and living together, and that of the latter through the establishment of vast international or multiracial cities like Alexandria where intellectuals mixed Judaism and Hellenism, translated the Bible into Greek, and later integrated ancient philosophy into Christianism. Nevertheless, the class of foreigners remained separated from the natives: even in Alexandria, Greeks married among themselves and foreigners did not belong to the polis. In Delos, there were alliances between Athenians and other groups, but foreigners did not vote. Roman Egypt was an exception, as has been pointed out; there, through the device of "mixed bodies," foreigners were allowed to administer the community at the local level. As to Panhellenic unity between city-states, it was accomplished less through one city merging with another than by means of federations (like that of the Cyclades) guaranteed by a powerful monarchy that dominated all.

One should note, among the political signs of cosmopolitan relaxation, the attitude toward those of "mixed blood." In the third century, so-called half-castes—who were not considered citizens—were nevertheless above the metics; thus, in Rhodes, where they were called *matroxenoi*, they were inferior citizens but were a part of society. As early as the second century, maternal lineage gave civic rights. The children of those mixed families could be naturalized, but they mainly constituted a new category, the *stateless*, separate from that of foreigners. Provided he submit to Greek education, the Hellenistic stateless person appears to have had better chances than the foreigner. Even gymnasia, traditionally closed to foreigners at the end of the fourth century, opened their doors to them: first in Delos, an international port, then in Athens. The rosters of epheboi, however, distinguished between Athenians, who came first, and the Romans, who were next, and finally the foreigners (until the second century in Delos). In Athens, foreign epheboi were never mixed with the others.[34]

More a center for spreading culture than a framework for political integration, the Hellenistic polis disseminated, along with its cosmopolitanism, Greek civilization more than politics. This means that the foreigner did not, during the Hellenistic age, enjoy a new status: the foreigner was still the citizen's other. But his role in the polis increased; this marked a retreat, specific to Greece at that time, of legal-political features as opposed to what is distinctive of an ideology, a mentality, or a way of life, which also, and in increasingly better fashion, define Greekness. Without for that matter wanting to speak of a reduction of the political, let me say that accepting foreigners in the polis led to establishing among the members of a community identifying criteria that transcended politics by putting forward cultural and symbolic factors. With such criteria, and availing itself of the scope of the ancient city-state itself, Christianism was founded by preaching to foreigners, merchants, and fringe elements. But nascent Christianism was no longer located within the bounds of the city; instead, it appealed to an invisible spiritual community: *the Ecclesia took the place of the Polis.*

For its part, however, biblical monotheism had included the foreigner in the divine Alliance. Contrary to the too easily accepted picture of the chosen people's ostracism against others, the Hebrews had for thousands of years, at the founding of their kingdom, enlisted those foreigners able to accept the divine covenant.

3 The Chosen People and the Choice of Foreignness

Foreigner or Convert

The covenant with God turned the Jewish people into a chosen people (especially after Jacob and the flight from Egypt) and, if it established the basis of a sacred nationalism, it nonetheless harbors in its very essence an inherent inscription of foreignness. There are numerous sections of the Bible that affirm the choice of the Jewish people to the exclusion of others: "I will establish my Covenant between myself and you," Yahweh said to Abraham, "and your descendants after you, generation after generation, a Covenant in perpetuity, to be your God and the God of your descendants after you."[1] Those who are opposed to such a covenant or are not a party to it shall be forcefully rejected: "Thus speaks Yahweh Sabaoth: 'I will repay what Amalek did to Israel when they opposed them on the road by which they came out of Egypt. Now, go and strike down Amalek; put him under the ban with all that he possesses. Do not spare him, but kill man and woman, babe and suckling, ox and sheep, camel and donkey' ";[2] "In particular: we will not give our daughters to the natives of the land nor take their daughters for our sons';[3] "No bastard[4] is to be admitted to the assembly of Yahweh. No Ammonite or Moabite is to be admitted to the assembly of Yahweh, not even their descendants to the tenth generation may be admitted to the assembly of Yahweh, and this is for all time; because they did not come to meet you with bread and water when you were on your way out of Egypt, and because they hired Balaam son of Beor from Pethor in Aram of the Two Rivers to curse you. But Yahweh your God refused to listen to Balaam, and Yahweh your God turned the curse into a blessing for you, because Yahweh your God loved you. Never, as long as you live, shall you seek their welfare or their prosperity."

Other kinds of foreigners, however, are accepted: "You are not to regard the Edomite as detestable, for he is your brother; nor the Egyptian, because you were a stranger in his land. The third generation of children born to these may be admitted to the assembly of Yahweh."[5]

Exclusive as it may be, and while basing that exclusiveness on the moral misdeed of those who are despised, the Jewish people's covenant with its God is an outgrowth not of favoritism but of choice founded on ordeal; this implies that, constantly threatened, the covenant is always to be conquered and its object remains the continuous improvement of the chosen. According to one tradition: "Why did the Holy One (let Him be blessed!) choose Israel? Because all the other people repudiated the Torah and refused to accept it, while Israel accepted and chose the Holy One (let Him be blessed!) and his Torah."[6]

Furthermore, a biblical universalism comes to light, which allows the possible dignity of humankind in its entirety to emerge, and the foreigner himself might chance to be God's unwonted although inevitable unveiler. In the eyes of rabbis, the Torah would eventually be destined for all mankind.[7] Thus "Moses expounds the Torah in sixty-six languages";[8] "You must keep my laws and my customs. Whoever complies with them shall find life in them."[9] One may conclude that *whoever* obeys the Torah, even a pagan, is equal to the high priest. "And *is* this the manner of man, Lord Yahweh?"[10] This is interpreted to mean that it is not the manner of priests, Levites, or Israel but of all men.[11]

Since all men were made in the image of God,[12] the precept, "You must love your neighbor as yourself,"[13] applies not only to the immediate neighbor, one of the same family or the same people, but to "man, the beloved";[14] "Just as it has been said, with reference to the man of Israel, you must love your neighbor as yourself, the same expression is used with reference to the foreigner."[15]

There are several texts that stress even more clearly the respect due to foreigners as such: "You must not molest the stranger or oppress him, for you lived as strangers in the land of Egypt."[16] A pagan can claim the same rights as the Jew if he espouses monotheism. The Torah ceaselessly dwells on the duties of Jews toward foreigners, and it may be noted that no other commandment (circumcision, dietary taboos, prohibition against lying and stealing) is repeated as often. The Talmud goes further: "If a convert comes to learn the Torah do not say to him, the mouth that has eaten impure animals, worms, and reptiles, would like to learn the Torah that has been given to us by God."[17] Furthermore, the fact of having been "strangers in the land of Egypt" is not interpreted as a sufficient reason assuring the kindness of Jews toward foreigners: is it not true that the bitterness accumulated in the exile's soul might express itself through the persecution of another exile. God alone watches over all foreigners, and the remainder of the stay in Egypt induces greater humility into the "chosen people" who might thus view themselves as having once been part of an inferior group. Justice rather than mercy seems to rise from that verse. One will recall another passage with similar meaning; "If a stranger lives with you in your land, do not molest him. You must count him as one of your own countrymen and love him as yourself—for you were once strangers yourselves in Egypt."[18] "Love the stranger then, for you were strangers in the land of Egypt."[19] Abraham himself is considered as the first "convert":[20] commentators emphasize that he has left his country behind, his fatherland and his father's house, and all the other peoples of the world, in order to proceed toward the land that God has shown him, as does the convert who has chosen Israel.[21]

The universalism of the prophets, from Amos to Jeremiah, asserts even more strongly the idea that all mankind is respectable in its intrinsic dignity—and this even before Greek philosophy and Stoic cosmopolitanism. The poor, widows and widowers, orphans, servants, foreigners are greeted with equal justice: "If ever I have infringed the rights of slave / or maidservant in legal actions against me—/ what shall I do when God stands up? / What shall I say when he holds his assize? / They, no less than I, were created in the womb / by the one same God who shaped us all within our mothers. / . . . No stranger ever had to sleep outside, / my door was always open to the traveler."[22]

The Hebrew term *ger*, meaning "stranger," is not without posing problems. Literally, it signifies "the one who has come to live with" or "resident," and it includes the idea of "convert." This very word, in the Bible as well as the Talmud or Midrash, is translated either by "proselyte" or by "stranger." Two sub-sets are generated from the same notion: on the one hand, *ger-tochav*, resident foreigner, on the other hand, just *ger*, which refers to conversion-naturalization. The *ger-tochav* maintains his identity as a foreigner but, whether or not he resides in Israel, he obeys Mosaic laws; these are moral laws that are indispensable to society; they endow one, in the spirit of Judaism, with a spiritual dignity equal to that of the Jew himself. Thus the *ger* is a foreigner who belongs to the Jewish nation-religion. Many rabbis of the Talmudic period, among whom one counts the famous Rabbi Arciba (second century, revolt against Rome), were converts.[23]

Some Talmudic or Midrashic texts, however, do not conceal their rejection or mistrust of converts. R. Helbo says, "Proselytes are as deplorable [for Israel] as a plague."[24] Such statements merely represent individual opinions, with the majority on the contrary identifying with the spirit of hospitality. Without proselytism, Jewish religion appears to candidates for conversion as highly demanding, but it subsequently offers its welcome to those who have accepted the ordeal of the covenant. Thus, all candidates for conversion are given solemn warnings concerning punishments following breaches of precepts, but they are also told about the rewards. "Nevertheless, he must not be excessively deterred"; [25] likewise, "In the presence of a proselyte, even after ten generations, do not insult an Aramean." [26]

Such demands, where the integration of the foreigner is concerned, which may disturb the modern ideal of tolerance and seem excessive, are still not fundamentally different from those imposed upon foreigners by other religious or moral doctrines (Stoicism, Christianity); the latter, although they claim to be universal, accept into their midst only those who adopt the *same* universality. It will be noted, moreover, that in the spirit of Judaism, the complete integration of the foreigner in the Jewish community is the counterpart of the idea of the "chosen people": I have been "chosen," but the privilege of being chosen is nevertheless "accessible to any individual, at any given moment"; hence a "hybrid conception of choice that includes heredity *and* the free joining of any individual or collective consciousness." Witness this extract from the Talmudic treatise, Pessahim 876: "Eleazar also said: 'God, blessed be His name, has exiled Israel from among the nations solely with the aim that proselytes might join Him.' " [27]

Exemplary in that respect, the story of Ruth the Moabite shows that unity can be achieved only if an exterior, an "outside of," is joined to the "same."

Ruth the Moabite

"In the days of the Judges famine came to the land." The Talmud characterizes that period of ordeals when "the Judges ruled" as a chaotic moment in Jewish history. Lacking a king, [28] everyone followed his own idea, no leader being able to obtain the people's allegiance. In fact, during the three centuries that

separate the arrival of Israel in the promised land and the time of
Ruth, the Law was degraded, forgotten. If Judge Ivtzan is the
same person as Boaz[29]—something not explicited in the Bible—
his marriage to Ruth occurred in the year 2792 (968 B.C.).

On two separate occasions the theme of foreignness is inscribed in this story. First, a venerable man called Elimelech left
his country, the land of Judah, instead of helping it in times of
distress, and dared to settle in the land of Moab—a foreign
kingdom and, what was worse, banned from the covenant for, as
we have seen, its people did not assist the Jews when they fled
from Egypt.[30] This exile amounts to treason and will be punished: Elimelech died and so did, later on, his two sons, Mahlon
and Chilion, leaving no heirs. Their mother Naomi survived
along with the two daughters-in-law Orpah and . . . Ruth. The
divine sentence coming down on such a betrayal-exile is obvious
and harsh, but it is not lacking in ambiguity, as the continuation
of the story shows; not only was Ruth saved but she became the
matriarch of Jewish royalty, the ancestor of David's line. And
who was Ruth?

A princess of Moab, she never would have married a Jew had
Elimelech not emigrated. The reprehensible immigration is thus
inverted into a necessary condition for the accomplishment of
Ruth's destiny. According to one interpretation of the Law, only
male Moabites were banned from the covenant and not the women,
but that interpretation remained unknown until the time Ruth
came back to Judea after her husband's death.[31] This means that
for Boaz and his compatriots Ruth was first a foreigner. Was she
already a convert? According to some, the Moabite princesses
would not have become converts in order to marry the two Jewish
brothers, Mahlon and Chilion, immigrants in their land—and
this amounts to an additional sin for the latter ("They neither
converted them nor ritually immersed them").[32] Moreover, had
her daughters-in-law been converted, Naomi would not have had
the right to send them back to their idolatrous country, as she
did. According to others, the conversion really took place, for the

two brothers were powerful men and could perfectly well impose their religion on the two young foreign sisters, princesses though they might have been. If that had not been the case, the text would not refer to Naomi as their "mother-in-law," nor would it speak of Ruth's submission to Levitic marriage rules.[33]

At any rate, Orpah alone, "she who turns her head" (*oreph*, "nape"), returned home (and, generations later, Goliath, the descendant of Orpah, was bested by David, the descendant of Ruth), while Ruth insists on accompanying her mother-in-law back to Bethlehem. Her words certainly show a devotion to Yahweh, but even more so a loyalty—that one might call passionate—between the two women: "Do not press me to leave you and to turn back from your company, for / 'wherever you go I will go / wherever you live I will live. / Your people shall be my people, / and your God, my God. / Wherever you die, I will die / and there I will be buried. / May Yahweh do this thing to me / and more also, / if even death should come between us!' " (Ruth 1:16–17).

Having no Hebrew roots, the name of Ruth has been the object of many pseudo-etymological interpretations that attempt a symbolic reappropriation of her story. One has thus supposed that *rut* comes from the root *rao*, "to see," "take into consideration" —the words of her mother-in-law (Ruth Rabba 2, 9); or from "saturate"—because she was the ancestor of David who showered God with hymns and prayers until he was saturated (Berchat 7b); it has also been said that the letters forming *Ruth* signify from the esoteric point of view *(Rut—Tor)* the dove ready to be sacrificed before the altar, like Ruth entering the divine Covenant (Zohar Chadash); or that the numerical value of the name is 606, and this coincides with the Torah, which contains 606 commandments in addition to the seven commandments given to Noah, which also concern non-Jews; finally, if the letter *H* represents God, Ruth is related to it and, by means of literal play and permutation, one obtains *Ruth = Thorah*.

Henceforth, Naomi's duty—her name according to the Mid-

rash signifies "agreeable," "pleasing," "for her deeds were pleasing and sweet"—was to find Ruth a "redeemer" who must be,
according to the levirate rules, the closest relative of the dead
husband, for whom he is substituted when the widow has no
children. The first in line was Tov, Elimelech's brother and Mahlon's uncle. The second was Mahlon's cousin, Boaz. In those
days, Jews considered it a moral obligation to give offsprings to
the widow, even if not, as the law strictly demands, through the
agency of the dead man's brother.

The initial meeting between the couple, Boaz and Ruth, which
was not lacking in innocent wile and seductiveness, is branded by
a strange destiny, guided—one must remember—by the desire
of the attractive Naomi: "So she [Ruth] set out and went to glean
in the fields after the reapers. And it chanced that she came to
that part of the fields which belonged to Boaz of Elimelech's clan"
(Ruth 2:3). One should note, along with Rabbi S. R. Hirsch[34]
that the Jewish idea of "what happens" is foreign to the idea of
"chance" and refers to those moments in life that man does not
control but they control him—moments of the divine message.
Boaz, then eighty years old, was perfectly warned by his servant
that Ruth was a Moabite, but he accepts her in his field, under
his protection, and, while calling her "my daughter," lets her do
the work of an ordinary gleaner,[35] perhaps so as better to observe
her and put her to the test. " 'Listen, my daughter, and understand this. You are not to glean in any other field, do not leave
here but stay with my servants. Keep your eyes on whatever part
of the field they are reaping and follow behind. I have ordered
my servants not to molest you. . . . Then she fell on her face,
bowing to the ground. And she said to him, 'How have I so
earned your favor that you take notice of me, even though I am
a foreigner?' " (Ruth 2:8–10). Boaz seemed to imply that the
law authorizing union with Moabite women had just been recognized and that Ruth, who therefore must not have known it,
deserves more spiritual credit for leaving her own land in order
to come to the Jewish people.[36] He therefore already suggested

that her reward would be *perfect*: "May Yahweh reward you for what you have done! May perfect recompense be made to you by Yahweh, the God of Israel, to whom you have come, to find shelter beneath his wings" (Ruth 2:12). One cannot help emphasizing, as several commentators have done, that Ruth's merit will be more sound than that of Abraham, and therefore worthy of a *perfect* reward. Could this be because Abraham left his father's house in answer to a call from God, while Ruth the foreigner did it on her own initiative?[37]

What followed in the narrative continues to reveal the charm of the Moabite's discreet but firm independence. Always obedient to her mother-in-law, Ruth becomes the representative of her desire. Thus, following Naomi's advice, she washed, anointed herself, hid beneath her cloak, and lay at Boaz's feet. Captivated for the second time, the old man (whose ordeal, in this instance, has often been considered harder than that of Joseph with Potiphar's wife) dwells not on the foreigner's obvious physical charm but on her "piety" or "benevolence, mercy, kindness" *(hesed)*: first, she obeyed her mother-in-law, then she selected an old man —"For this last act of kindness of yours is greater than the first, since you have not gone after young men, poor or rich. Have no fear then, my daughter, I will do whatever you ask, for the people of Bethlehem all know your worth" (Ruth 3:10–11).

Boaz nevertheless wishes to accomplish the law of the levirate and give Ruth to Tov, the closest relative. When the latter declines to do so (it would have deprived him of his own name and of his inheritance as well, to the benefit of the dead man's heirs), Boaz asks the people of Yahweh to be his witnesses, and then he marries Ruth: "So Boaz took Ruth and she became his wife. And when they came together, Yahweh made her conceive and she bore a son" (Ruth 4:13). This was not a wedding according to the true levirate rules: Boaz "took" Ruth and had the wedding sanctioned, a ceremony that was not required since, according to the levirate, the widow is normally meant for the closest relative. According to tradition, Boaz died the very night of the wedding's consummation, while Ruth immediately conceived and took her place in Jewish history. If her name received no further mention, Ruth nevertheless enjoyed an exceptional longevity, since she was to have her descendant, Solomon, rise to the throne.[38] Her child, whose birth was favored by Naomi's desire and the affection she showed Ruth and Boaz, became part of Jewish lineage from the moment of his birth. As for Naomi, she was recognized as that child's mother—we would say a symbolic one: "And the women said to Naomi, 'Blessed by Yahweh who has not left the dead man without next of kin this day to perpetuate his name in Israel' " (Ruth 4:14). Ruth's conversion inscribes the child's name in the history of the Jewish people and portends an illustrious destiny for him. It was Naomi, however, who took the child to her bosom and raised him; the Talmud makes quite clear that Ruth bore him and Naomi raised him (Sanhedrin 19b). "And the women of the neighborhood gave him a name. 'A son has been born for Naomi,' they said; and they named him Obed" (Ruth 4:17). Obed is the one who "serves" God: he served as go-between for two peoples and two mothers so as to insert himself in the symbolic lineage of Boaz and Naomi. His descendants would be a line of kings: "This was the father of David's father, Jesse" (Ruth 4:17). There follows the whole of David's paternal line, which goes back to Pharez, son of Judah, but nevertheless omits the embarrassing story of Judah and Tamar, mentioned in 4:12 (instead of marrying her young brother-in-law after her husband's death, Tamar conceived Pharez with her father-in-law, Judah).

Besides, this insertion of foreignness at the very root of Jewish royalty is somewhat disturbing: "For how long are they to speak to me wrathfully, saying: is he not of unworthy lineage? Is he not a descendant of Ruth the Moabite?" David beseeches, addressing himself to God.[39]

Nevertheless, the place of foreignness is not exceptional in that chosen lineage. Saved from Sodom's destruction, Lot and his daughters, who believe themselves to be the only survivors on earth, produce two sons through their incestuous relationships, Ammon and Moab. Ruth the Moabite is thus a descendant of that fruit of incest. The transgression committed by Judah and Tamar has also been alluded to. After the time of Ruth, Naamah the Ammonite became the wife of King Solomon.

Foreignness and incest were thus at the foundation of David's sovereignty. The biblical narrative suggests that being chosen is paid and deserved by the possibility of transgressing strict obedience and taking the risk of deviation—provided the latter is subordinated to a global design. It also assumes a conception of sovereignty based on the rejected, the unworthy, the outlaw. According to tradition, the letter *dalet* signifies "poor": *David* is twice poor, and his ancestor Ruth the foreigner is there to remind those unable to read that the divine revelation often requires a lapse, the acceptance of radical otherness, the recognition of a foreignness that one might have tended at the very first to consider the most degraded. This was not an encouragement to deviate or proselytize but an invitation to consider the fertility of the other. Such indeed is the role of Ruth—the outsider, the foreigner, the excluded. Nonetheless, if the one "outside-the-covenant" accepts the moral rules of the covenant, the latter finds therein its mainspring, its vital momentum, its sovereignty. Perhaps damaged, worried at any rate, that sovereignty opens up—through the foreignness that founds it—to the dynamics of a constant, inquisitive, and hospitable questioning, eager for the other and for the self as other.

The faithful devour the foreigner, assimilate him and integrate him under the protection of their religion's moral code, which both integrator and integrated support. Covered by such religious ideals, devouring fantasies are not expressed and the guilt they might give rise to is avoided. Even more so, under the protection of the moral ideals that are characteristic of religion, the assimilated foreigner works on the faithful himself from the inside but as a "double"—calling for an identification with the "base," the "excess," and the "outlaw," which is continuously presented to the believer and stimulates the dynamics of his perfection. If David is *also* Ruth, if the sovereign is *also* a Moabite, peace of mind will then never be his lot, but a constant quest for welcoming and going beyond the other in oneself.

4 Paul and Augustine: The Therapeutics of Exile and Pilgrimage

Paul the Cosmopolitan

"I made myself a Jew to the Jews, to win the Jews; [. . .] To those who have no Law, I was free of the Law myself (though not free from God's law, being under the law of Christ) to win those who have no Law. [. . .] I made myself all things to all men in order to save some at any cost."[1]

Thus did Paul express himself. A Jew from Tarsus, in Cilicia, a polyglot, an untiring traveler of the eastern Mediterranean between the years A.D. 45 and 60, he changed the small Jewish sect called primitive Christian Church into an *Ecclesia*. Adapting the word of the Gospels to the Greek world the *Ecclesia* apposed to the community of citizens in the polis a community that was other: a community of those who were different, of foreigners who transcended nationalities by means of a faith in the Body of the risen Christ.

There was first the strangeness of Paul. His portrait, in a Sicilian mosaic of the twelfth century resembles that drawn by Seneca's Roman friends—"stunted" but "visionary," bald, with a rather large nose, linked eyebrows, hollow cheeks, a pointed beard . . . A few frescoes, in the catacombs, represent him with bulging eyes; on others he squints—and this seems a recall of "the splinter in the flesh," an expression the apostle used.

This Pharisee, waiting with others for a messianic era, a "Jew born of Jews" as he defines himself, is a Roman citizen and proud to be so ("of a city not without reknown"). Paul's mother tongue was Greek and he was brought up in a Hellenistic environment but was not imparted a Greek, classical culture. As a disciple of Gamaliel he had a rabbinical training and Christ speaks to him "in Hebrew," that is, in Aramaic, a language he uses while learning to be a scribe. Such a heterogeneous character is not exceptional. Was not Paul born in the Greek city of Tarsus? That crossroad of the Roman Empire, where Asia Minor and Syria meet, is a melting pot of Mediterranean traditions under Hellenistic sway, as the early Paulinians show: Joseph, known as Barnabas, was a Levite from Cyprus; Manahen, Herod's foster brother, was brought up in the Hellenistic tradition. Everything—including the name he assumes, "Saul, also called Paul . . . "—testifies to that double part one loved to play among the better families of Syria, Cilicia, or Cappadocia. A native part with a native name, a Greek part with a Greek name.[2] But the choice of that name also signifies allegiance to Quintus Sergius Paulus, proconsul of Cyprus, a convert to Christianism (Paul assumed Paulus' cognomen only after his stay in Cyprus).

To such a polymorphic world Paul adds an additional unbalance: the journeys. A *first mission* to Cyprus in 47–48 (or 43–45); to Pamphylia, Pisidia, and Lycaonia; returning to Antioch and going to Jerusalem. *Second mission* from 49 to 51 (or 46 to 51): Asia Minor; Alexandria; Macedonia, in Philippi and Thessalonike; Athens; Corinth; Ephesus and Antioch. *Third mission* in 52–58: Galatia and Phrygia; three years in Ephesus; Corinth again, and then Macedonia; return journey, *Captivity voyage* in 60–61 . . . until his execution in Rome in 62, 64, or 67.[3]

Those routes confront Paul with the Jewish diaspora, and his teaching is focused on the synagogues. But the eastern religions (Isis, Attis, Adonis . . .) were spreading all over, and conversion was a trend of the times. His audience came from that part of the population that was "marginal to the civic body": merchants, sailors, or "exiles," the most frequent travelers of antiquity.

Paul's accomplices? Lydia at Philippi, in Thracia, a former slave from Lydia, in Asia Minor, a "purple-dye merchant" who is more of a modest shopkeeper than a wealthy merchant, Aquila and Priscilla, Jews from Asia Minor who settled in Rome and came back to Corinth, whence they accompanied Paul to Ephesus. Itinerant doctors such as Luke, who wrote the Acts of the Apostles. Women, whom the Acts describe as "ladies of quality." Such marginal people, women, foreigners who remained bound to their native culture, nevertheless created among themselves *bonds* of solidarity, mutually welcoming each other in holy places where, precisely, the foreigner was safe from any affront, while he had, as we have seen, only very few rights in the polis.

Paul first preached in Asia Minor to a population that was outside Greek cultural structures and whose mysticism, isolated from traditional Hellenic centers, seemed to him perhaps more receptive to his own novelty. He next confronted the traditional Greek world, particularly in Macedonia, Athens, and Corinth, but he then relied on the set of foreign merchants. And with the third journey (52–58),[4] when Ephesus was his base, Paul dealt with a city that is certainly Panhellenic but without dogmatism, a polymorphous city mixing Jewish exorcists with followers of Artemis' cult. Paul adopted, developing it to the highest degree, an essential feature of the spirituality characteristic of a place teeming with foreigners: hospitality. What is remarkable is that he makes it free—priests do not beg and do not make a career out of religion but work with their own hands (Paul is an artisan, either a weaver or a tent maker). What is more: as the foreigner is Christ himself, to welcome him is to be welcomed in God.

The Pauline Church thus inherited the *cosmopolitanism* specific of late *Hellenism*, which already offered material and legal conditions more favorable than before to foreigners and their beliefs. Paul relied on such predispositions to break with the nationalism of Jewish communities[5] and the regionalism of Eastern worships. Present in Jewish mysticism and in the tradition of Ruth and of David, those universalist tendencies were perceived as a threat by Jewish orthodoxy and by Roman authorities as well—the latter probably fearing that the framework of the polis itself might be shattered as a result of such an ethical cosmopolitanism, which created a new alliance cutting across the political community. The Pauline Church emerged as a community of foreigners, first from the periphery, then from the Greco-Roman citadel, united by a statement that challenged the national and political structure: "Do not forget, then, that there was a time when you who were pagans [. . .] you had no Christ and were excluded from membership of Israel, aliens with no part in the covenants with their Promise; you were immersed in this world, without hope and without God. But now in Christ Jesus, you that used to be so far apart from us have been brought very close, by the blood of Christ. [. . .] So you are no longer aliens or foreign visitors *[xenoi kai paroikoi]*: you are citizens like all the saints, and part of God's household."[6] *Paroikos*, which renders the Hebrew *ger,* refers to the foreigner in Israel. For Paul there were no longer Jews nor Greeks, but "a new creation."[7]

This new dimension where the former foreigners found their cohesion at last became the foundation of the Pauline *Ecclesia.* The meaning of that word, in Paul's writings, evolves from "political assembly" to "ideal community."[8] Finally meaning the meeting of the community and the set of communities, the term brings together the meaning of "local Churches" and that of a universalist vocation. Then, as J.-R. Armogathe has demonstrated, *Ecclesia* conflicts with the Greek word *laos* (people). Of course, pagan ethnic groups and nations were already distinct from the people. What mattered to Paul, however, was a new opposition: the nations and the people refashioned so as to constitute an original entity: the Church. The well-known messianism of the Jews was changed into a messianism that includes all of humankind: the *Ecclesia* was to be the universality of the "people" beyond peoples, gathered in the isolation and solitude of the desert in order to receive the words of a new Alliance.[9]

The New Alliance

What was there in the ecclesiastical community thought up by Paul that could have sufficient appeal to weld the foreigners of that heterogeneous universe? What was there that made it seem more appealing than the official institutions of Greco-Roman jurisdiction, which allowed exiles a certain affluence? Or more appealing than the introversion of Eastern religions, which provided them with mystical evasions? One thing among others is striking in the Pauline conception of the *Ecclesia*. Beyond the material unease of foreigners, Paul spoke to their *psychic* distress and he proposed, instead of an insertion in a social set aimed at satisfying their needs, a journey between two dissociated but unified spheres that they could uncover in themselves: a journey between "body" and "soul," if you like—a "transubstantiation," as one would say later on. As for Paul, he spoke of the Body of Christ as Risen, that is, as having come from death to life. He identified Christ with the Church: their merging is erotic, nuptial. To that dyad he added a third equivalence, the Eucharist: to Commune with Him was to share in His Body.

Such a threefold equation between the risen Christly Body, the Church, and the Eucharist is not merely a theological subtlety. In that respect, to be sure, it must be credited with tackling gnosticism and transposing the Jewish image of an Adam created by God into a transcendence, making of the new man not a created being but a "life-giving spirit,"[10] always already occupied by the Other. But in order to understand the power of the ecclesiastical community one must ponder the unit made up of Church, risen Christ, and Eucharist. That unity enables one to recognize in the transition going from real to symbolic (and vice versa) a logic that takes hold of and soothes the foreigner's psychosis. Better than the legal solutions that were aimed at neurosis, or the Eastern immersion in the bosom of the mother goddess, the Pauline church assumed the foreigner's passion-inspired division, deeming his being torn apart between two worlds to be a split less between two *countries* than between two *psychic domains* within his own impossible unity. Foreigners could recover an identity only if they recognized themselves as dependant on a same heterogeneity that divides them within themselves, on a same wandering between flesh and spirit, life and death. Now is that not what is laid down in their personal experience by the Resurrection of Christ, *His* Transfiguration, and *our* Eucharist?

There will be a possible *we* thanks only to that splitting that all wanderers are urged to discover within themselves and in others, after they first recognized themselves in Christ. Paul is not only a politician. He is a psychologist, and if the institution he sets up is also political, its efficiency rests on the psychological intuition of its founder. It is based on the logic of desire in which one is led to identify with a splitting that henceforth is no longer dangerously set (like the foreigner's melancholy distress), but is, thanks to Christ, experienced as a transition toward a spiritual liberation starting from and within the concrete body. The splitting that has become a link is called Resurrection or Eucharist. The word that stages them becomes a *therapeutics of exile and distress*. At this point of victory over psychosis, the rediscovered community is not the arithmetical addition of units that are always more or less incompatible (Jew, Greek, barbarian, slave, free man, and so forth), it is a new community following upon a logic of subjectivity, and it is continuously undone and redone, its very transmutation being precisely the "new creation": "You have stripped off your old behavior with your old self, and you have put on a new self which will progress toward true knowledge the more it is renewed in the image of is creator; and in that image there is no room for distinction between Greek and Jew, between the circumcised and the uncircumcised, or between barbarian and Scythian, slave and free man. There is only Christ: he is everything and he is in everything."[11]

Echoing Jewish messianism, this emerging of the subject of desire, through the splitting that is generative of catastrophic anguish, was to be experienced as a *journey*. The experience involved is not that of a material tourism, but a *theory* in the sense of spiritual contemplation and mutation.

One notes with John the Evangelist another painful and proud reference to strangeness. It is Jesus himself who defines himself as a stranger on this earth: he does not "belong to the world," and it is only in going back to the Father that he regains "that glory I had with you."[12] Surrounded by hostility,[13] the Johannine community finds its home only in heaven ("There are many rooms in my Father's house").[14]

The foreignness of Jesus would thus have been the basis of Paul's cosmopolitan *Ecclesia*.

Civitas Peregrina

As the Jews, captive in Babylon, dreamed of returning to Jerusalem, Augustine, faithful to the Psalms, contrasted a City of oppression with a City of freedom. The adventure he advocated could not do without the two focuses: estrangement and reunion, want and desire—and never the one without the other. It was a pilgrimage: "We, too, must first become acquainted with our captivity, then with our liberation, we must know Babylon [. . .] and Jerusalem [. . .]. Those two cities taken in the literal sense are two real cities [. . .]. Those two cities were founded at a given time in the past in order to be the symbol of those two 'cities' that were there at the beginning and will remain until the end of time";[15] "Now, brethren, let us listen and sing; let us aspire to the city of which we are citizens [. . .]. Because of our desire we are already there, we have already cast our hope like an anchor on these shores [. . .]. *What I sing is over there and does not originate here:* for I sing not with my flesh but with my heart [. . .]. The citizens of Babylon hear the voice of the flesh, he who founded Jerusalem hears the song of our heart."[16]

Tearing oneself away from flesh to heart, from despondency to enthusiasm constituted a true transubstantiation, which Augustine precisely called a pilgrimage. Transforming the foreigner into a pilgrim did not, of course, solve his social and legal problems. But he found, in Christianity's *civitas peregrina*, both a psychic momentum and a community of mutual assistance that seemed like the only solution to his uprooting, with neither rejection nor national assimilation, the religious element preserving the ethnic origin, which it dominated at the same time through the availability of a psychic and social experience that is other: "People of God, Body of Christ, noble race of pilgrims [. . .] you are not from this world but from elsewhere . . ."[17] At the core of the transitional logic called for by the Eucharist, the Resurrection, and the Church, the difference between communities was not only recognized but demanded as the place that was necessary for the transformational event: "They are nevertheless distinguished by saintly desires that animate them."[18]

Differences in love are not to be erased but forgiven ("*Ordinate in me caritatem*" is what the *City of God* sings, like the bride in the Song of Songs). Differences between the worthy and the unworthy, the faithful and the unfaithful, the good and the bad—and even the heretics: those are not to be reconciled but brought together through the possibility of giving and the acceptance of what is given. The pilgrim gives and receives, his wandering having become gift is an enthusiasm: it is known as *caritas*.

Caritas

The alienation of the foreigner ceases within the universality of the love for the other. For if the believer in the Bible must love his neighbor as he loves himself, the neighbor, with Augustine, is explicitly "any man": "You are alone and your neighbors are many. Indeed, mark this well, your neighbor is not only your brother, your relative, your marriage relation. Any man's neighbor is any other man. One considers oneself close between father and son, son-in-law and father-in-law. But there is nothing closer to a man than another man."[19] The otherness coming from blood and ethnic or national origin was transformed into love for one's fellow man in the image of Christly love. Identification with the absolute subject, Christ, brings foreigners together: "Your soul is no longer yours alone, but it belongs to all your brethren whose souls also become yours, or rather whose souls and yours constitute just a single soul, that is to say, the unique soul of Christ."[20]

The *unlimited* aspect of *caritas* allows us better to understand why, going beyond ordinary feelings and drawing its inspiration from a superior model, it is not dependent upon reciprocity and cannot be understood in the realm of debt, dependency, and gratitude. *Caritas* is infinite, it grows, goes beyond itself and ourselves, thus welcoming foreigners who have become similar in their very distinction. "It is a debt that is not wiped out when paid. Even though one discharges it one still owes it and there is no specified time when one is no longer indebted. It is a treasure one does not lose when giving it back, but increase twofold, as it were, through the very return one makes. It is a feeling that grows in the heart of man as he gives evidence of it and increases all the more as more people are its object."[21]

Nonetheless, the absolute aspect of this religious bond soon collided with human needs as well as with the demands of States and soon afterward those of nations. The fate of the foreigner in the Middle Ages—and in many respects also today—depended on a subtle, sometimes brutal, play between *caritas* and the *political jurisdiction.*

Peregrine Hospitality

A spiritual reality, to be sure, pilgrimage just the same became a fully practical activity. Travelers would throng toward churches, monasteries, and holy places. Christianism was led to elaborate not only a hospitality code in order to receive them, but also a real lodging industry. The *peregrini propter Deum*, protected by authority of the Church, maintained a privileged status all through the Middle Ages and modern times. In other civilizations, too, pilgrims enjoy similar favors. Belonging to the Moslem *umma*, for instance, theoretically insures equality among political groups and special consideration for the pilgrim going to Mecca. Those who, likewise, commune at Lhasa, Varanasi, or some other holy place in Asia enjoy the same hospitality.

During the early centuries of Christianity, the welcome provided by individuals was not sufficient, inns *(tabernae)* were useful but disreputable. Next to *hospitia*—the hotels of the time—Basil of Caesarea thought of instituting shelters for pilgrims and the first Nicene council (325) demanded that every town have its *hospitia* or its *xenodochia*. Thus did the *xenon* or *xenodochium* become the place of assistance specially planned for the support of the poor but above all of the foreigners. *Xenodochia* were built by the entrance to convents or close to churches. Bishops, on account of their hierarchical responsibilities, and monks, naturally, felt a calling for hospitality, but special stewards were entrusted with the duty to handle the heavy and complex maintenance of the *xenodochia*. Those bachelors whose responsibility was to accommodate foreigners were considered the holiest of priests. But laymen, equally generous in hospitality, emulated their initiative by founding *diversoria peregrinorum*, or overdid it like the magistrates of Oxyrhynchus, along the Nile, who sent men to the gates of the city to intercept foreigners and offer them the necessary care according to the principles of Christian hospitality. John Chrysostom, Ambrose, bishop of Milan, and others distinguished themselves in the practice of that hospitality whose exercise they preach. "One knows more than enough," John Chrysostom wrote, "that there is a common house of the Church known as *xenodochium*. But one should act on one's own, go sit at the gates of the town, and spontaneously welcome the newcomers. On the contrary, one relies on the resources of the Church."[22]

Nevertheless, such generosity had its limits: it was meant solely for Christians. For the Christian, in short, the foreigner was not excluded if he was a Christian, but the non-Christian is a foreigner Christian hospitality cared little about. The practice of "letters" illustrates that limitation in a manner both under-standable and grotesque. As a foreigner, I must attest that I am a Christian, for the right to hospitality is mine only if I can show a Christian passport. The use of such passports, which goes back to apostolic times, became generalized in the fourth century, per-haps because of an upsurge in the struggles against heretics. They were called *litterae communicatoriae* or *literae formatae*, and *epistolae* for ordinary laymen. With the prevalence of mistrust, the bishop ended up brushing priests aside and taking upon himself alone the right to issue such letters.[23]

Here one reaches the borderlines—which, as can be imagined, may become constricting and abusive—of religious hospitality. A means of proselytism, or even of pressure, such hospitality when all is said and done forced the pilgrim to be a pilgrim of Christ, and forced every wandering person to become a Christian. Dogmatism raises its head in the unfolding of that universalism, which was real nevertheless and was able to go beyond the political particularisms of antiquity. But as soon as it reached its golden age in the fourth and fifth centuries, and while displaying that breadth of mind that endowed it with its early seduction and strength, Christian cosmopolitism bore in its womb the ostracism that excluded the other belief and ended up with the Inquisition.

Moreover, within feudal society, the lord—who maintained his independence from divine matters and ruled on the rights of men here below—had the final say in deciding the fate of the foreigner. One was an *aubain* [resident alien], hence a foreigner, when he was not born on the lord's land. It was possible, under certain conditions, to accede to the lord's unity; this shows indeed that the *foreigner's being* was decided by considering not Chris-tian universality but one's belonging to the lord's estate, that is, in the final analysis, the hereditary belonging to an economic and legal set. Consequently the Middle Ages experienced two atti-tudes where foreigners were concerned: one, Christian, with its advantages and abuses, now protective, then persecutive; and the other, political, which was modified along with the evolution of feudalism toward a centralized feudal State, and which submitted the foreigner to economic demands according to the views of the local political powers (either, "the foreigner is in excess," or, "we need the foreigner").

The Late Empire: Integrating the Peregrines

Thus the notion of foreigner in the sense of "peregrine" became blurred in the Late Empire. Beginning with the moment when "Rome no longer was in Rome," one grants more and more the right to be established in the city to a great majority of inhabitants who came from elsewhere. "Citizens and peregrines are welded in a common obeisance to the ruler."[24] The assimilation of peregrines into the Republic, but especially into the Roman Empire, has often been compared with the integration of peoples into the French Republic, an Empire between 1795 and 1814: through the process of annexation France almost immediately imposed the French law upon most of the vanquished.

The word "peregrine," which lost its legal meaning to acquire a mystical drift,[25] finally refers to the traveler—certainly as a consequence of the thrust of the Germanic people during the fourth and fifth centuries and their gradual settling in. *Peregrinus,* as early as the mid-fourth century, no longer contrasted with *civis romanus* but with *civis* and referred to one coming from another province or city, Thus in the Constitution of Valentinian I in 364 that word referre not to the foreigner but to a person from the provinces. The notion of foreigner being, as has been pointed out, antithetic to that of *civitas,* when the City was replaced with the Empire "the concept of peregrine lost its meaning."[26] Nonetheless, foreignness persisted during the Late Empire but under the guise of the barbarian and the heretic.

The barbarians of the fourth and fifth centuries became integrated into the Empire, which welcomed them and granted them various statutes, without for all that feeling threatened by the "barbarian fury" that would later cause it to break up. Just the same, the discrimination in legal statutes between *Romani* and *Barbari* indicates an evolution in the way in which foreigners were confronted. Considered useful because they were good soldiers and good plowmen on abandoned land, barbarians were either *deditices*—defeated people forcefully taken to Gaul, Italy, or the East, having an uncertain legal status, but subjected to the tax on peregrines—or *feoderati*, whose essential obligation was to fulfill their military service, who enjoyed tax exemption and saw their status evolve toward hospitality, "distinct but equal to the Romans." The *laeti* seem to fit in between those two; they were perhaps freed barbarian prisoners. The *gentiles* (or *gentes*) were considered inferior to the *laeti*,[27] but they were granted concessions along the borders "in exchange for military service and the upkeep of the *limes*" [fortified frontiers]. During the fourth and fifth centuries barbarians earned the right to accede to military and civilian offices, thus circumventing the principle— one that seems to go without saying everywhere and up to the present time—banning the foreigner from any public office. As the army was in large part made up of barbarians, these often became military leaders—auxiliaries but also generals, even reaching, according to circumstance, the rank of dictator. Constantine and Julian promoted barbarians to public offices, and there are cases when well-known barbarian leaders became, like Dagalaiph, *magister equitum;* the Frank Merobaud, who assumed the regency between Valentinian I and Valentinian II, became consul and king of the Franks; also notable are the names Bauto, Arbogast, Alaric, but especially Stilicho, who became dictator, and Athaulf, who would have liked to "rehabilitate the Roman name through Gothic might." This practice has been compared with other appointments of foreign leaders, which were too rare not to be emphasized: Islam calling on Christians or Jews before the Crusades; Chinese emperors naming foreigners to public offices; medieval India integrating its *para-disi* ("men from another land") . . .

The ambiguity of this near-assimilation of barbarians is never-theless revealed in the case of mixed marriages, which are, about 370, forbidden in the strongest terms in the Constitution of Valentinian I. Prudentius, however, deems that they are common at the beginning of the fifth century.

Such a change in the status of foreigners, which seems to have resulted in an interpenetration of populations, found its accom-plished expression in the fourth century in the notion of *Ro-mania*. Witness to the fragile balance between Romans and those who were assimilated, such a notion refers to a civilization that is often identified with the Roman Church and conflicting, by its very nature, with the barbarians outside as it did with the heretics inside. That being the case, one understands that the concern to protect themselves became, for the Romans, a theological rule: there was a strong mistrust of pagans. The Jew was deemed a foreigner, but he remained under the protection of the Roman law, except in cases of proselytism. Penal steps, however, were taken against heretics, especially after Gratian and Theodosius imposed Roman Catholicism on the whole Empire. The antiher-etic legislative activity, which remained intense up to the begin-ning of the fifth century, transformed heretics into foreigners in their own country: they could serve neither in the administration or in the army; they had neither the right to bear witness nor to inherit; they were sometimes forbidden to engage in any com-mercial transaction.

Whereas faith was initially a means of transcending the politi-cal differences that afflicted foreigners, it eventually turned out that dissidence within the faith was perceived as a political threat against this new, certainly fragile unit, which was no longer the polis but the empire—this civilization resting solely on the unity of the new religion. Religious transcendency was not absolute: it was, from the start, subjected to the political interests with which one religion identifies as against the others. One foreigner drives out the other.

The Elusive Foreigner in the Middle Ages

The *aubain, alibi natus,* was someone born in another seigniory.[28] Having left his native land he has settled in another, without for that matter making an oath of fealty to the new lord. Nevertheless, the flexibility of feudal society determines the imprecision of the *aubain's* status. If the social group he came into —even if it were that of a very small seigniory—turned out to be closely knit and intolerant, the newcomer from the neighboring village was to be considered an *aubain.* On the contrary, if the lord's power was well established over his land, one peasant's moving from one area to another did not turn him into a foreigner, for the lord was in a position to guarantee his origin.[29]

One has laid considerable emphasis on the *aubain's* precarious status: burdened with heavy taxes, he was mainly forbidden to marry outside the seigniory or without the lord's permission, and could not bequeath his property. The marriage restriction was gradually changed into a tax payment, which in France disappeared in the sixteenth century.[30] Now, since those interdictions were similar to those affecting the serf, one came to the conclusion that the *aubain* was a serf. Nonetheless, for the Carolingian world, the *aubain* is a free man;[31] thus, a charter granted by Louis the Pious forbids to levy taxes on free men, *aubains* among others, living on the domain of Notre Dame of Paris (*"neque de aliis liberis hominibus vel incolis quae rustici albani appelantur"*). The fact remains that beginning with the thirteenth century, when servitude became generalized, the *aubain* who had not made his oath would fall into serfdom within "a year and a day," unless, of course, the foreigner involved was a clerk or a nobleman. The *aubain* became *homo de corpore regis,* serf to the king, but this does not necessarily imply that the category of serfs absorbed the *aubains,* since in the thirteenth, fourteenth, and fifteenth centuries a special legal status is reserved for the "foreign man."[32]

Under such conditions, what did the *oath* mean? Such a "rule of feudal administration" obliged everyone to be attached to a seigniory, lacking which one's body and possessions were fully exploitable by the lord of the land where one had settled. The oath varies. What has often been called an oath of bourgeoisie was a recognition of freedom; the oath of serfdom became widespread toward the thirteenth century. Actually, beginning at that time, the *aubain* fell into servitude if he did not obtain any protection. Some lands led to servitude and the *aubains* who settled on them lost the possibility of transmitting their possessions to their sons if it could be shown—as was the case in some lawsuits—that the father, although born free, had made no oath. The inheritance then fell to the king in accordance with the rules of mortmain.

Let us also note that the distinction between visiting and settled foreigner remained. As early as the twelfth century, canon law distinguished the *peregrini*—visiting foreigners—from the *advenae*, those who were almost domiciled in the diocese or the parish, since they resided there for the better part of the year. Shifting from one category to the other took about six months, while the delay was one month in some Greek city-states.

Nevertheless, the complexity of hierarchical bonds and the diversification of powers in feudal society became unified and centralized as centuries went by. The king gradually became the sole lord, and the rights of *aubains* were affected: jurists claimed the benefit of servitude for the king in case the lord concerned had neglected to do so;[33] later, homage to the king became mandatory.[34] The kingly offensive to take over the *aubains* was intensified toward the end of the thirteenth century, going through compromises with the feudal lords (Philip IV The Fair) or surrenders (Louis X before the noblemen of Normandy, Burgundy, Champagne, and others). But as early as the fourteenth century the king's counts asserted themselves. As a consequence, the notion of *foreigner* was no longer conceived in relation to the lord and his land but in relation to the kingdom. The *aubain* was no longer one liable to servitude but the one whose inheritance, being in abeyance or in escheat (no inheritable relatives), falls back to the king but only on this account. Only the inability to bequeath remains, but the *aubain* is no longer a foreigner in the kingdom. The report written for queen Jeanne then distinguished between strays (foreign to the kingdom) and *aubains* (foreign to the seigniory).[35]

The French Revolution abolished "for ever" the *droit d'au-baine* (law of August 6, 1790), but the step remained ineffective, for reciprocal action on the part of other countries was lacking; it was only in the nineteenth century that international agreements —already made in the sixteenth—were brought into harmony and the *droit d'aubaine* was done away with.

5   By What Right Are You a Foreigner?

At this stage of our journey through the historic images of the foreigner, we might try to bring out an overall legal status of foreigners throughout history and to sketch out a comparison with the present situation.

Jus Soli, Jus Sanguinis

Who is a foreigner?

The one who does not belong to the group, who is not *"one of them,"* the *other*.

The foreigner, as it has often been noted, can only be defined in negative fashion.

Negative with respect to what? The other of what group?

If one goes back through time and social structures, the foreigner is the other of the family, the clan, the tribe. At first, he blends with the enemy. External to my religion, too, he could have been the heathen, the heretic. Not having made an oath of fealty to my lord, he was born on another land, foreign to the kingdom or the empire.

The foreigner was defined mainly according to two legal systems: *jus soli* and *jus sanguinis,* the law according to soil and the law according to blood. Are then considered to belong to the same group those who were born on the same soil (a system that is still maintained by U.S. law, which grants American citizenship to any child born on U.S. soil); or else the children born of native parents (in this case patrilinear and matrilinear systems are in conflict, according to this or that civilization, when granting the right of membership). With the establishment of nation-states we come to the only modern, acceptable, and clear definition of foreignness: the foreigner is the one who does not belong to the state in which we are, the one who does not have the same nationality.

If the foreigner concentrates upon himself the fascination and the repulsion that otherness gives rise to, any simple difference does not, however, endow one with the attributes of foreignness. Differences involving sex, age, profession, or religion may converge on the state of foreignness, support it or add to it: they are not one and the same. The group to which the foreigner does not belong has to be a social group structured about a given kind of political power. The foreigner is at once identified as beneficial or harmful to that social group and its power and, on that account, he is to be assimilated or rejected. Either *rechtlos*—without a single right—or enjoying certain rights that the political power from which he is excluded is willing to grant to him, the foreigner is thought of in terms of political power and legal rights. Such a condition, which, in spite of its variations, has never been belied throughout the course of history, may be observed in all its purity today.

Here one comes up against a paradox. If political regulations or legislation generally speaking define the manner in which we posit, modify, and eventually improve the status of foreigners, they also make up a vicious circle, for it is precisely with respect to laws that foreigners *exist*. Indeed, without a social group structured about a power base and provided with legislation, that externality represented by the foreigner and most often experienced as unfavorable or at least problematical would simply not exist. Consequently one notices that it has been the lot of philosophical (Greek and Latin Stoicisms with their cosmopolitanism) and religious (Proto Christianism) movements, going beyond the political definition of man, to grant foreigners rights that are equal to those of citizens; these rights, however, may be enjoyed only within the city of the beyond, in the bosom of a spiritual city. Such an absolute solution to the discomforts of foreignness proposed by some religions clashes, as one knows only too well, with their own dogmatism, and lo and behold the fanatics point to a new set of foreigners, those who do not share in their faith, for new exclusions or persecutions. Political jurisdiction then appears a safeguard, until its own machinery jams, at a given moment, under the pressure of such and such a social group or political power. One will then call upon moral or religious cosmopolitanism, and the rights of man will attempt to preserve the few rights that citizens have deemed appropriate to grant non-citizens. Such checks and balances are the best that democracies have found in order to face foreigners, who have the fearsome privilege of causing a State to confront an other (other State, but also out-State, non-State . . .), and, even more so, political reason to confront moral reason.

Man or Citizen

The rights of man *or* the rights of the citizen?

That conflict, the genealogy but also the deterioration of which Hannah Arendt has delineated—the one that gave rise to totalitarianism (see chapter 7 below)—shows up distinctly in the approach to the "problem of foreigners" in modern societies. The difficulty engendered by the matter of foreigners would be completely contained in the deadlock caused by the distinction that sets the *citizen* apart from the *man*: is it not true that, in order to found the rights that are specific to the men of a civilization or a nation—even the most reasonable and the most consciously democratic—one has to withdraw such rights from those that are not citizens, that is, other men? The process means—and this is its extreme inference—that one can be more or less a man to the extent that one is more or less a citizen, that he who is not a citizen is not fully a man. Between the man and the citizen there is a scar: the foreigner. Is he fully a man if he is not a citizen? Not enjoying the rights of citizenship, does he possess his rights of man? If, consciously, one grants foreigners all the rights of man, what is actually left of such rights when one takes away from them the rights of the citizen?

Expressing the modern problem of foreigners in such deliberately paroxistic terms does not necessarily presuppose an anarchistic claim, libertarian or "leftist." This simply points out that, from a legal standpoint, the problem of foreigners follows from a classical logic, that of the political group and its peak, the nation-state. A logic that, amenable to improvement (democracies) or degeneration (totalitarianism), acknowledges its being based on certain exclusions and, consequently, surrounds itself with other structures—moral and religious, whose absolutist aspirations it nonetheless tempers—in order precisely to confront what it has set aside, in this case the problem of foreigners and its more egalitarian settling.

In today's circumstances of unprecedented intermixing of foreigners on earth, two extreme solutions are taking shape. Either we are heading toward global united states of all former nation-states: a process that could be contemplated in the long run and that the economic, scientific, and media-based development allows one to assume. Or else the humanistic cosmopolitism shows itself to be utopic, and particularistic aspirations force one to believe that small political sets are the optimal structures to insure the survival of humanity.

In the first hypothesis, citizenship is called upon to integrate the rights of man to the fullest extent and be dissolved in them, for if they assimilated the ex-foreigners the nationals would necessarily lose many features and privileges that defined them as such. Other differences would undoubtedly take shape, giving rise to the multinational kaleidoscope of the global united states: sexual, professional, religious, and other differences.

On the contrary, if the nation-states were still to survive a long time, as the fierce preservation of their own interests seems to indicate presently, the unbalance between the rights of man and the rights of the citizen would produce a more or less subtle or brutal equilibrium, similar to what can be observed in France according to political situations. It would then become necessary to institute a statute for foreigners, to be protected from abuses on both sides and to specify the rights and obligations of all concerned. Such a statute would have to be temporary, progressive, and adapt itself to changes in social needs and attitudes.

Without Political Rights

Whatever differences there might be between one country and another, it is possible to generalize in the following manner the rights of which foreigners are deprived in contemporary democracies in contrast with those that citizens enjoy.

First, the foreigner is excluded from *public service* in all periods and in all countries, barring a few exceptions. In France, the naturalized ex-foreigner could, until recently, accede to public service only after five years.[1] For *mixed marriages*, which come under *jus connubii*, there have been various solutions in the past, the economic necessities of a political group weighing diversely toward exogamy or endogamy. If some religions, such as Islam, proved very strict in this matter (a Moslem woman cannot marry a man who is not a Moslem, a Moslem man may acquire a non-Moslem woman as an object), contemporary Western countries do not, in principle, raise actual obstacles to mixed marriages, they merely lay down formal restrictions.

The right to own *real estate* is variously handled but generally denied non-natives. In Athens, *metics* could not own real estate while in Rome *peregrini* could, with some restrictions and differences in comparison with natives. The *aubain* in France was able to own real estate since the end of the Middle Ages; in the cities, on the other hand, the bourgeois put obstacles in the path of their purchase by foreigners. Presently, countries that have adopted the Code Napoleon make no objection to such ownership.

The *right of inheritance* presents other complex problems concerning the foreigner. Passive inheritance: what is to be done with the estate of someone who dies in a foreign country? Active inheritance: is it possible for a foreigner to inherit the estate of a native? The *droit d'aubaine* is well-known in this respect: it authorized the lord, and the king after the fourteenth and fifteenth centuries, to claim the property of an *aubain*, whether he had heirs or not.

The right of *non arrestando* is seldom granted to foreigners who, unlike natives, may be seized before judgment is rendered; access to courts is allowed to them only if securities are given (various guarantees and assurances). The testimony of a foreigner, sometimes denied, is of lesser weight when admitted.

While it is possible to sum up in such fashion the major, nearly universal penalties that foreigners incur, one has to note that essential variations remain between one country and another, one period and another, without one's being able to single out specific social structures that might determine this or that relation to foreigners. Nonetheless, one has been able to point out that "individualistic civilizations,"[2] among which the Western civilization of the nineteenth and twentieth centuries, show themselves to be more sympathetic to foreigners. Thus, in France today, foreigners enjoy a *social protection* equal to that of the French. Article 7 of the Civil Code, however (the text is that of the law of June 26, 1889), is of fundamental importance to foreigners: "The exercise of civil rights is independent of the exercise of political rights; the latter are acquired and preserved in accordance with constitutional and election laws." In practice, this means that the foreigner and the citizen come closer with respect to their civil rights (which corresponds roughly to personal law) but remain clearly differentiated with respect to political rights. Thus article 11 of the Civil Code pertains explicitly to civil rights alone and not to political rights: "The foreigner shall enjoy in France the same civil rights as have or will have been granted to Frenchmen by the laws of the nation to which that foreigner belongs."

To conclude, one sees that the ethics of Christianity and the Rights of Man, strengthened by the economic necessities of the contemporary world, grants to the foreigner those rights that are granted to all men by the contemporary moral consensus. Nevertheless, there remains the thorny problem of denying him political rights, particularly the right to vote. In this conflict, which holds no easy solution, the arguments on both sides are well known. "Foreigners eventually remain loyal to their country of origin and can be harmful to our national independence" is the contention of some; "Foreigners share in the building of our economic independence and consequently should enjoy the political rights that endow them with the power of decision" is what others answer.

A Second-Rate Right?

No matter what side one is led to take in this difficult question, one will have to recognize that in the course of time a number of rights that might be said to belong to the political domain, such as the right of professional association, have been granted foreigners. The fact nevertheless remains that the denial of the right to vote actually excludes foreigners from *any decision*—political or legal—that might be taken with respect to them, be it favorable or unfavorable. As Danièle Lochak notes, the foreigner is thus reduced to being a passive *object*.[3] Foreigners do not vote and participate neither in the State, nor in Parliament, nor in government, they are "alienated with respect to the legal realm —as they are with respect to the political realm and the whole of the institutions of the society in which they live" (p. 216).

One could add to that observation that the foreigner's status implies a denial of "subjective right": "To enter the territory of the welcoming country, to maintain a residence there, to work there, sometimes even to speak out [. . .] the foreigner must ask

a permission from the appropriate authorities" (p. 208). Moreover, such permissions and other regulations pertaining to subjective rights stem from the opinion such and such a government
has arrived at concerning the country's economic and political
interest, and this endows the objective rights granted to foreigners with a very peculiar legal status. Indeed, as jurisprudence is
truly never absolutely independent of politics—even if, ideally,
it should be—one witnesses, in the case of foreigners, an "in-
strumentalization of the law" (p. 211). Contradictory and muddled, as it reflects the uncertainties of the political leadership and
is nevertheless subordinate to its objectives, fluctuating as they
may be.

Finally, the power given to the administration to assess, to
interpret, or even to modify through *regulations* and *decrees* the
current legislation, leads to changing the rights of foreigners into
"second-rate rights" (p. 216). In fact, the freedom allowed to the
administration to take steps "that it deems appropriate, depend-
ing on considerations the pertinence of which it alone assesses"
(p. 217), can lead to an arbitrary exercise of administrative power
with respect to foreigners.

One should also note, along with Danièle Lochak, that foreigners find themselves excluded from the "symbolic effects of the
law": abstract judicial symbolism's investment in the subjective
imagination—with its consequence that, in the mind of any
citizen, the law possesses a "sacred" hence affective value, more
real than realistic—no longer holds with foreigners. They do not
participate in the legal process that leads to the adoption of laws.
Furthermore, the legal existence of the foreigner is administered
not by a law but by the least dignified forms of regulation,
executive provisions being substituted for parliamentary legislation (p. 214).

To the welcomers' symbolic and legal holding back of the
foreigner, the latter respond with a tendency not to accept the
legislation in force. This is expressed not only through various
infringements of the law (lack of a residence permit, several

breaches of the labor laws, and so forth), often caused by material constraints (the foreigner who cannot return to his country must, come what may, survive in the welcoming country), but also by a refusal—often basic with contemporary foreigners—to accept the symbolics of the law, as well as the culture and civilization of the welcoming country. Cultural values, symbolic but also legal, have remained over there, in the other country, and, when one does not forget them, one still adheres to them—either by reconstituting on the spot the authorities (religious ones, for instance) of the old country; or by submitting to them silently, and the more easily as those original authorities are not there to demand obedience. Such an attitude does not seem to be simply a spontaneous response to the legal, cultural, and psychological discrimination undergone by the foreigner: "One does not give me a place, therefore I shall keep my place." Within the crowd of foreigners—on the increase in the contemporary world—who either do not wish or cannot either become integrated here or return where they came from, a new form of individualism develops: "I belong to nothing, to no law, I circumvent the law, I myself make the law." This stance on the part of the foreigner certainly arouses the conscious commination of the natives; just the same it attracts the unconscious sympathy of contemporary subjects—unbalanced, wanting everything, dedicated to the absolute, and insatiable wanderers.

In that sense, the foreigner is a "symptom" (Danièle Lochak): psychologically he signifies the difficulty we have of living as an *other* and with others; politically, he underscores the limits of nation-states and of the national political conscience that characterizes them and that we have all deeply interiorized to the point of considering it normal that there are foreigners, that is, people who do not have the same rights as we do.

Thinking the Commonplace

The political and legal response inevitably borders on the philosophical conceptions the contemporary world has of the foreigner when it is not inspired by them. Let us then pursue our journey by approaching a few key moments in the history of contemporary thought that have been nourished by the confrontation of national man with the diversity of men.

People will object, however, that when an overflow of immigrant workers humiliates French suburbs, when the odor of North African barbecues offends noses that are used to other festivities, and the number of young colored delinquents leads some to identify criminality with foreignness—there is no point in poring over the archives of thought and art in order to find the answers to a problem that is, when all is said and done, very practical, one might even say commonplace.

And yet, do we have any other recourse against the commonplace and its brutality except to take our distance by plunging into it—but in our minds—confronting it—but indirectly? Facing the problem of the foreigner, the discourses, difficulties, or even the deadlocks of our predecessors do not only make up a history; they constitute a cultural distance that is to be preserved and developed, a distance on the basis of which one might temper and modify the simplistic attitudes of rejection or indifference, as well as the arbitrary or utilitarian decisions that today regulate relationships between foreigners. The more so as we are all in the process of becoming foreigners in a universe that is being widened more than ever, that is more than ever heterogeneous beneath its apparent scientific and media-inspired unity.

6 The Renaissance, "so Shapeless and Diverse in Composition". . .

Dante the Exile: From "Salty Taste" to "Golden Mirror"

At the threshold of the modern era there lived an exile, Dante (1265–1321). The author of *The Divine Comedy* wrote his *entire text* in exile, after the war between the Guelphs and the Ghibellines compelled him to leave his native Florence. The Guelphs, loyal to the Pope's authority, were already long opposed to the Ghibellines who supported the emperors' political primacy, and the conflict increasingly took on the shape of hostilities between the bourgeoisie and the nobility. At the time of Dante's birth, the power shifted over the Guelphs, and the Ghibellines were conclusively defeated. The Guelphs themselves, however, became divided into Whites and Blacks, with Dante taking the side of the Whites. In the Councils of the Republic he represented the moderate, anti-expansionist tendency, devoted to Florentine national independence (the Whites), against those whose aim was to liberate trade by eliminating the shackles comprised of the small Tuscan States (the Blacks). The nobility having lost the right to participate in public affairs, Dante, who was born to the lesser nobility, enrolled in the professional corporation of the *arts*, which included doctors, apothecaries, librarians, and poets, and this restored the possibility of his participating in political life. In 1301 he left for Rome on a mission to see Pope Boniface VIII, who favored the Blacks, in order to plead the cause of the

Whites. In the meantime the Blacks seized Florence, banished Dante from the city, and condemned him to be burnt at the stake should he return to his native land. Up to the time of his death in Ravenna Dante would be indignant with the intrigues of Boniface VIII, whom he held responsible for his exile, and his status as a refugee would not cease affecting his thought.

Thus, among the many keys that enable one to read his complex work, exile is not the lesser one. One notes how favored Ulysses is in that work, for although in Inferno, where, being a pagan, he must reside, he is worthy of being praised for his "virtue and knowledge"—and the poem conjures up the "haughty law," the divine law that, nevertheless, should apply neither to the Inferno nor to Ulysses. Unless, precisely, Dante admired himself in the person of that ancient wanderer and adopted as his own the "pure, lofty ideals" of the travelers whose only homeland was an ethics.

Moreover, it is at the heart of Paradise that the exile's destiny is presented. Threats and bitterness do not prevent the lot of foreignness, located in the paradisiacal heavens, from asserting itself as the condition for the journey toward divine love, whose light enraptures the end of *The Divine Comedy*:

> *You will leave everything loved most dearly;*
> *and this is the arrow*
> *that the bow of exile shoots first.*
> *You will learn how salty the bread tastes*
> *in others' houses, and how hard*
> *is the going up and down of others' stairs.*
> *And what will weigh heaviest upon you*
> *will be the evil and senseless company*
> *into which you will fall in this valley,*
> *A company which, ungrateful, mad, and impious,*
> *will turn against you, but soon they,*
> *not you, will blush for it.*
> *Their ways will give proof of their brutishness*
> *so that it will be well for you*
> *to have made a party by yourself.*

[. . .]
I perceive clearly, Father, how Time
rushes toward me to give the blow
that falls heaviest on him who is most heedless.
Therefore I must arm myself with foresight,
so that if the dearest place is taken from me
I may not lose others through my verses.
Down in the world eternally bitter
and on the mountain from whose fair summit
I was lifted by my lady's eyes,
And afterward in heaven from star to star,
I have learned things which, if I relate them,
will have for many a bitter taste.
And if I am a timid friend of Truth,
I fear to lose life among those
who will call this time "ancient."
The light in which the treasure smiled
that I had found there flashed
like a golden mirror in the sunlight.[1]

Finally, today's foreigner easily imagines that this consummate poem, which embraces the whole of the universe—ranging from individual passions to political conflicts, from the quiverings of the landscape to the mysteries of theology, from the pains of hell to the ecstacies illuminated by Beatrice—is an extraordinary device, for Dante, for endowing himself with a *universe* at the very moment when his *own and proper place* is lacking. The deprival of an anchorage seems, with Dante, to have liberated the entire imagination, so that, owing nothing to any tribe, but supported by a Christian universalism that he embraces with the fullness of his faith, he fashions in the shape of a poem the most complex universe possible, infinity itself molded into a world.

His political writings, particularly *On Monarchy* (1311), express in more prosaic terms Dante's universalism. While its major objective was to support the emperor against the papacy, it is characterized by assertions drawn from Christian and Stoic ethics, from Averroes as well as Aquinas, and, while extolling the virtues of monarchy, it heralds the ideal of a human universality

—an ideal that, with individualism, founded the Renaissance: "There is thus a certain process characteristic of all men together, with the aim of which, I say, the whole of mankind becomes organized in such a large multitude; a process that is amenable neither to man alone, nor to the family alone, nor the village, nor the city, nor the kingdom taken separately from the others. And the nature of the process will be obvious if it appears as the end set forth for the power of mankind as a whole [. . .] A multitude must prevail in mankind through which all of that power will be carried out [. . .] The proper task of mankind taken as a whole is constantly to carry out all the possible power of its intellect."[2]

So, from *The Banquet* up to *The Divine Comedy* and including *On Monarchy*, Dante shows himself to be a monarchist. Surrounded by bourgeois and republican nationalists, this Christian mystic is led, against the new political wave, to wish for another universality—a Catholic one. Attainable in peaceful fashion, it is nevertheless centered not in the papacy but in the uniqueness of the monarch, a man who is the intermediary between divine unity and the world here below and whose Christian soul achieves the immanence of the religious within the political. Lay power and religious power are separate but the Empire, in *The Divine Comedy*, rises to the task of spiritually reforming the Church and insuring the salvation of the entire universe (thus it is the imperial eagle that proclaims the truth on predestination).[3] Superseded in time, the Empire, with Dante, is essential as the desire for a just, eternal City, beyond historical contingencies. The retrograde follower of the Empire, at the dawn of the Renaissance, appears, when all is said and done, as the visionary advocate of a universe of small communities harmonized within a spiritual design.[4] The exiled monarchist was a poet who sought salvation in the paradise of writing and the bliss of the Catholic "smile of the universe."

The Machiavellian State

Universalism salvaged from tradition, on the one hand, individualism characteristic of the new conquerors of techniques and territories on the other were to converge into this crucible of ideas that was to found the Renaissance State. Machiavelli (1469–1527) was its wily, cynical, or simply Janus-headed alchemist, who quickly abandoned virtues for the sake of the effectiveness of power. The *Discourses on Livy* (1513–1520) take the Roman republic as an example in order to show how the passions of private individuals can be repressed by the laws to which citizens submit, but also to denounce modern Italian States, which are just as much unaware of inner dynamics as of outer expansion and condemn themselves to factional struggles, banishments, and exiles. Far from being an internationalist, Machiavelli nevertheless suggested a balance of those relationships that one would today call *international law*, but without any concern for international justice and merely to insure the prosperous development of states.

On the other hand, if he recognized that virtue was the necessary recourse in the face of the corruption of political mores and that early Christianity as well as Roman religion guaranteed the ethics of the city, Machiavelli, condemning the corruption of the Church in his day, is particularly pessimistic concerning the Italian State, simply proposing, at times, the recourse to "extreme force." The democrats of the Enlightenment selected his *Discourses* and his republican utopia—addressed to the people and not to the princes—in order to contrast them with *The Prince* (1513); but all will see, in the two major works of the politician, the prophecy of the *nation-state* and of the *power-state*.

The contemporary idea of state control is a Machiavellian idea. Indeed, *The Prince* offers us—by means of naturalist metaphors, concepts in the form of an open chain of rings, and various sarcasms concerning the papacy—the portrait of the "new principality." This new ruler, lion and fox, frees his imagination in order to bypass the restraints of ethics, and Machiavelli pleads for a national unity, an "organicness" founded on the characteristics of the prince and of his fortune. While it is easy to contrast this treatise with the previous republican *Discourses*, to understand why the Huguenots rejected it and the Jesuits appreciated it, nevertheless one notes a certain unity of thought in the two works. The point is, finally, to reinforce the state: republican or princely, it owes it to itself to be organic, in other words strong, and this national state control, which is only minimally concerned with diplomacy and geopolitics, remains the precursor of the modern nation-states' ideology.

In fact, Machiavellism is nothing more than patriotism. This does not mean that *The Prince* is, as Rousseau claimed, one of "the great lessons for nations"; but it was in the name of a finally united and consolidated Italy, shielded from the lords' intrigues and the barabarians' assaults, that Machiavelli gives his advice, which lacks virtue only because it aims at effectiveness. Exiled from Florence (when the Medici abolished Savonarola's republic, for which Machiavelli had been a clerk in the chancery, and later a member of various diplomatic missions) and tortured, Machiavelli retired to the countryside; there, he did not, like Dante, dream of universal Christianism but of a powerful national state. Breaking off his thoughts on the Republic, he convinced himself that only a prince could establish such a nation-state, and he dedicated *The Prince* to Lorenzo II de' Medici: "The opportunity, then, for Italy at last to look on her deliverer, ought not to be allowed to pass away. With what love he would be received in all those Provinces which have suffered from the foreign inundation, with what thirst for vengeance, with what fixed fidelity, with what devotion, and what tears, no word of mine can declare."[5] The kernel of his remarks is an "exhortation to seize Italy and liberate it from the Barbarians." "*Fuori i Barbari!*" is what Machiavelli shouts in the name of Italian unity, persisting in his will to convince the Holy See (between 1513 and 1514) to build up a unified Italy around Rome and

Florence, against the mercantile, antidemocratic Venice, against Spain, the spoilsport of Christendom, for an alliance with France. A Machiavellian diplomacy is appended to nationalism. One understands that the author places action before ethics[6] and that he sets aside "international law" for the sake of the pragmatic necessity to occupy through strength and terror the conquered foreign territories.[7]

In a spirit that was far more positive and anthusiastic, the great humanists Guillaume Budé (*De l'institution des princes*, 1516) and Claude de Seyssel (*La Grand-Monarchie de France*, 1519) present their version of the new national state. Louis XII becomes the wished-for exemplar of the philosopher-prince capable of insuring the unity of a people. Jean Bodin (1529–1596) calls for giving dignity to the national language to counteract the exclusive use of Latin in schools, while Guillaume Budé (1467–1540) suggest, for the sake of national cultural health, the foundation of a trilingual college, a royal college that became the Collège de France (1530). The "pleasure" of Francis I (1494–1547) will do the rest: blending the Renaissance state with the power, less wily than elegant, of the enlightened prince. Open to Christianity and to its scientific and esthetic transformation, the French court became in this era a balance of Frenchness and cosmopolitanism that would remain one of the most prestigious traditions of the monarchy.

From Rabelais the Marvelous to the Marvels of the World by Way of Erasmus

"As we raised and emptied our glasses, good weather has been raised likewise," Pantagruel said during a marvelous feast on the island of Chaneph, that is to say the island of Hypocrisy and Intolerance. "Raising the weather": rising above the constraints of history that are accumulating around 1550, after the period of play and knowledge of the "substantial marrow" that was still possible before, toward 1530. "Raising the weather": taking advantage of the clearing weather to speed up the journey of that *Fourth Book* that Rabelais (1494–1553) wrote at the end of his life, between 1548 and 1552, and which leads us, beyond the picture of a voyage probably inspired by the model of Jacques Cartier (1494–1554), who discovered Canada, within the secret exhilaration of an inner quest for the strange in the bosom of the "secret garden." "Raising the weather": dreaming, imagining, pushing reality to the point of fantasy, for better and for worse.

The *Fourth Book* is a masked book that narrates the journey of Pantagruel's companions—Friar John, Panurge, and the others —to visit the Oracle of the Holy Bacbuc, located "near Cathay, in Upper India." Let there be no mistake about it: this expedition toward China, very much in keeping with the spirit of the times, is actually a journey toward myth, dream, ideal, wealth, and happiness, but passing by, in the same volume the strange world of excesses. Rabelais said so: he would not "take the ordinary Portuguese route," past the Cape of Good Hope, but took a circular course around the Pole Star "in a westerly direction." We read this as meaning that, neither Protestant nor Catholic but surely an evangelist like Erasmus, Rabelais was seeking another way. And if his conclusion leads to an Epicureanism that is both Christian and Erasmian,[8] which the themes of eating, drinking, and elevation-delight in time proceed to unfold, this land of plenty was reached by going through a strangeness that was indeed made up of marvels, but above all woven with excessiveness and obscurantism.

Allusions to religious excesses are obvious: Sneaks' Island, where King Lent rules, a stupid and sterile monster, "master of illness," is an indictment of bigotry; the Chitterlings, on Savage Island, display only too well some of the Protestant features in opposition to King Lent; the Papimaniacs and Popefigs are clear references to the papacy and its opponents, allowing one to see, on the other hand, that Pantagruelism means independence; the "scholars of Trebizond" give us an inkling of Rabelais's mistrust of occult sects; and so forth. Other strangenesses are added: the poorly matched "alliances" of affectation and snobbishness, upon which Rabelais pours jokes and obscenities, on Ennasin Island, the island of "noseless people"; that of the courts of law and their corruption (the land of Clerkship, inhabited by the Bumbailiffs); the monstrous spouting whale, ghostly being or windbag, more frightening than dangerous, an allegory of prejudice; the conceited dreamers who "live on wind," on the Island of Ruach—a "poet" who should be brought down to earth; and so forth. There is no lack of fantastic elements through excessive opulence and gratification: such is Medamothy, "or Nowhere Island," a land of fabulous wealth, a utopia stuffed with miraculous objects displayed at the time of the great fairs and worthy of the best-known merchants of Asia and Africa, a land of illusions where one merely believed one's eyes instead of judging; such is the Island of Cheli, "large, fertile, rich, and populous," on the occasion of which victuals and gluttony are appreciated—and mocked . . . ; and one should obviously not forget the island of the Gastrolaters and its absolute ruler, Messer Gaster; "all for the sake of the belly!" is what this "true master of all the arts" proclaims. Nor do the travelers, caught in the mesh of outlandishness, omit a certain foretaste of disquieting strangeness [uncanniness]: the Isles of Vacuum and Void—the abode of absurd deaths, symbols of our ephemeral destiny; the Storm—the risks attendant to a quest more inner than geographic; the Isles of the Macreons where, "violating the whole order of Nature," comets, meteorites, earthquakes, signal the death of an exceptional being —an allusion to the taste of the times for monsters and omens . . . and, to wrap things up, a finale that is not a finale—the *Fourth Book* is a journey without arrival, an infinite quest . . .[9]

Rabelais has only to transpose into the framework of a geographic investigation his notion of human strangeness, and at once the "secret garden" fills with marvels, absurdities, or monsters. Beyond the critical picture of the period, what is outlined here is, ahead of its time, a glance at Freud's *Unheimliche* [the uncanny]. And one is surprised to see that even the positive minds of the earth's conquerors appear to have taken the inner voyage as a truthful indication on the reality of the foreign people at the antipodes.

The *Fourth Book* actually takes up again an old and particularly fruitful tradition in the writings of the thirteenth- to sixteenth-century explorers, such as Marco Polo's accounts of the *Kingdoms and Marvels of the East*, Jourdan Cathala de Severac's *Mirabilia Descripta*, or *The Travels of Sir John Mandeville* in the fourteenth century. To the actual discoveries they had made, these explorers would add Western or Islamitic legends, even seeing the inhabitants of the new lands as fabulous birds, or as people "without buttocks or digestive system," or simply endowed with "gold, rubies, and an infinite amount of other wealth."[10] As for Rabelais, he strongly emphasized the extent to which those *mirabilia* had their source in our own world, in our dreams and political conflicts. Nevertheless, even later, the burgeoning ethnographic discourse had difficulty freeing itself from the phantasmal bent of the observers without falling into another, just as ethnocentrical, reduction that amounted to bringing down the foreigners' strangeness to the same universal logic that Western tradition had brought to the fore.[11] André Thévet and Jean de Léry have organized their dicourse on *other* peoples by freeing themselves—*but not without effort*—of that strangeness within ourselves that Rabelais exposes under veils and with humor. Ethnological discourse (see "Voyages, Cosmographies, Missions," below) rises up from those fantasies: one eventually perceived, not without difficulty, that other peoples do not correspond to our intimate strangenesses, but that the other is simply . . . other.

The "voyage" that has us meet strange foreigners remained nevertheless a privileged means for showing our individual flaws or the political weaknesses of our own countries. The grating humor of Jonathan Swift (1667–1745) haughtily illustrates such a literary genre: who has not been shaken and filled with wonder by Gulliver's encounter with the Lilliputians or those unpronounceable horses, the Houyhnhnms, that ruled over degraded humanoids, the Yahoos . . . ? Closer to our times, Edgar Allan Poe (1809–1849) or Henry James (1843–1916) have become the explorers of strange ghosts lurking within our absurd or commonplace frenzies. And one cannot leave out James Joyce (1882–1941), that peculiar Irishman, himself an exile, who gave the name of Ulysses the sailor to the strangest novel of our own times, roaming through a divided culture—Greek, Jewish, Christian—in a quest of his elusive singularity.

As for Rabelais, he was an inner cosmopolitan. The contemporary reader sees the water over which he sailed as an image of the course of a psychic investigation: blurred or odd, it was changed into a mysterious "Trink!" Would happiness arise from a reconciliation with our marvels and our monsters? "Raising the weather!" for later or never. Rabelais heralded Montaigne.

But he also displayed the comical, French version of the placid, somewhat despondent lucidity of Erasmus (1467–1536)—the laughing double of his dialogical universalism, made up of adages and precepts, but, as both were, open to all new ideas.

Erasmus, the evangelist who extolled free will against Luther's "will in serfdom" and even in the extreme *(ultima ratio)* wished for just wars (against the Turks, for instance) to unify Europe and the Christian Church, was equally able to write *The Praise of Folly* (1515) and *On the Purity of the Church* (1533). And his *Colloquia*, which he constantly reworked, gave expression to the strange aspects of his time: prostitutes, beggars, an ignorant priest and an intellectual woman, scoundrels and crooks of all kinds, old people and school children, clerics and laymen. Erasmus' universalism, which, in his writings and through his acts, *in fact* united a Europe shaken by religious wars, actually rested upon an amused recognition of the human comedy.

Erasmus and Rabelais: two complementary "cosmopolitans" . . .

Thomas More: A Strange Utopia

Nevertheless, elegant and ironical, written in meticulous, concise Latin, but in a steadfastly democratic or indeed communist spirit, bewildering on account of its ambiguities, Thomas More's *Utopia* (1515) towers above the times and still disturbs the contemporary reader. A friend of Erasmus, a convinced Catholic, the faithful Lord Chancelor of Henry VIII, who did not want to subject ethics to politics, and who for that very reason died on the scaffold, has left us with this true manifesto of a "Christian humanism" written against a background of sea journeys, geographic discoveries, and myths involving "good savages." Influenced by Plato's republic (*Laws*, IV, 321) as much as by the memory of the Happy Island of the Sun that the Greek Iambulus claimed to have visited south of Ceylon, this essay-romance by Thomas More was directly influenced by the voyages of Amerigo Vespucci (which took place between 1499 and 1504). The main character, Raphael Hythloday, born of More's imagination, was of the explorer's generation and it is while relating his own observations that he outlines the model for the utopian state: the Utopic State.

Thus, on the island of Utopia, meaning nowhere, which he supposedly visited, people abhor tyranny, share all wealth, abolish private property, work no more than six hours a day, skillfully administer social assistance and leisure, respect culture and religion. The human spirit naturally tends toward Christianity, even before having been given Revelation, for Raphael was the first to speak of Christ in Utopia. On the other hand, utopian cynicism does not fail to surprise us: resolving overpopulation by means of colonialism or even imperialism doubtlessly shows a lack of charity; the ascendency of the collectivity over the individual seems gruelling, the practice of war brutal; moralism and abusive planification foreshadow Orwell . . .

Was More suggesting that the futuristic romance becomes inverted into a tyrannical idealism, one that is ambitious and totalizing, totalitarian? Or is that a modern reading, a too modern one? Thomas More's message, ironical and complex, does not cease to question itself: is it a matter of carrying a generous project and its dead ends to their limits in order better to appreciate the political and moral difficulties peculiar to England and to Europe at the time? Utopia, in short, as a means and not as an end?

Let us note that a number of key words in the text are etymologically negative: the Achoriens are a people without a territory; Anyder is a river without water; the chief city, Amauratum, is a mirage; Adamus is a prince without a people; and Hythloday himself is one who "lets inventions shine." The purpose of this negative rhetoric is surely to indicate that we are dealing with a work of the imagination not a piece of reporting. But perhaps it also suggests that Raphael Hythloday, the man who abandons roots and homeland, boards the "ship of fools" when he loses his national, historic soil. Indeed, the first chapter, written after the second, portrays characters out of contemporary society who have nothing utopic about them (Peter Giles, Cardinal Morton, and More himself). Are we invited to navigate between national imperatives and universalist fantasies? Would ethics be a dream allowing one to escape from actual political distress but one that can also turn into a nightmare if one does not respect national, concrete political necessities? It is impossible to decide the meaning of an irony that indeed leads nowhere—unless it be to show the dead ends of all excesses and to throw light on Berdiaeff's observation (used by Aldous Huxley as the epigraph to his *Brave New World*, 1932): if all utopias seem attainable today, if modern life is about to achieve them, perhaps we should try to avoid them in order to recover a non-utopic society, less perfect and more free . . . But how can one be free without some sort of utopia, some sort of strangeness? Let us therefore be of nowhere, but without forgetting that we are somewhere . . .

Michel de Montaigne's Universal Self

> Authors communicate with the people by some spe-
> cial extrinsic mark; I am the first to do so by my
> entire being, as Michel de Montaigne, not as a
> grammarian or a poet or a jurist.
>
> Each man bears the entire form of man's estate.
> —*Essays*, Book 2, chapter 2

At a time when the great navigators open up the earth for mankind, which was already skeptical and just the same filled with wonder at the discovery of new civilizations, mentalities, languages, or races, the Renaissance was showing itself, on the one hand, to be nationalistic and individualistic, and on the other, cosmopolitan. The model for binding those two features together might well be the subtle uncertainty of Montaigne (1533–1592). Nothing indeed fastens his individuality exclusively to the Bordeaux Parliament, nor to the courts of Henry II, Francis II, or Henry III, any more than it did to the retinue of Henry of Navarre, who acceded to the French throne under the name of Henry IV. He was called a "dilettante"; but between Rome and the Reformation, this friend of Henry of Navarre remained a Catholic and preferred to die with the rites of the Church, faithful to his choice of a national religion—at the same time criticizing the king's politics in the name of a demanding concept of justice that did not hesitate to take on the very symbols of the nation. There may have been a civil war, strife between the Huguenots and the [Catholic] League, the Saint Bartholomew massacre, the plague, and so forth; Montaigne endured, went by, administered, but always anchored in a kind of strangeness that he perceived as slightly eccentric and that turned out to be less the "library" of his tower than the very presence of his self.

Indeed, Montaigne expressed for the first time this major fact that we each have our own self, worthy of interest—deficient and amusing, blurred and nevertheless substantial, to the extent of transcending contingencies through the mere desire to know ourselves: "If I study, I seek only the learning that treats of the knowledge of myself."[12] Thus oriented toward a region that must indeed be called "self-centered" *[moïque]*, and while remaining loyal to his judicial and political duties, Montaigne nevertheless displayed a new sort of man in his *Essays*. From friendship to speculation, including fondness for erudite, concise, and clear expression, the counselor in the Parliament of Bordeaux moves about within a universal gamut that could be called psychic or political, or both at the same time, but whose tight-wire performance lacks neither graceful flavor nor scathing moralism. There the individual can be understood in its universality—he could be neither a foreigner not a judge of foreigners,[13] except in brief, spicy details pertaining to food, clothing, or the beauty of those women he saw during his journey toward Italy or in that country, which *The Diary of Montaigne's Journey to Italy* offers as curious variations of our common condition.

"Constant Cheerfulness"

A weak and puny self, "so sluggish and so quiescent" as to move the author himself to pity and contempt: so be it. But his serene enjoyment, just the same, was the ultimate hallmark of wisdom.[14] Piecemeal, forgetful, devoted to his pleasure and "bent" rather than to the effort of "judgment," Montaigne, however, never ceased judging himself—stern, without leniency, but not without fondness for his weaknesses, overtly proud to discover that he was ruled by desire. To know such a rule of desire and to say it without embarrassment, that is the originality claimed by the *Essays* as they for the first time compelled one to accept a vision of the self beyond good and evil: "I stand up well under hard work; but I do so only if I go to it of my own will, and as much as my desire leads me to it [. . .] Otherwise, if I am not lured to it by some pleasure, and if I have any other guide than my own pure free will, I am good for nothing. [. . .] And all I needed was to enjoy pleasantly the good things that God in his liberality had placed in my hands."[15]

Nevertheless, it is on the *other* that the self relies for suste-
nance and trust: "Our mind moves only on faith, being bound
and constrained to the whim of others' fancies."[16] Inscribed at
once within the framework of the other's attention, when it is
not a well-tempered friendship whose apex, with La Boétie, is
well-known. Montaigne's self depended on the "fantastic" opinion of the other,[17] the self knows it is "other": "That other life
of mine that lies in the knowledge of my friends" (pp. 474–475);
"But we are, I know not how, double within ourselves" (p. 469);
"Myself now and myself a while ago are indeed two" (p. 736).
Consequently, aware of its splitting, the self perceives no certainty apart from its mobility and singularity. Instead of asserting, "I am dubious," it questions, "What do I know?" And
mindful of the particularity of each existent thing—name, object,
or person—it carries out a real escalation of the notion of difference: "He does not find so much difference between one animal
and another as he does between one man and another" (p. 189—
in reference to Plutarch). "There is more distance from a given
man to a given man than from a given man to a given animal"
(p. 189); "We are all patchwork, and so shapeless and diverse in
composition that each bit, each moment, plays its own game.
And there is as much difference between us and ourselves as
between us and others" (p. 244).

An affirmation of concord banning oddness and marginality
proves possible if, and only if, such an apology of universal
difference is asserted: "Any strangeness and peculiarity in our
conduct and ways is to be avoided as inimical to social intercourse, and unnatural" (p. 123).

Of Cannibals and Coaches

What followed, probably in the most natural way, was respect
for the seeming strangeness of others, at once included in the
universal naturalness of this enlarged, diversified, and tolerant
region of the self. So, when Montaigne in 1562 met Brazilian
natives who had come to Rouen,[18] he was at first dubious of our

ability to take in the immense world, no longer in the manner of the ancient philosophers but such as it offered itself to modern experience: "I had with me for a long time a man who had lived for ten or twelve years in that other world which has been discovered in our century, in the place where Villegaignon landed, and which he called Antarctic France. This discovery of a boundless country seems worthy of consideration. [. . .] I am afraid that we have eyes bigger than our stomachs, and more curiosity than capacity. We embrace everything, but we clasp only wind" (p. 150). Montaigne deems those "nations" to be close to "the laws of nature," "very little corrupted by ours;" innocent, pure, and simple—"a happy state of man" that reminds one of the Golden Age and foreshadows Rousseau—those foreign men know of "no contracts" (p. 153). They are unpolished, unlike ourselves, occasionally cannibalistic, nevertheless not lacking common sense in that very ritual, nor were they without poetic talent in their folklore; they were, alas, not inclined to small talk— Montaigne cannot help observing them, but he hesitates to call them "barbarians": "So we may well call these people barbarians, in respect to the rules of reason, but not in respect to ourselves, who surpass them in every kind of barbarity" (p.156).[19]

Moreover, the humility instilled by a reading of ancient writers is first changed into uncertainty concerning the author's own speech; embarrassed by his regional accent, he went so far as to criticize his particular use of the French language.[20] Afterwards, such a "barbarity" acknowledged in himself was added to the general sense of humanism and led him to greet with an often emphatic curiosity and kindness the differences in others, henceforth precisely freed of "barbarisms": "There are infinite other differences of customs between countries, or, to put it better, there is almost no resemblance between one country's customs and another's" (p. 590).

Montaigne the dillettante was then able to change into a dispenser of justice. He condemned the forced conversions of Portuguese Jews: "a horrible spectacle" (p. 36). The colonial policy of Spain and of the Church also incurred its first, violent criticism. Not only do the American Indians have no cause to be jealous of us as to ability, "But as for devoutness, observance of the laws, goodness, liberality, loyalty, and frankness, it served us well not to have as much as they" (p. 694). The massacres carried out by colonizers in Peru and Mexico were an "indiscriminate butchery," "a horrible and unheard-of calamity" (pp. 696, 697). Montaigne defended religions and races against the excesses of religions and races: would the "puny" self be the first antiracist? The first anticolonialist?

A suspicion, however, forces itself upon the contemporary reader: is such a generous acceptance of "others" by Montaigne's nimble, sensuous self a recognition of their *particularities*, or on the contrary a leveling absorption; even though performed in good faith, might it not salvage the natives distinctive features to the benefit of a humanism capable of swallowing everything surprising and unknowable?

Nevertheless, for and through the self that knows it is also barbarous, a natural human universality is in the process of taking shape, which impugns supremacy without erasing distinctions. Friendship and conversation are proffered to all: it is up to each one to prove . . . his rhetoric.[21]

Whether or not they could have had the spirit of Montaigne or been able to take advantage of his writings, I imagine the great travelers, ethnologists, and explorers of the Renaissance developed in like manner. One must indeed first be securely grounded in oneself, be cognizant of one's wretchedness and one's glory, be able to talk about them in straightforward manner—without banality or pathos. Then, the self that has thus been created, rather than such and such a land, religion, court, or policy will become the port of departure for that other Renaissance, which, beyond the nations that are taking shape, draws comparisons, makes relative, renders universal. A new cosmopolitanism is being born, no longer founded on the unity of creatures belonging to God, as Dante conceived, but on the universality of a self that is fragile, casual, and nevertheless virtuous and certain.[22] Montaigne's self, which never ceases to travel in the self is already an invitation to explore the world and others with the same uncompromising kindness: "I want to be seen here in my simple, natural, ordinary fashion, without straining or artifice; for it is myself that I portray. My defects will here be read to the life, and also my natural form, as far as respect for the public has allowed. Had I been placed among those nations which are said to live still in the sweet freedom of nature's first laws, I assure you that I should very gladly have portrayed myself here entire and wholly naked./Thus, reader, I am myself the matter of my book; you would be unreasonable to spend your leisure on so frivolous and vain a subject./So farewell. Montaigne, this first day of March, fifteen hundred and eighty."[23]

Voyages, Cosmographies, Missions

The number of "geographical" publications increased: a reading public, more numerous than before, first wanted to know the Orient (many works were sold about the Turks, who often stood for all Moslems); the new world of the Americas only came next. The Wars of Religion did not cause such curiosity for an increasingly widened universe to dry up: between 1593 and 1604 more geographical works were published than from 1550 to 1559, the Renaissance's peaceful years. And, from 1605 to 1609, as many geographical books were published than had been brought out since the beginning of printing in 1550.[24] The leading item of that literature, completely forgotten today is Les Voyages du Seigneur de Villamont, which between 1595 and 1609, went through thirteen printings! One should mention above all the unusual but very much appreciated in its time Cosmographie et singularités de la France antarctique (1557) by André Thévet,[25] and Le Voyage au Brésil (1578) by Jean de Léry, a Protestant, who compels recognition as one of the best writers in the field, the Lettres of Francis-Xavier, written from the Indies, and even the Histoire de la Nouvelle-France (1609) by Marc Lescarbot,

who writes, "If only out of consideration for mankind, and because the people we are to discuss are men just like us, there is
enough to prompt our desire to understand their ways of life and
their mores."[26] Such works represented and shaped a modern
taste and mentality, henceforth directed more toward a new image of the world and men than toward the previous fictions.[27]
One discovered "atheistic peoples," one idealized the goodness of
the "savage," one was astonished, delighted, or shocked by the
nakedness one did not imagine possible in society, but one was
always eager to read about the "Antipodes" (which is what, in
the sixteenth century, men living in distant lands were called).

Apparently incompatible with cosmopolitanism, *nationalism*
may also perhaps have benefited from it: is it not true that if
those discoveries chip away at the authority of Antiquity, one
might rightfully substitute for them if not the authority of the
"good savage," which is indeed more tardy, at least that of the
naturalness and excellence . . . of French culture? There follows
the *Défense et illustration de la langue française* (1549). The
political problem would thereafter be stated in the following
terms: how can one reconcile the dignity of a nation-state in the
process of expansion with the diversity of the world and the
universalism of the philosophy that stems from it?

In 1664 François Charpentier wrote a report on French trade
with the West Indies and concluded that France could not remain
restricted to Europe but had a duty to spread her civilization to
the most barbarian peoples. Undoubtedly colonialism was already
beginning, but the initial intent was a cultural expansion of which
all men are worthy. The brutality of colonizers has been emphasized to such an extent that one should point out, on the other
hand, this other design of universalist explorers who, on the
contrary, balanced their own culture with the thought of a "concord of the terrestrial globe"—such a person was Guillaume
Postel (1510–1581), the "cosmopolitan Gaul," as he like to call
himself.

A Cosmopolitan Gaul

A polyglot with an international reputation, Guillaume Postel is considered by some as the forerunner of comparative philology: did he not imagine that all languages were tied to a common origin—Hebrew? Such linguistic concerns, however, gave way, during his sparkling career, to the passion of a visionary missionary, unless linguistic knowledge be a condition of religious and moral tolerance. Having visited Turkey and the Holy Land, familiar with Arabic and Moslem civilization, Postel often proclaimed their superiority, but he nevertheless insisted that it was necessary to include all religions and civilizations within the orbit of Christianity, of which France would be the inspirer and the ruler. As a Jesuit he taught at Sainte Barbe but was later banished by the Company of Jesus; he was hostile toward the papacy without challenging its principles and an enemy of the Protestants but coming closer to them in the second half of his life—although they exposed him as a deist; he taught at the Collège de France but fell out of grace with Francis I (around 1542) and was again welcome at the court under the protection of Princess Marguerite, sister of Henri II, when Charles IX viewed him as "his philosopher"—but this did not prevent his spending the last eighteen years of his life in jail. Such a strange character has left a number of works, the most cosmopolitan undoubtedly being *De Orbis Terra Concordia* (Basel, 1544), the ideas of which he takes up again in his other writings. An apostle of tolerance in the midst of the Wars of Religion, dreaming of a world united by Catholicism, Postel actually professed a faith that was so unorthodox that his adversaries at times had him not only condemned for heresy and thrown into jail but they quite simply found him "insane."[28] One is indeed puzzled by the "feminism" of this cosmopolitan Gaul: in Venice he became enamored of the religious virtues of Dame Jehanne and upon her death asserted that the spiritual body and sensible substance of that "mother" now resided in his own body, so that "presently it is she and not I who lives in me."[29] An abyss of learning he surely was; nevertheless Postel the scholar was something of a visionary—did not this Gallic Faust claim to possess a mysterious elixir of long life? . . .

It is to be noted that such a cosmopolitanism, of which Postel probably embodied the paroxystic stage, one that was not rare, especially during the first half of the sixteenth century, was based on a new philosophical judgment: the relativity of national and religious values. Foreshadowing the "philosophies" of the eighteenth century, this thought produced the image of the "good savage"—natural man at the foundation of universal mankind. Even if he often could be cause for laughter, the "good savage" was close to us just the same—and consequently he showed himself to be liable . . . of access to our civilization. Our own values, however, lost some of their arrogance when confronted with the national pride of the Chinese and their invention of writing, for instance. In its turn, the authority of the Classics was soon lessened when one discovered their ignorance, a discovery brought on particularly by the new geographic knowledge provided by explorers. Starting from that, and at the same time as national consciousnesses awakened before reaching their classical phase, in the following century, in the political aspect of monarchic absolutism, a cosmopolitan politics saw the light of day. Thus, *supranational bodies* were beginning to be conceived on the basis of the new geographic and political reality. Sully suggested the formation of a European Federation to fight the Turks, while Eméric Crucé wrote *Le Nouveau Cynée, ou Discours d'Estat représentant les occasions et moyens d'établir une paix générale et la liberté du commerce par tout le monde* (1624).[30] A "new world" was being conceived—one that was nationalist and eager to join with others. Communication or domination? Exchanges or wars? The nation-state was destined to be a colonial state.

7 On Foreigners and the Enlightenment

The Enlightenment, and the French Revolution as well, has spawned a wealth of ideas about such concepts as nation and foreigners, mankind and the masses; these have become more and more complex, for we are still living with that inheritance—its dignity, its contradictions, its tolerance, and its pitfalls—and can project our present sensitivities onto them. As we pick out just a few of those aspects that are inherent in what I shall, to simplify matters, call the cosmopolitanism of the Enlightenment, let us think of how these fragments appeal to our contemporaries when facing the perplexing question that still seems utopian: is a society without foreigners possible?

Beginning with Montesquieu's neo-stoicism and including Diderot's pantomime of human strangeness or the cynicism of cosmopolitans rebelling against all sacred values, the eighteenth century was to hand down to the Revolution an ideology of human equality that, from the "rights of man" to the "rights of the citizen," proved hard to manage when facing the onslaughts of political passions, war, and the Terror.

Montesquieu: The Fully Political and the Private Sector

Without dodging the problem of our antagonisms but in opposition to Hobbes who posited a state of war inherent in nature and in human society, Montesquieu (1689–1755) affirmed the notion of *human sociability* at the outset of *The Spirit of the Laws* (1748). More timorous than malevolent, human beings would nevertheless join together naturally, and their political constructs could hardly be the art of "building iniquity into a system" but on the contrary would succeed in working out a "moderate form of government." Such a sociability has forerunners with Cartesianism (the jurist Jean Domat), Christian theology (Fénelon), English neo-stoicism and empiricism (most particularly with Locke and Shaftesbury). It found its anchoring in the economic history of the eighteenth century, which Montesquieu attentively scrutinized and described as a period of increasing wealth, of unprecedented expansion of trade, and of an economic and political liberalism that, in his eyes, would insure the possibility of social peace. Whether it be Christian charity, or the ideal of the whole of mankind achieving the satisfaction of all, or the liberal trade economy of the time—there are numerous, heterogeneous factors that, with Montesquieu, come together and enable *The Spirit of the Laws* to be founded on such an intrinsic sociability, which government policies should both make explicit and guarantee. One can argue as to whether such a position leads to conservatism or on the contrary to social dynamism, whether it is purely sociological, adumbrating the stance of modern social sciences, or necessarily philosophical, laden down with the writer's masonic humanism.[1] I shall, for my purpose, extract from the still not too apparent complexity of Montesquieu's thought his concern for *totality* and one of its major consequences—his *cosmopolitanism*.

A totality encompassing *nature* and *culture* ("climate" and "customs," for instance); *men* and *institutions*; *laws* and *mores*; the *particular* and the *universal*; *philosophy* and *history*. These are multiple series among which *mediations* are at work, the latter being able at the same time to insure the tempering of institutions and that of human beings; the latter, if they are thus fully political, embody a large number of political determinants that are brought to the level of ideality. Ernst Cassirer wrote, "One can say of Montesquieu that he is the first thinker to grasp and to express clearly the concept of 'ideal types' in history."

Indeed, "On Laws and the Relationship they Have with the Principles that Shape the General Spirit, the Customs, and the Manners of a Nation" is the title of the fundamental nineteenth Book of *The Spirit of the Laws*. Here an *ideality* has been posited (the "general spirit"), of which the stoic and Christian, natural and "liberal" genealogy has been pointed out, and which is a fundamental prospect of Montesquieu's political thought. It at once endows it with its moral essence (as Kant clarified this notion in his conception of what he saw as the indissoluble pair constituted by the "political" and the "ethical") in that, beyond climatic determinations, for instance, it emphasizes a *contingency* in which both the course and the fatality of history are carried out, and in which the exercise of political freedom is precisely located.

This *fully social*, which is also considered here on the level of the nation, nevertheless reaches its climax when Montesquieu's thought tackles the *totality of the species*. His thinking is then weighed down with fatalistic determinism (particularly climatic) and conceives the political fabric of the globe on the basis of the sociability and "general spirit" that govern the human species finally restored to its actual universality through the modern expansion of trade. The nation's burden, so often acknowledged, is then transposed in order to be absorbed at the heart of a *borderless* political philosophy dominated by the concern for politics understood as the maximal integration of mankind in a moderate, attainable ideality.

Traces of it may be found in the less technical text of his *Thoughts*. To be sure, Montesquieu asserted, "I love only my

homeland."² But also: "When I traveled in foreign countries, I
became attached to them as to my own; I shared in their lot, and
I should have liked them to be in a flourishing state."³ His
political reflections, national as they may be, were not nationalistic: the good State was conceived for others, for all. Moreover,
he noticed that national feelings have waned in the course of
history.⁴ Finally, there is the famous statement: "If I knew
something useful to myself and detrimental to my family, I
would reject it from my mind. If I knew something useful to my
family but not to my homeland, I would try to forget it. If I
knew something useful to my homeland and detrimental to Europe, or else useful to Europe and detrimental to Mankind, I
would consider it a crime."⁵

Mankind, thus united by the ethic will of the political thinker
becomes nevertheless *historically* specified as an international
society made possible by the development of trade, dominated by
Europe, and dependent on a moderate regulation of the flow of
goods and currency. "Now that the universe nearly constitutes
only one nation, that each knows that of which it has too much
and that which it lacks, and tries to acquire the means to receive
it, gold and silver are extracted everywhere from the earth, those
metals are transported everywhere, every nation obtains them
and there is not a single nation whose gold and silver capital does
not increase every year, although more promptly and more abun-
dantly with some than with others."⁶

We should note this observation, astonishing for its modern
tone: "Europe is no more than a Nation made up of several
others, France and England need the richness of Poland and
Muscovy as one of their Provinces needs the others; and the
State that thinks it increases its power through the downfall of
its neighbor, usually weakens along with it."⁷

Such a universalizing argument, which, as I pointed out, is
based on reflections related to a nation's economic and social
policies, both foreign and domestic, surprisingly leads to a pre-

mature warning (which foreshadows Hannah Arendt's position) against distinguishing the "rights of man" from the "rights of the citizen"; for it is indeed true that with Montesquieu any political policy, in the full sense of the term, is implicitly a cosmopolicy because it includes the totality of human beings, the "general spirit": "All particular duties cease when they cannot be accomplished without offending human duties. Should one consider, for instance, the good of the homeland when that of mankind is at stake? No, *the duty of the citizen is a crime when it leads one to forget the duty of man.* As it was impossible to place the universe within the same society, this has caused men to be foreigners to some, but such a division did not stipulate against primary duties, and man, everywhere a creature of reason, is neither a Roman nor a Barbarian."[8]

Montesquieu's cosmopolitanism was more than the outgrowth of a naturalistic rationalism that might have been derived from the stoics. That pattern undoubtedly followed the outlines of an epistemological process that was specific to Montesquieu himself. In that sense, *cosmopolitanism* would be the metaphor of *political thought itself* when it has succeeded in dialecticizing the highest determination of the human within its own concept, and when it unfolds, ruled by a need for periodic homeostasis rather than for stability. Nevertheless, concurrently with the birth of modern political thought, a historical necessity has taken shape, which the nationalism of the two centuries that followed Montesquieu's time has bypassed, but whose urgency, for us, he has heralded. If *The Spirit of the Laws* is to remain faithful to the fundamental sociability and the moderatable ideality that the distinguished political thinker had presupposed, nation-states must give way to higher political systems.

Now, assuming that such a cosmopolicy is the expression of the associative and integrative spirit that governs Montesquieu's political thought, it goes hand in glove—need this be restated? —with setting up a safety network that should prevent the brutal integration of difference (and, to begin with, that of the *social* and the *political*) into a totalizing, univocal set that would eliminate any possibility of freedom.

The separation of powers, the preservation of a constitutional monarchy whose possible excesses would constantly be checked by a reasonable judiciary, the very belief in a social peace based on the freedom of individuals and obtained by upholding the dichotomy between the social and the political that is represented by the organic enactment of power in the royal figure—those are the strong features of Montesquieu's thought, which resurfaced in the liberal, post-revolutionary conservatism of Benjamin Constant or Alexis de Tocqueville; they constitute the safety network I just referred to and should be pondered in the light of his cosmopolicy.

Not that they should be taken up again as they were; rather, they should induce us to think that, within the judiciary that would insure the *rights of men* for all, beyond the *rights of citizens*, the obliteration of the very notion of "foreigner" should paradoxically encourage one to guarantee a long life to the notion of . . . "strangeness." It is from such a viewpoint that it is essential to respect what is *private*, or even *secret*, within a fully social domain that would not be homogeneous but preserved as a union of singularities. The singular should not be confined only to the figure of the monarch, who might be tempted—a rationalist vertigo—to embody perfect legality, but above all in the "weakness" and "shyness"[9] of his subjects, who are subject to cosmopolitical laws only when their rights to concord are recognized on the basis of their singularities, which cannot in themselves be harmonized. Beside the *political* and the *social*, there would then emerge, in a dignity that cannot lawfully be bypassed, the *private* domain (matters recently brought up in ethical debates concerning genetics are no more than its contemporary extension). At the same time, the level of political power, already curbed by the judiciary but more and more removed from its sacred pedestal by the impact of economics and the technical requirements of its administration, would find itself scaled down in its intrinsic use and distributed between the *social* and the *private* sectors. That implies not only that "heroes" and "great leaders" in politics are vanishing, as deplored today by disgruntled and sacramental people, but, above all, that there is a new concept of politics, understood as an attempt to harmonize what is irreducible through an interplay of diversified systems and stratums (political, social, private). Let us not forget that Montesquieu's cosmopolitism was the consequence of his fundamental concern to turn politics into a space of possible freedom. His "modernism" is to be understood as a rejection of unified society for the sake of a coordinated diversity.

The Foreigner: The Alter Ego of the Philosopher

Within that frame of mind, the image of the "good savage" that had already been coined by the Renaissance underwent a metamorphosis. What comes into view is a *foreigner*, as odd as he is subtle, and who is none other than the alter ego of national man, one who reveals the latter's personal inadequacies at the same time as he points to the defects in mores and institutions. Beginning with Montesquieu's *Persian Letters* (1721) and including Voltaire's *Zadig* (1747) and *Candide* (1759), to mention only the most famous works, philosophical fiction became peopled with foreigners who invited the reader to make a twofold journey. On the one hand it is pleasant and interesting to leave one's homeland in order to enter other climes, mentalities, and governments; but on the other hand and particularly, this move is undertaken only to return to oneself and one's home, to judge or laugh at one's limitations, peculiarities, mental and political despotisms. The *foreigner* then becomes the figure onto which the penetrating, ironical mind of the philosopher is delegated—his double, his mask. He is the metaphor of the distance at which we should place ourselves in order to revive the dynamics of ideological and social transformation.

This apology of the "private" and the "strange," including "idiosyncracies"—which, however, does not cease being the leaven of a culture when the latter is aware of and transcends itself— reaches a power that still enthralls us today in the writing of Denis Diderot (1713–1784). The pinnacle of those peculiarities that other eighteenth-century writers had depicted under national colors, *Rameau's Nephew* (written in 1762, published in German in 1805, in French in 1821) internalized both the discomfort and the fascinated recognition aroused by the strange and carried them to the very bosom of eighteenth-century man. If he were to wander to the end of his passion for altering, dividing, knowing, modern man would be a foreigner to himself—a strange being whose polyphony would from that moment on be "beyond good and evil."

The Strange Man, the Cynic, and the Cosmopolitan

1. Rameau's Nephew Between Diogenes and *Myself*

When Diderot "allows [his] mind to rove wantonly," a henceforth famous partner answers him in an open dialogue, without synthesis; it is a text the cynical, "Menippean" derivation of which has often been emphasized. That partner is one of those "peculiar characters," one of those "eccentrics," held in little esteem by the philosopher, who nonetheless lets him dominate the conversation—Rameau's Nephew.

Who is the Nephew? The philosopher's opponent or his hidden self? The opposite other or the nocturnal double that comes to the surface? A clear-cut answer to the question would bring the pantomime to an end and betray the "mental trollops" that Diderot, in an extraordinary flight of polyphonic fancy, presents in fact through the confrontation between *Myself* the philosopher and the strange *He*. Different and accomplices, others and same, *Myself* and *He* are in conflict, agree, even change places (*He*, insolently, all of a sudden extols virtue . . .). Rameau's Nephew *does not want* to settle down—he is the soul of a game that he does not want to stop, does not want to compromise, but wants only to challenge, displace, invert, shock, contradict. Negation, this is understood, not only of conscience and morality but of the will as passion: a twisting of sexuality—and then a negation of such negations. Take the episode at Bertin's house: the free-loading Nephew is expelled, because, he says, he has been per-ceived "as an other" [*comme un autre* = like the next man], while it is precisely because he is other, singular, peculiar, and, as such, makes the boring virtuous people laugh, that the latter invite him! The Nephew is conscious of his strangeness, and he is aware of that consciousness; [10] he claims it against himself—gathering from it a wounded personal dignity that surprises *Myself*[11]—and against society—deeming that those "others" deny his otherness while taking advantage of it; whereas he himself prefers not to be like "others," who actually represent only the abject consen-sus, the perverted mass.[12] He believes his strangeness to be essential,[13] and considers that its one and only accomplishment, beyond the contradictory challenge to accepted values, is witti-cism and pantomime: "All I could do to avoid the ridicule in-curred by my isolated applause was to throw in a few ironic words, which gave it a contrary interpretation."[14]

Witticism? The Nephew has quite simply and for once spoken "common sense." For instance: the Abbé who today enjoys being at the head of Bertin's table will daily "go down one cover." The frankness he displays is a turning inside out of deceitful words, the correction of a falsehood. Within the gyre of this negativity (true/unspoken/everyday falsehood/restored truth), the Nephew experiences the meaning of his words as a liberating process: clash of opposites, pleasure springing up, truth of laughter. The host and Mademoiselle Hus, on the other hand, incapable of that estranging motion, become judges and indignant. In short, witti-

cism would exist as such only for a consciousness on the move
that becomes estranged to itself in order to have another meaning
come forth, by way of the same, but also to bring forth the other
of meaning, the explosion of pleasure.

Pantomime? The Nephew mimes those he talks about, but he
also mimes his own feelings, displaying the objects and subjects
of his discourse by means of spasmodic, climactic gestures, thus
refusing to assume the single viewpoint of the relaxed speaker
but breaking out in a spate of attitudes. Foreign to the consensus
of others, he splits into many facets, first representing the *characters* that he mimes, next reverberating through the varied
intonations and intensities of his speech, finally insinuating himself into the very *syntax* of Diderot's sentence, which, from
parataxis to holding in suspense, integrates in turn the strangeness of the pantomime: "What is amusing is that while I was
saying this, he was acting it out in pantomime. He was prostrate
at my feet, his face on the ground, and seemed to be clutching in
both his hands the tip of a slipper. He was crying and sobbing
out words: 'I swear it, my dear Queen, I promise, never will I do
it again, never, never, never.' Then suddenly jumping up . . ."[15]
As for his voice: "He jumbled together thirty different airs,
French, Italian, comic, tragic—in every style. Now in a baritone
voice he sank to the pit; then straining in falsetto he tore to
shreds the upper notes of some air, imitating the while the stance,
walk and gestures of the several characters; being in succession
furious, mollified, lordly, sneering. First a damsel weeps and he
reproduces her kittenish ways; next he is a priest, a king, a
tyrant; he threatens, commands, rages. Now he is a slave, he
obeys."[16]

This articulation of opposites, this dislocation of identity contaminate even Diderot's sentence, in which the syntax loses its
subject to the benefit of the fragment-objects of the polyphonist
musician's body, which invade the narrative and replace it with a
fragmented image of the playing body. "*He.* 'Ah, you won't, eh?
But I say you will and they will, it works—' Saying which, he

had seized with his right hand the fingers and wrist of his left and was bending them this way and that, until the tips touched the forearm and the joints cracked and I was afraid the bones would be dislocated."[17]

Such a strategy of strangeness, played out at the same time in an uncontrolled and knowing, spontaneous and conscious manner, has a genealogy, a biology, a sociology.[18]

As to genealogy, the Nephew himself suggests it when he places his discourse, at the very beginning of the satire, under the aegis of Diogenes and ends it with a new mention of the Greek cynic.[19] Neither Cesar, nor Marcus Aurelius, nor Socrates; nor will he "Catonize": "No, I should like it better between Diogenes and Phryne. I am as cheeky as the one and often visit the sisters of the other." "What a consummate dog I am,"[20] he says further on, thus claiming for himself the symbolic animal of the cynics. Diogenes of Sinope (412–323 B.C.), the eccentric dog-man, rancorous and scornful toward Alexander as the Nephew was with respect to Rameau, was looking for a man from the threshold of his barrel before taking refuge in it if he was disappointed in his expectations. Posterity has remembered the incisive expressions of the cynics: their art of argumentative paradox, whereby they assume the position of their opponents and uphold in turn two contradictory points of view; their mockery of vices and social conventions, which leads to an ethics of naturalness and licentiousness, both aggressive and wanton. Eccentric, if not insane, the cynic displays the *other* of reason; foreign to social conventions, he discredits himself in order to have us face our shameful otherness. Thus, a *high* cynicism, aspiring to a mystique of human purity, is linked to a *low* cynicism that—in order to reach it (but does one not often forget the ends when one gives oneself over to the means?)—displays an alienated, debased man. Diderot, who wrote the "Cynic" article in the *Encyclopédie*, often mentions Diogenes as a model to identify with.[21] But the Nephew counterfeits Diogenes: his cynicism is an "effrontery," a sham that scoffs at the philosophical loftiness

eventually chosen by Diogenes. He replaces the cynic virtue of
the Ancients with infatuation, flattery, glibness, and material
ease. The Nephew is the cynic's cynic: he experiences its rhetoric
and carries it to its peak, remaining up to the end foreign to
ethical identity, even that of the cynic. In that sense, the Nephew
is closer to a cynic who left his imprint on literary genres by
inventing a new model of satire—Menippus of Gadara, who,
besides, was a corrupt usurer and ended up hanging himself.
Diderot speaks of him in his article on the "Cynic": "Menippus
[. . .] was one of the last cynics of the ancient school; he made
himself more commendable for the kind of writing to which he
gave his name than for his morals and his philosophy." Bakhtin
sees him as the founder of dialogism and of that rhetorical polyphony out of which the western novel arose.[22] Outside of the
ethical heroism of Diogenes, who succeeded in submitting the
passion-inspired strangeness of natural man to a moral imperative, the Nephew, and Diderot too, leave such asceticism to Rousseau; they adopt only its acceptable portion—the play in language, the logical violence that destroys and does not cease being
aware even of its own disappearance. The Nephew's pantomime
is faithful only to Menippus' rhetoric, not to Diogenes' virtue.
Diderot never conveyed so drastically the fact that the ethics of
his day could only be a given language: a cultivation of strangeness to the very end, without finish or conclusion.

Such a scouring of apparent identities—ethical or logical—is
supported by a biological model. The strangeness of the uncom-
mon, exceptional, but frank person—in Diderot's satire "frankness" takes the place of any Catonizing apology of "truth"—
unfurls within a polyphonic rhetoric that is the visible facet of a
spasmic, convulsive nature, centered in the nervous system discovered by the physicians of the time, and which Diderot adopted.
From Albrecht von Haller to Whytt, from William Cullen and
John Brown to Kaau Boerhaave, without forgetting the French
physicians Louis de Lacaze, Bordeu, Fouquet, and Menuret de
Chambaud (who wrote the article on "Spasm" in the *Encyclopé-*

die), the medical currency of Diderot's day was to discover the spasm everywhere.[23] Diderot shows himself to be very mindful of it in his *Eléments de physiologie*. He goes so far as to view any sensation as bound to "organic convulsions."[24] Indeed, when the Nephew reaches the climactic frankness of his pantomime, he reveals his "thoughts," which are at the same time sensations, through a language made up of spasms, convulsions, and starts. Strangeness, which we have seen as rhetorical (cultural), would be neurological in nature (organic): "There is not the slightest difference between a wide-awake physician and a dreaming philosopher,"[25] as long as both scrutinize the strange.

Surreptitiously, strangeness is also political. A rhetorician with peculiar nerves, the Nephew could not have come from a single place, a single side, a single country. From the very outset he regrets—which is to say, admires—that men of genius "don't know not what it is to be citizens";[26] and they are precisely the ones he wants to resemble, they are an exceptional model not to be imitated by the crowd. Putting citizenship aside, what would then be the vessel for the unrestrained pantomime performed by such a convulsive harpsichord player? *He:* "I look about me and take my positions, or else I entertain myself watching others take theirs."[27] The stance is temporary, movable, changing—if steady, it is artificial; provisional, it is wandering. Original, it strays from the origin, it knows neither root nor soil, it is traveling, foreign. "In the whole country only one man walks—the King. Everybody else takes a position." The strange Rameau is surely not the King. But is the King still sovereign at the time the dialogue takes place? "One has a homeland, under a good king, none under a bad one," Voltaire asserted.[28] *Myself*, who often really embraces at full tilt the logic of *He*, and even forestalls it, believes that even the king postures before his mistress and before God ("Whoever stands in need of another is needy and takes a position").[29] But in such a case, there would not even be a king? Nor would there be a kingdom, since it would lack a king? Therefore nothing works, because there is no sovereignty, beginning with the kingdom? The strange man, spasmodic and pantomimic, would be the inhabitant of a country without power, the sociological symptom of a political transition. If he claimed strangeness to the point of idiosyncracy ("The older the institution the more the idioms; the worse the times become, the more the idioms multiply"),[30] would it not also be because political institutions that are undergoing a crisis no longer insure the symbolic identity of the power and the persons? *Myself* the philosopher generalizes human instability, which he suspects lies with all as soon as there is dependency on the other. More pragmatic, however, the Nephew comes out with it: the king must walk if the kingdom is to be. Or else—and *Myself* confirms the royal poverty—there no longer is a kingdom where to stand. Relieved of political power, the posturing man is the same as a man without kingdom. Being frank to the point of strangeness reveals modern man on the political level as a man without a country. His pantomimic positions could only be assumed by cutting through the kingdom, by going across the borders of wobbly sovereignties. Into cosmopolitanism.

2. Fougeret de Monbron, a Cosmopolitan
"with a Shaggy Heart"

A "lumpen-intelligentsia" thus emerged above nations, refusing to belong to phantom kingdoms and ravaged countries. "Cosmopolitan" reverberates like a challenge, if not like a mockery. Jaucourt's article in the *Encyclopédie* points out that "cosmopolitan" or "cosmopolite" is used sometimes jokingly to refer to one "who has no fixed abode" or one "who is nowhere a foreigner." The definition repeats that of the 1721 *Dictionnaire de Trévoux*: a "cosmopolitan" is a man "who has no fixed abode or a man who is nowhere a foreigner." The first text to bear the title *Le Cosmopolite ou le citoyen du Monde*, in 1750, is signed by Fougeret de Monbron.[31]

Who is he? Diderot ran into him at the Opera.

We didn't know Pergolesi then; and Lulli we considered sublime. In the rapture of my ecstasy I grabbed my neighbor Mont-

bron by the arm and said to him, "You will agree, Sir, that this is beautiful." The man with a sallow complexion, black, bushy eyebrows, fierce, covert eyes, answered, "I don't appreciate that."
"You don't appreciate that?"
"No; I have a shaggy heart . . ."
I shudder; I move away from the two-footed tiger.[32]

It has often been suggested that *Rameau's Nephew* might have been inspired by this cosmopolitan who described himself to the philosopher as having a "shaggy heart."[33] An angry text, scoffing at all nations (beginning with the English and the Turks, including the Spanish, the Italians, and of course the French, and so on) and even more so all beliefs, *Le Cosmopolite* advocates, in an offhand way and not without skill, hatred and selfishness as antidotes to ambient hypocrisy. Except for the art of pantomime —which is essential—Monbron's creed cannot be distinguished from that of the Nephew. Thus: "I most readily and sincerely admit that I am worth precisely nothing, and the difference there is between others and myself is that I am bold enough to take off the mask"; "I am isolated in the midst of wanderers." In the spirit of the prevailing neo-Stoicism Fougeret borrows his epigraph from Cicero: "*Patria est ubicumque est bene*" (*Tusculanes*, V); but he vitiates the cosmopolitanism of the ancients by showing the vices of each nation as being the mainspring of his passion for travel. Fougeret's cosmopolite is shrill, bitter, full of hatred. A character trait or a rhetorical figure—or undoubtedly both at the same time—such malevolence is truly dynamite that destroys borders and shatters the hallowed legitimacy of nations. One reads this *Cosmopolite* with the embarrassment provoked by the pathology of excesses. And yet, upon a second reading, even though one will not condone so much irascible selfishness, one cannot help recognizing that a great deal of violence and paroxysmal iconoclasm was necessary before a man of the neoclassic century or even of the enlightenment could tear himself away from the most primal and seemingly most trifling covenant— belonging to the country "tribe." "The Universe is a kind of book, of which one has read no more than the first page when one has seen only one's country" is what Fougeret said when he was freed after having been arrested in November 1748. "I leafed through quite a few, which I found almost equally bad. Such a perusal did not prove fruitless. I hated my homeland, and all the uncivilities of the various peoples among whom I lived have reconciled me with it. If I had reaped no other profit from my travels save that one, I should regret neither their cost nor the strain they caused."[34] Byron remembered the beginning of those lines for his epigraph to *Childe Harold*. But the "patriotism" of the repentant cosmopolitan is deceptive. There was soul-searching, musing over the personal wound and, therefore, extolling of that which is one's own, surely—but certainly no patriotism. Beliefs, even territorial ones, hardly hold the attention of the negativist who knows, ironically, that he has a "shaggy heart." Citizen of the world out of scorn for all countries, Fougeret indeed does not admit of belonging to any nation.[35] Statements such as "My restless imagination could not sympathize with methodical order,"[36] or, "I warn you that my wilful spirit knows no rule and that, like the squirrel, it leaps from limb to limb without settling on any one,"[37] might indeed have been spoken by the Nephew. Subjectivistic relativism, hatred toward others and oneself, and the feeling of being empty and fallacious, govern the impossibility of settling down and the acid laughter of such a cosmopolitan.[38]

Fougeret's malevolent cosmopolitanism, which is certainly ridiculous, in fact discloses the violence and strangeness of the subjective facet of cosmopolitanism—not the neutral serenity of philosophical wisdom that remains above borders, but the passionate tearing away that shakes the identity of one who no longer recognizes himself in the community of his own people. The drama of the foreigner, tossed from his bruised narcissism to a fascinated hatred for the other, could find its expression in this embittered text, the excessiveness of which suggests, across the centuries, Zeno's *Republic* and Menippus' cynicism. Diderot's genius changed such intentions, straightforward to be sure but brutal and immoderate, into a rhetoric that is also emancipated and yet composed with an art that endows drives with adequate signs. To Fougeret's exultation Diderot appends—more than he opposes . . .—culture. Nonetheless Fougeret's style lacks neither precision nor savor: it tends toward its consumption into truth, even if it remains essentially a record of complaint and scorn. Renowned readers have appreciated it and used it: besides Byron, there is Lessing, Voltaire, Goldsmith,[39] and Stern.[40]

The pejorative meaning of the word "cosmopolitan" was undoubtedly enhanced by such provocations that further irked the protective feeling for the nation, jealous of its prerogatives. "Whoever does not adopt his homeland is not a good citizen," as the *Dictionnaire de l'Académie* notes in 1762, in the article "Cosmopolitan." And Rousseau among others: "Any partial society, when it is close and well-knit, becomes alienated from the larger one. Any patriot is hard on foreigners; they are mere men, they are nothing in his eyes. This drawback is inevitable, but it is slight. The essential is to be good with the people one lives with. [. . .] Beware of those cosmopolitans who seek far off in their books duties they fail to accomplish close by."[41]

Montesquieu all the same—as we have seen—asserted along with Shaftesbury a positive value for cosmopolitanism, in a century where many famous cosmopolitans can be mentioned, among which Charles Pinot Duclos (*Considérations sur les mœurs de ce siècle*, 1751), the Prince de Ligne, and also Grimm, Galiani, Bonneval, Casanova, Caraccioli. "Although one should love one's homeland, it is just as ridiculous to speak of it with prejudice as it would be of one's wife, birth, or property. How foolish vanity, wherever it is shown!"[42] "If I knew something useful to my homeland and detrimental to Europe, or else useful to Europe and detrimental to mankind, I would consider it a crime."[43]

With its raging reverse and generous obverse, between Fougeret and Montesquieu, cosmopolitanism henceforth appears as an audacity, utopian for the time being, but which must be taken into account by human beings who are conscious of their limita-

tions and aspire to transcend them in the organization of social
bonds and institutions.

3. The Nephew with Hegel: Culture as Strangeness

When, in its dialectical motion, the world of the Spirit becomes
foreign to itself,[44] Hegel deems that two parts of the spiritual
world start facing each other: actuality and pure consciousness.
"But the existence of this world, as also the actuality of self-
consciousness, depends on the process through which self-consciousness divests itself of its personality, by so doing creates its
world, and treats it as something alien and external, of which it
must now take possession."[45] This process is, as Hegel saw it,
constituted by culture *(Bildung)*—political, economic, social, intellectual . . .—as *estrangement* of the natural being. The transition of the *thought-constituted substance* to *concrete actuality*
is thus effected, as, conversely, that of *determinate individuality*
to its *essential constitution* (Jean Hyppolite comments: the individual becomes universal at the same time as universal substance
increases in actuality).

This argument, the maze of which cannot be traced here, takes
as its horizon and object seventeenth- and eighteenth-century
French culture, coming to a head with the enlightenment. It
relies on *Rameau's Nephew* to illustrate the notion of culture as
estrangement of the individual into the universal, and vice versa.
The strangeness collected at Diderot's font takes on three aspects:
—individuality becomes stable only by giving up the self for the
universal: that is the role of *Myself* the philosopher. Lacking
such an accomplishment, there is only a "pretence of individuality," individuality is "mere presumptive existence" and passes
"simply for what it is," for a kind of being, an *espèce*. Here
Hegel takes up the French word and recalls the meaning given to
it by *Lui* in *Rameau's Nephew:* "The most horrible of all nick-
names, for it signifies mediocrity, and denotes the highest degree
of contempt"; [46]
—still relying on the Nephew's experiences, particularly the

episode at Bertin's house, while trying to extract from them a dialectic of abjection between patron and client (p. 543), Hegel brings out the logic of the French monarchy as another illustration of self-estrangement. The power of the State becomes alienated in an individual and a name—"Louis" ("state-power becomes, by the self-abasement of the noble consciousness, a universal that renounces itself, becomes [. . .] the empty name"—p. 535). What follows is "the heroism of flattery," where language becomes alienated in turn as a pure appearance in order to seek an empty power, for it is wealth that constitutes true power. Cultural self-estrangement is here revealed through the historical reality of courtly culture—which is mere seeming, hypocrisy, and appearances, and against which the inverted strangeness of the Nephew will assert itself by claiming frankness;
—finally, the "distraught utterance" is the major representation of cultural estrangement. Through an ultimate reversion, it does not become frozen into the "placid consciousness" of a self that is unaware of its underlying contradiction but on the contrary abolishes the distinction between "noble" and "base," confronts wealth with the inner abyss, expresses a "rebellion that repudiates its own repudiation" (p. 540), knows its naturalness, its flattery, or its abjection; in short, to each of its moments it attaches its opposite. This is "pure self-consciousness," which ends up, like the speech of Rameau's Nephew, "in absolute and universal inversion of reality and thought." But that is precisely *"pure culture"* (p. 541): "The distraught and disintegrated soul is, however, aware of inversion; it is, in fact, a consciousness of absolute inversion" (p. 543).

This sort of strangeness, which Hegel also describes as "self-transparent" and "distracted" (p. 544) or as "a universal deception of itself and others," becomes the "greatest truth" on the very account of the "shamelessness manifested in stating this deceit" (p. 543). One is struck by Hegel's faithfulness to that cynical polyphony of culture as embodied by the Nephew.[47] He raises it above "that simple, placid consciousness of the good and the true," characteristic of the philosopher *Myself*, who can "say nothing" and is "merely an abstraction," barely capable of gathering "into a trifling form the meaning of what spirit said" (pp. 544–545). Nevertheless, this strangeness of culture, even though it be highly appreciated, remains yet with Hegel a "perversion" that, as scintillation of the spirit and all the more so of witticism, must be transcended. The polyphony of Hegel, a careful reader of Diderot, gives way before the triadism of his dialectic. The world of Culture will be surpassed by that of Morality before finally turning into that of Religion and absolute Spirit, for only the latter will be able to replace the simple "presentations" of culture's perverse language with thoughts (p. 549). Indeed, Culture in Hegel's sense, in its scission and essential strangeness, proceeds by way of *disunion* and *contradiction*, which it unifies in its wrenching discourse; but the latter merely judges "by reducing everything to the self in its aridity" and cannot grasp the substantial content of thought.

Might Culture Be French?

Out of the many implications of such remarks on cultural estrangement as opposed to moral and religious conciliation, one might consider a few concerning the novel, the imagination, and their present shape—the mass media. The perversion that sets up the opposites in human signification facing each other, with neither synthesis, nor internalization, nor supersession—that is indeed novelistic culture in the polyphonic sense of the French eighteenth century. It still underlies the great imaginary syntheses, religious in inspiration, of the nineteenth century, such as Dostoyevsky's dialogism, which shattered the believer's virtue by dint of idiocy.

One might well ask if France has not preeminently continued to be the area of culture—in the sense of Hegel's "perversion"; one might ask if it has not identified with culture, and if culture, defined in such a manner, is not definitively French. Nowhere else indeed, is political power—as if it continued a form of despotism, weakened to the point of being merely an empty appearance—experienced as factitious to such a degree. One goes along with it out of custom, one manages it or submits to it, but it has neither the moral authority of Anglo-American governments, always ready for impeachments, nor the despotic firmhandedness of totalitarianisms. In the same way, media-based culture—as it does elsewhere but perhaps in a more disrespectful manner—scoffs at and takes advantage of it, shuffling the cards of "pluses" or "minuses," ready to exchange winners and losers according to the excellence of their pantomime, as they would in an ersatz of *Rameau's Nephew*. The good is bad, the bad is good, they live together . . .

Within this context of living together, of conflicting shams, the weighty role of the "foreigner as such" becomes neutralized. Indeed, culture (as defined above) forces everyone to take into account a value *and* its opposite, the same *and* the other, the identical *and* its alien. When the perverseness of values establishes the subtle norm of a culture conscious of its reversibilities, one could not insist in assuming all by one's self the univalent role of the *Foreigner*, whether it be positive (a revealer of the tribe's hidden significance) or negative (an intruder who destroys the consensus). The romantic or terroristic seriousness of strangeness in itself becomes dissolved in this glittering of polymorphic culture that returns everyone to his or her otherness or foreign status. Nor does such a culture, however, assimilate foreigners; it dissolves their very being as it dissolves the clear-cut boundaries between same and others. Alas, it does not always withstand the dogmatic attempts of those—economically or ideologically disappointed—who restore their "ownness" and "identity" by rejecting others. The fact remains nonetheless that in France such attempts are immediately and more than elsewhere seen as a betrayal of *culture*, as a loss of *spirit*. And even if, at certain times in history, such a healthy cultural reaction tends to be forgotten, one feels like counting on it so as to maintain France as a land of asylum. Not as a house of welcome but as a ground for adventure. There are foreigners who wish to be lost as such in the perverseness of French culture in order to be reborn not with a new identity but within the enigmatic dimension of human experience that, with and beyond belonging, is called freedom. In French: culture.

The Rights of Man and Citizen

During the meetings of the National Assembly between August 20 and August 26, 1789, the *Declaration of the Rights of Man and Citizen* was debated and adopted. Two centuries later, it remains the yet unsurpassed touchstone for those freedoms to be enjoyed by any human being on our planet. One has often admired the conciseness and lucidity of a text that succeeds within a few pages to foresee abuses and threats, and to guarantee the reasoned exercise of freedoms. Those who composed it were heirs to the Enlightenment, and to the philosophers' reflections on natural and political man. Their text does not conceive "the natural, inalienable, and sacred rights of man" as being outside the "social body" but, on the contrary, endeavors to make *all* members of the social body aware of "their rights and their duties." The *Declaration* was thus drawn up in order to affect the existing political institutions, to modify them so that they might show respect for "simple and indisputable principles." Consequently, basing itself on a universal human nature that the Enlightenment learned to conceive and to respect, the *Declaration* shifts from the universal notion—"men"—to the "political associations" that must preserve their rights, and encounters the historical reality of the "essential political association," which turns out to be the *nation*. Let us read (the emphasis is mine):

> Article I. *Men are born and remain free and equal of right;* social distinctions may be founded only on the common usefulness.
> Article II. The aim of any *political association* is to preserve the natural and inalienable rights of man; these are the rights of liberty, property, security, and resistance to oppression.

Article III. The principle of all sovereignty lies essentially in the *nation;* no group, no individual may have any authority that does not expressly proceed from it.

Thus, man is political and his national identification is the essential expression of his sovereignty. What a slap in the face of those—king or social groups—who would assume the privilege of sovereignty! The legal basis for everyone's equality before the duties of the national political community is thus set forth, and one can only admire the boldness and generosity of that position. Far from proclaiming a natural egalitarianism, the *Declaration* at once inserts equality in the grid of "political" and "natural" human institutions and more precisely within the scope of the *nation.* The national political body must act for all.[48]

The progressive and democratic aspect of that principle strikes the commentator and yet questions him. In fact, it is within the once constituted national grouping that all persons can remain free and equal of right. Thus the free and equal man is, de facto, the citizen. In article VI of the *Declaration,* moreover, the term "man" that opened article I is replaced with "citizen"—the latter being necessarily called for after the overview of the social and national nature of his humanity, which was clarified and gradually introduced by the preceding articles:

Article VI. The law is the expression of the general will; all citizens have the right to work toward its creation; it must be the same for all, whether it protects or punishes.

One will note the talent of the drafters: the word "citizen" appears in a sentence where *rights* turn out to be civic *duties*— citizens will "work toward." And it is on account of this give-and-take of obligations and enjoyments that *man,* having become a *citizen,* will be protected as well as, in case of an offense, punished. The general will specific to the nation, a phrase again borrowed from Rousseau, asserts itself here, including the poor, workers of all stations, sex and age being indifferent . . . Never has democracy been more explicit, for it excludes no one—*except foreigners . . .*

In fact, "natural" man is immediately *political,* hence *national.* This slippage in the argument was to lead, with the economic development of Western societies, to the creation of nation-states and, by derivation or deviation, to the explosion of nationalism in the nineteenth and twentieth centuries. Nevertheless, one will note the caution, often called abstract—by Edmund Burke to start with[49]—involved in dissociating the being of the *national citizen* from that of the *universal and natural man.* Defined by the French *Declaration,* which links them to nature, these rights of man consist in "liberty," "protection of property," "national sovereignty." Related to God in the American *Declaration,* they are called "life," "liberty," and "the pursuit of happiness." It may be regrettable to find such a duality—"man"/ "citizen"—at the very heart of a maximal demand for equality. It may be regrettable to find a lack of precision as to the foundation—"divine" or "natural"?—that underlies such human equality. Nevertheless, after the dreadful experiences of contemporary history, one can only admire the ethical and political intuition that set aside an *inalienable horizon,* irreducible to that of national political conscience and its jurisdiction, and this beyond the historical necessity that consisted in recognizing men's *national* political essence. But before returning to the advantages of such a splitting, let me note some of its drawbacks.

Indeed, the man supposedly independent of all government (in article I) turns out to be the citizen of a nation (articles II-VI, etc.). About such an identification of man with the citizen, subsequent history has suggested those questions that Hannah Arendt did not fail to raise. What happens to peoples without an adequate government to defend them (the Napoleonic expansion comes to mind, for instance)? What happens to peoples without a homeland (the Russians, the Poles, victims of the destruction of their state; or, in more radical fashion, the Jews)? Generally speaking, how are those who are not citizens of a sovereign state to be considered? Does one belong to mankind, is one entitled to the "rights of man" when one is not a citizen?

The spreading of the French Revolution's ideas over the continent triggered the demand for the national rights of peoples, not the universality of mankind. As for the monstrosity of national socialism, one may wonder if it is merely a deviation and pathological distortion of "normal" nationalism under the pressure of economic developments, or if it is affiliated upon traditional nationalism. While emphasizing the break that such a monstrosity represents in political thought and institutions, Hannah Arendt is right in thinking that the national legacy served as guarantee for Nazi criminality, at the beginning at least; one was thus prevented from detecting crimes against humanity under a terminology whose previous history and tradition one thought familiar.

The world of barbarity thus comes to a head in a single world composed of states, in which only those people organized into national residences are entitled to have rights. The "loss of residence," a "loss of social framework" worsened by "the impossibility to find one" are characteristic of this new barbarity issued from the very core of the nation-state system. The modern world —I refer to Nazism and its aftermath—includes people who are no longer recognized as citizens of any sovereign state, thus do not belong to any sovereign community nor, by extension, to any community whatsoever.[50] If national needs do not require it, "nobody wants even to oppress them"; "nothing they think matters anyhow";[51] "deprivation of human rights is manifested first and above all in the deprivation of a place in the world which makes opinions significant and actions effective."[52]

To these agonizing observations Hannah Arendt nevertheless adds a spontaneous response that shows mixed feelings—sympathy for the resurgence of nationalism, whereby those who have lost their residence attempt to reconstruct their own homeland, and an implicit condemnation of the notion of rights of man, which is seen as having been unable to stand up to the national confinement that rejected the "stateless." "The world found nothing sacred in the abstract nakedness of being human [. . .].

It seems that a man who is nothing but a man has lost the very qualities which make it possible for other people to treat him as a fellow-man."[53] And thereupon Hannah Arendt surreptitiously comes round to Burke's views, which she had previously criticized, and deplores the "abstraction" of the rights of man and sets against them either the past, the "entailed inheritance" (Burke contrasted the "abstract" rights of the French Revolution with the "rights of an Englishman," the "rights which one transmits to one's children like life itself"), or a transcendental, divine guarantee of the principle of humanity.

Now it is possible to separate, in the spirit of eighteenth-century humanism, its *principle* from its *content*. While it is true that the content is wedded to the abstract notion of human nature, reduced in a now outdated manner to "liberty," "property," and "sovereignty" (article I of the *Declaration*), the principle does remain, and it has a twofold bearing. On the one hand it inherits the stoic and Christian tradition of universality, and postulates its immanence here and now in speaking beings. On the other hand it has the pragmatic advantage of being centered in the reality of political institutions, without being limited to them. The idea is to postulate an ethical value without confusing it with historical society and its vagaries.

The principle of the rights of man is the Faith of the Enlightenment—in the sense in which Hegel understood that term as an antidote to the Terror.

It is only by maintaining the *principle* of that universal dignity —without scattering it among new national, religious, or private regionalisms—that one might consider modifying its *content*, taking into consideration what the behavior of human beings reveals as to their humanity. One would notice, in addition to the social propensity for association and life, murderous surges, jouissance of death, pleasures of parting and narcissism, carrier waves of the social fabric's fragmentation but also that of the very identity of the individuals' body and their psychic space. The destructive tendencies of society come together with those that destroy human nature as well as human biology and the individual's identity. Being aware of that infernal dynamics of estrangement at the core of each entity, individual, or group certainly distances one from eighteenth-century optimism but without calling the principle into question. Maintaining the dignity of the human being as principle and aim allows one to understand, to care for, perhaps to modify its founderings. The Nazis did not lose their humanity because of the "abstraction" that may have existed in the notion of "man" ("the abstract nakedness of being nothing but human").[54] On the contrary—it is because they had lost the lofty, abstract, fully symbolic notion of humanity and replaced it with a local, national, or ideological membership, that savageness materialized in them and could be practiced against those who did not share such membership. Had they abandoned it because it was "abstract" to the point of lacking meaning or, on the contrary, because in that so-called "abstraction" there was a symbolic value that went against the desire to dominate and possess others under the aegis of a national, racial, or ideological membership that was considered superior? Confronting Nazi nationalism with another nationalism betrays an unconscious surrender to the same thought. On the other hand, the distinction set forth in the *Declaration* between "humanity" (whether it is "natural" or "symbolic" is a moot point) and "citizenry" maintains the requirement of a human, trans-historical *dignity*, whose content nevertheless needs to be made more complex, beyond the eighteenth-century's optimistic naivety. Such a modification, however, is not within the competence of the courts of law alone: it implies not only *rights* but *desires* and *symbolic values*. It falls within the province of ethics and psychoanalysis. It thus appears that while the *Declaration* is destined to remain untouchable, the practical fulfillment of human rights that will remain faithful to its spirit—and not to its letter—must presuppose two considerations.

First, a progressive and reasonable adjustment of the rights and duties of citizens with respect to non-citizens shall attempt to balance in the best possible manner the status of the former and the latter. Such a process, initiated through international law in developed countries, seems, in spite of clashes and wars, destined to become widespread.

Second (and in inseparable fashion, as a necessary lining, never to be isolated from the first), there must be an ethics, the fulfillment of which shall depend on education and psychoanalysis. Such an ethics should reveal, discuss, and spread a concept of human dignity, wrested from the euphoria of classic humanists and laden with the alienations, dramas, and dead ends of our condition as speaking beings. Individual particularistic tendencies, the desire to set oneself up as a private value, the attack against the other, identification with or rejection of the group are inherent in human dignity, if one acknowledges that such a dignity includes strangeness. That being the case, as social as that strangeness might be, it can be modulated—with the possibility of achieving a polytopic and supple society, neither locked in to the nation or its religion, nor anarchically exposed to all of its explosions. The interbreeding of nations is accompanied by the liberation of their political institutions and social structures— which goes from emancipated competition to self-management and always presupposes respect for one's "own distinctive features" *taking into consideration* the "different." Such an adjustment, which may be described as a cosmopolitanism interior to the nation-states, appears indeed to be the middle way that democratic societies are already capable of following, before dreaming the utopia of a society without nations.

Foreigners During the Revolution

1. Universal Brotherhood and the Birth of Nationalism

The cosmopolitan trend, heir to certain ideas of Montesquieu or Rousseau, was powerful at the beginning of the Revolution and found concrete political fulfillment in many decrees and other judicial actions. Thus Guy-Jean-Baptiste Target, a moderate member of the National Assembly, suggested on April 30, 1790, that all foreigners having resided in France for five years and owning some property be naturalized. Approved without discussion, the proposal became a decree unprecedented in its liberalism.[55] The decree stipulates as follows: "All persons having been born of foreign parents outside the kingdom and who have settled in France will be recognized as French and, after having taken the civic oath, allowed to exercise the rights of an active citizen, after residing five years in the kingdom, provided they have furthermore acquired real estate or married a French woman, or founded commercial establishments, or received from some cities letters patent or burgess, contrary regulations notwithstanding, which are hereby abrogated." The Constitution of 1791 repeats this text in article 2 of title II. After that, foreigners constituted private societies in which they gathered according to nationality, or they became integrated into French clubs.[56] There was for instance the Nicolas de Bonneville Social Circle, affiliated with the Masonic Lodge of the Union of Foreigners. Its cosmopolitan program proposed to establish a Confederation of the Friends of Truth throughout the earth, abolishing war by doing away with nations and choosing democracy. For his part, Pierre-Jean-Berthold Proly, a Belgian, founded an explicitly cosmopolitan newspaper, which was even entitled *The Cosmopolitan or Historical, Political, and Literary Journal* (later *The Cosmopolitan or the Universal Diplomat*) and lasted from December 1791 to March 1792. He tried to prevent war but after it broke out he was suspected of treason and fled. Eventually captured, he went to the guillotine with Hébert.

Pacifist at the beginning, the Assembly had proclaimed on May 20, 1790, that it would never undertake any conquest nor use force against any people. In that spirit, the support of an international elite for revolutionary ideas could only be applauded. After the abortive flight of the king, who was stopped at Varennes, and the Declaration of Pillnitz by the King of Prussia and the Emperor of Austria and in order to fight the accord of the

European monarchies against the revolutionaries, the Girondists chose cosmopolitanism as the trump card in their political battle. They were hoping that the principles of human rights would contaminate neighboring people and incite uprisings against the tyrants. Refugees and political exiles were then encouraged, and the Legislative Assembly legalized the formation of foreign legions.

Those policies were not even modified on the eve of the war. Foreigners had never been better treated in France than when the government was getting ready to fight their countries of origin.[57] Thus, on August 24, 1792, a group of men of letters, led by the dramatist Marie-Joseph Chénier, brother of the poet, requested the Legislative Assembly to adopt, as "allies of the French people," a set of foreign writers whose works were already supposed to have abolished "the foundations of tyranny and prepared the way for liberty." To put it plainly, "these benefactors of humanity" were to be elected deputies. For the first time in the history of mankind, a statute of (honorary) integration was voted, which, in the name of human universality, recognized as *French* those who had done the most for mankind. Marie-David Alba, known as Lasource, Jacques-Alexis Thuriot, and Claude Basire were opposed to it, but, following a report by the Girondist Marguerite-Elie Guadet, a decree was approved on August 26, as proposed by Chénier, conferring the title of French Citizen to those foreign writers and learned men who, "in various areas of the world, have caused human reason to ripen and blazed the trails of liberty." Among those who were "adopted": Joseph Priestley, Thomas Paine, Jeremy Bentham, William Wilberforce (British politician and humanitarian, who successfully fought the slave trade), Thomas Clarkson (English abolitionist), Sir James Mackintosh (who, at first, had defended the French Revolution against Burke), Anacharsis Clootz, Johan Heinrich Pestalozzi (the Swiss educational reformer), George Washington, Alexander Hamilton, James Madison, Friedrich Gottlieb Klopstock, Thaddeus Kosciusko, Friedrich Schiller.

The course of events, however, particularly the launching of the Revolutionary Wars, did change the climate. Cosmopolitan ideas and their promotion, quite obviously, had not led European countries to line up under the revolutionary banner. As the time of armament arrived, foreigners appeared embarrassing, if not suspicious or guilty. Some foreign groups must have been "infiltrated" by the enemy. On that basis, an overall suspicion spread against all foreigners, to the point of making them liable to be sent to the scaffold, where many of them did perish.[58]

It is worth noting that henceforth the Hébertist faction became the defender of patriotic foreigners, while at the same time coming out for a fight to the death against the European coalition. Refined cosmopolitans did thus paradoxically move about in the extremist camp of *Père Duchesne* (the newspaper edited by Hébert), and some were sent to the guillotine when the Hébertists fell.

As bad news came from the battlefields, "foreign agents" were made responsible. On March 18, 1793, Bertrand de Barère demanded in the name of the Committee on Public Safety a repressive law against foreigners, whom the Republic was henceforth urged to banish. Pierre-Joseph Cambon asked that "all foreigners be made to leave the territory of the Republic." In each commune or section a twelve-member committee was established in order to collect statements by foreigners on the basis of which it would decide which one "must leave the commune within twenty-four hours and leave the territory of the Republic within eight days."[59] Having started with foreigners, those committees would soon extend their watchfulness to all other suspicious persons. On April 5, 1793, Robespierre asks the Jacobins "to expel all foreign generals whom we have unwisely entrusted with the command of the army."

After the events of May 31st involving a conflict between the National Convention and the Paris Commune, which resulted in a shift of power from the Girondists to the Mountain, both sides accused each other of being agents of William Pitt and the Duke of Saxe-Coburg, as foreigners inevitably became suspected of political scheming. With the financial situation going from bad to worse, Cambon blamed foreigners for the economic crisis that increasingly shook up the Republic (report to the Committee on Public Safety, dated July 11th). At once, reprisals against foreigners were organized, as they were against the European governments of the First Coalition. "Let us drive the English from our territory!" the Committee on Public Safety was urged. "All of them! All of them!" the representatives shouted. They asked that the road to Paris be blocked and suspects arrested. The National Convention declared: "Foreigners originally from those countries with which the Republic is at war and who had no domicile in France prior to July 14, 1789, will be arrested at once and seals placed on their papers, crates, and belongings." Many foreigners were imprisoned in town houses and requisitioned state buildings. It was proposed that "hospitality certificates" be created, which would be given by municipalities to those foreigners having successfully passed the "civics examination"; they would then wear an armband bearing the name of their country of origin and the word "hospitality." Fabre d'Eglantine laid stress on having all foreigners in France arrested and their possessions confiscated to the benefit of the Republic. A Hébertist asked, to no avail, that an exception be made for political immigrants who had come to defend the cause of liberty.

Two parties appeared to be forming: the Dantonists, who favored increasing harshness in the treatment of foreigners but were in favor of peace; and the Hébertists, who defended the immigrant patriots but pressed for an uncompromising war against Europe. Fabre d'Eglantine was particularly conspicuous in denouncing foreign plots. François Chabot and Claude Basire uncovered a conspiracy. Well-known foreigners were arrested: two Germans, the financier and ex-adviser to the Emperor of Austria Junius Frey, his brother Emmanuel, and their secretary Diedrichsen; two bankers from Brussels, Simon and Doroy as well as four other men who were employed by Hérault de Séchelles and found guilty of being secret agents.

One specific circumstance was injected into this hunting down of foreigners—and such a hunt, after all, was understandable in time of war. Some of the foreigners (like Clootz and Proly) were dyed-in-the-wool atheists and participated actively, sometimes crudely, in the "dechristianization" drive then in progress. The reactions that such excesses could not fail to provoke led some to believe that the dechristianization movement was a counter-revolutionary scheme. In similar fashion, the ultra-revolutionary retaliations demanded by the Hébertists, the sans-culotte followers of *Le Père Duchesne*, divided and decimated Republican ranks while hampering the necessarily mediatory role of the government. "We know of only one way to stop the evil, and that is to sacrifice without pity, on the tomb of the tyrant, all who regret tyranny, all who would be interested in avenging it, all who might have it come to life again among us," Saint-Just asserted in one of those well-turned and contradictory sentences that can lead people to make strange amalgamations. Besides, the catchword "Amalgamate!" has been attributed to him.[60] Extremists who were blamed for shortages, instigators of rebellions in prisons, and others, were "amalgamated" with foreign agents.

The clubs of foreigners were disbanded. On December 25, 1793, Robespierre, in his *Report on the Principles of Revolutionary Government*, blames foreigners for all crises.[61]

Obviously, it would be difficult to distinguish patriotic foreigners and those who remained faithful to a country hostile to France; in most cases, they would all be viewed as plotters. The Jacobins were convinced that "a criminal faction, a party bribed by a foreign country wanted to destroy the National Convention and the Jacobins."

On March 12, 1794, the Committee on Public Safety, fearing it was being outflanked by extremists, decided to have the Hébertists arrested: the Terror swooped down on those who had promulgated it. "Hébert, Vincent, Momoro [. . .] were foreign agents pretending to be anarchists"—thus was their arrest justified before the special meeting of the Jacobins on March 14th.

Were anticlerical cosmopolitans wrongly "amalgamated" with the Hébertists, or were the two trends actually in collusion? It has been said that Hébert had no link with Clootz,[62] and indeed *Le Père Duchesne* saw "the prophet Anacharsis Clootz" as a "Don Quixote" who wanted to convert people to liberty by means of war. Nevertheless, Hébert advocated cosmopolitanism, which, after the wars, would allow one to found a "Society of Nations."[63] All in all, Hébert, who appealed to the working class, whose vocabulary was coarse, was perhaps more rational than the visionary Clootz, but they probably shared a similar cosmopolitanism: the Belgian Proly and his friend François Desfieux were among the leaders of the Hébertist party. Moreover, does not cosmopolitanism, eccentric by definition, tend toward extremism? The anarchism of *Le Père Duchesne* could hardly displease these refined—but rebellious—enemies of identities and values, and who perhaps recognized in the oubursts of the sans-culotte avant-garde the Nephew's embarrassing verve and Fougeret's gall.

The scaffold took care of the cosmopolitan's lot, while nationalism—perhaps "regretfully" and "reluctantly"[64]—became paramount in both minds and laws. The Committee on Public Safety, after some hesitation, drew up a new law on foreigners on April 25, 1794. All former members of the nobility and foreign subjects were forbidden to stay in Paris, fortified towns, or coastal cities, for the length of the war (exceptions were made for workers in arms factories, foreign wives of patriots, and all those whose services were deemed useful to the Republic). Former members of the nobility and foreigners were henceforth excluded from people's societies, watch committees, communal or sectional assemblies. Amendments allowed a few exceptions for foreigners in residence for more than twenty years and a few other categories. Consequently, Englishmen were interned, the others forbidden to stay. The possessions of Englishmen and Spaniards were impounded, foreign legions were disbanded, deserters sent to work on farms. All were *excluded from public service and public rights*. Any troublemaking foreigner became suspicious and could be brought before the revolutionary tribunal.

It should be noted, however, that those steps were not as harsh as those taken during the war of 1914 . . .

2. Anacharsis Clootz: The "Speaker of Mankind" Against the Word "Foreigner"

It is worth recalling the fate of two foreigners who became French out of universalist spirit and thanks to a text adopted by the National Convention.

Jean-Baptiste du Val-de-Grâce, von Gnadenthal, Baron Clootz, born in the Rhineland (then under Prussian rule) of Dutch ancestry, educated by the Jesuits, favoring the ideas of the *Encyclopédie*, calling himself "Jesus Christ's personal enemy," joined the Revolution at its beginning, and was active in the Jacobin Club. On June 19, 1790, he presented to the National Assembly a "mission of mankind" made up of thirty-six foreigners, proclaiming that the world supported the *Declaration of the Rights of Man and Citizen*. This "Speaker of Mankind," who took the name of the Scythian philosopher Anacharsis in order to show his rejection of Christianism, became an ally of the Girondists.

Speaking before the Legislative Assembly he extolled in vivid terms the Girondist policy of expanding the rights of man to include foreign peoples, who would thus rise against their tyrants under the aegis of France: "The tricolored cockade and the tune *Ça ira* will be the delight of twenty liberated peoples [. . .] Frenchmen, swaggering with the book of the Constitution, shall be invincible" (December 13, 1791). Elected to the National Convention from the Department of Oise, he ceaselessly proclaimed his cosmopolitan ideas and published several noteworthy works.[65]

After the Girondist spirit was defeated to the advantage of a surveillance policy that soon developed into the Terror, Clootz not only failed to object to the steps taken against foreigners but violently broke with his former Girondist friends, accusing them, as was fashionable at the moment, of being allied with "the Prussian, Dutch, and English tyrants." Was this the about-turn of a fickle visionary, or the tactical quest for a new party that might shelter his cosmopolitan ideas? Be that as it may, Clootz, having become the friend of Hébert, Pierre-Gaspard Chaumette, and Jean-Nicholas Pache, ceaselessly asserted his ideas in support of a universal Republic, even going so far as to challenge the very notion of "foreigner": "The 'foreigner' a barbarous term that is beginning to make us blush, and the enjoyment of which we shall leave to those savage hordes who shall be eliminated without effort by the plow of civilized men" (April 16, 1793). That diatribe, perhaps the first critique of the concept of "foreigner" in history, did not fail to cause, at the moment, ironic reactions in the audience.

Clootz' excesses could only strengthen the policies of Robespierre and the Committee on Public Safety against conspiracies. One should note that Chabot's denunciation of foreigners as "foreign agents" occurred the day after Anacharsis, Pereira, and Chaumette succeeded in convincing the Bishop of Paris, Jean-Baptiste-Joseph Gobel, to announce theatrically before the National Convention that he was abdicating his title (November 7, 1793). Shortly thereafter (November 10), the Festival of Reason took place; it was the high point of the dechristianization trend, which Robespierre, fearing violent opposition, wanted to check.

Clootz' ebullience brought him closer to the Hébertists whose excesses bothered the government, and he became a favored target of the anti-Hébertist struggle. "Clootz is a Prussian, he is the first cousin of the often denounced Proly," Camille Desmoulins wrote in the second issue of *Le Vieux Cordelier* (December 10), convinced as he was that foreignness was a most effective argument in proving the guilt of a former friend. Anacharsis defended himself: "I am from Prussia, a future department of the French Republic." But that was not enough and, with the Jacobins, Robespierre had the last word—his telling point also being Clootz' foreign origin: "Can we view a German Baron as a patriot? Can we view a man who has an income of one hundred thousand pounds as a sans-culotte? [. . .] Fellow citizens, no. Let us beware of those foreigners who try to appear more patriotic than Frenchmen themselves. Clootz, you spend your life with our enemies, with the agents and spies of foreign powers, like them you are a traitor who must be watched."[66] Emphasizing further on that Clootz prefers the title, citizen of the world, to that of French citizen, Robespierre concluded: "Therefore, as an unerring consequence, the foreign party is dominant in the midst of the Jacobins. Yes, foreign powers have in our midst their spies, their ministers, treasurers, and a police force [. . .]. Clootz is a Prussian [. . .], I have outlined the history of his political life [. . .]. The verdict is yours to deliver!"

Anacharsis vainly attempted to defend his ideas on dechristianization. The very Hébertist press henceforth remained indifferent to his words. Clootz became more and more isolated.[67] It was also decided that all foreign-born members of the National Convention would cease to be members; Clootz and Paine were ejected and arrested. Jailed on December 28, 1793, Clootz had to wait until March 20, 1794, before being accused of Hébertism. He was guillotined along with the Hébertist leaders on March 24th. He remained an atheist to the last, preventing his companions from calling a priest and preaching them materialism.

Clootz' verve, passion, visionary and prophetic behavior had earned him favorable reactions,[68] before arousing suspicions and rejections. On account of his ebullient nature and speech, Anacharsis reminds one of the Nephew—an eccentric cosmopolitan, obtrusive, refractory, he shared in the tradition that includes Zeno and Diogenes among the best, Fougeret for the worst. The exuberance, the strangeness, and fervency of cosmopolitanism were not to outlive the cutting edge of the Revolution.

3. Thomas Paine: The "Citizen of the World"
Wants to Save the King

Thomas Paine, also a colorful character, the son of an English Quaker and tradesman, was a convinced revolutionary and first-rate polemical writer. At first a staymaker like his father, he soon bound himself to the American revolution; he emerged as one of its founders and was the friend of Franklin, Jefferson, and Washington. In 1775, using "Humanus" as a pseudonym, he published an article entitled "A Serious Thought" later collected in the same volume as *Common Sense*, which, before the *Declaration of Independence*, attacked the British crown and asked for independence from Britain. In *Common Sense* he violently attacked the aristocracy and the monarchy of the parent country, insulted George III whom he called "the royal brute of England" —and "even brutes do not devour their young." The Loyalists were outraged, they would have liked to have Paine out of the way. He later was appointed clerk of the Pennsylvania Assembly and, with the nickname "Common Sense," he became a national hero. That was only the beginning of the adventures of an untidy personage, lacking in personal hygiene (according to some biographers), a heavy drinker, quick-tempered, suspicious, ungrateful, but also generous, friendly, tolerant, and fair: impossible to categorize.

Attracted to the ideas of the French Revolution, Paine made several visits to France; he powerfully answered Burke and his *Reflections Upon the Revolution in France* (1790) by publishing his *Rights of Man* (1791–1792). He was ironic about Burke's liberal ideas and his lyricism, himself writing in a clear and straightforward manner. Relating the events he had observed in France, as a journalist might, he propounded a social and democratic theory of government and education. In the name of intelligence and against the "rotten boroughs," against fanaticism and aristocracy, he spoke of his confidence in man and his optimism concerning the French Revolution. Paine was henceforth seen as a fellow-traveler of French radicalism, his arguments receiving support from only a few English nonconformists—Richard Price, Charles Stanhope, Mary Wollestonecraft. Translated into French, his book was of course received with more enthusiasm: Condorcet and Lafayette were fervent admirers. Paine struck up a friendship with François-Xavier Lanthenas, his translator, and especially with Nicolas de Bonneville—who was one of the founders of the Republican Club and its ephemeral journal *Le Républicain*. The support of Nicolas de Bonneville never failed, even during the years of persecution. His family accompanied Paine when the latter, toward the end of his life, left France for an inglorious return to America.

For the time being, however, Lafayette, who believed in constitutional monarchy, ordered the royal fugitives to be recaptured at Varennes—and Paine argues . . . in order to save the king's life. The virulent antimonarchist of *Common Sense*, the boisterous revolutionary ready to justify the excesses of the people in the name of democracy, suddenly taught French revolutionaries an exemplary lesson in antiterrorism; he was able to put hatred aside for the sake of revolutionary reason, which was here identified with the rights of man for all, including the king. Brissot de Warville acted as his interpreter, as did his Girondist friends, Condorcet, Lanthenas, and Baucal des Issarts. Following a favor also granted several other foreigners, Paine became a representative of the Pas-de-Calais area and pleaded for the king: yes, let him be imprisoned and banished; as for the guillotine, no.

Without claiming any sort of immunity for the sovereign but, on the contrary, strenuously emphasizing the human weaknesses of the monarch, Paine believed that if the nation showed compassion toward him, that should come as an effect of magnanimity: "But my compassion for the man who is in trouble, even if he is also an enemy, is equally keen and sincere." Moreover, he evoked the support given by the defendant to the American revolution . . . The National Convention voted the death of the king. "The decision made by the National Convention, in favor of death, has

filled me with a deep sorrow," Paine stated; not understanding
French, he had Baucal translate the sentence. An honorary French
citizen since 1792, this francophile, by the way, never learned the
language of his third country. Suddenly Marat rose: "I submit
that Paine is incompetent to vote on this question. Being a
Quaker, his religious principles run counter to the will to inflict
the death penalty!"

Thus the hour of the guillotine tolled at the same time as that
of religious and national discrimination. Such a trend kept grow-
ing in strength, and foreigners were more and more suspected of
treason. After the fall and execution of the Girondists, Paine was
arrested. Curiously—was it on account of influential friends?—
this happened only on December 28, 1793, along with Clootz and
others, and he was locked up in the Luxembourg prison. But—is
it because he was seriously ill or because he benefited by secret
intercessions?—he eluded the guillotine. Freed on November 4,
1794, when the new American ambassador, James Monroe, claimed
him as a U.S. citizen, after ten months of jail, weakened and
unwell, "Common Sense" returned to the National Convention
and participated in the discussions on the constitution. But he
expressed reservations about the bill, which he considered conservative and a step backward from the *Declaration of the Rights
of Man*. Isolated from his peers, he was soon ignored at the
National Convention. As no department asked for his nomination
for the new elections, his career as representative came to an end
. . . He wrote Washington a letter full of insults that was inter-
cepted at the last minute, but in the end he managed to send it to
the American president. He became an adviser to Bonaparte and
then was rejected by him. Nevertheless, he kept on writing works
on economic, political, and technical problems . . . In ill health,
Paine left France in 1802. His enemies published slanderous
books about him, describing him as an alcoholic, and he sank
further into melancholia. On bad terms with everyone, depressed, drunk, dirty, and foul-smelling, Paine died in America,

forsaken; alone with a Quaker and two blacks, Mme de Bonne-ville and her two sons attended his funeral . . .

Was he a "hippie ahead of his time"? Someone "denational-ized," like Marxist-Leninists in the twentieth century?[69] This "citizen of the world" was the enemy of Christianity. His book, *The Age of Reason* (1794–1796), took it out on the clergy as much as on institutionalized religion, which he deemed a source of superstition contrary to Reason. But Paine remained faithful to the notion of a spiritual bond that transcends all religious differences. Provocative, heir to the cosmopolitan free-thinkers who challenged sacred values, Paine, however, was not precise enough to satisfy Robespierre. His essay proved to be a disap-pointment for French revolutionaries; in America, "then in the midst of a religious revival,"[70] it found only rare radical follow-ers.

Paine remains a foreigner everywhere. When modern histori-ans discover him today, they are surprised to note that he is unknown in France, the country to which he devoted the best of his chaotic ardor and talent. Some wished that a Paris street would bear his name. Man of the street, indeed, is Paine never-theless a man of any place? Of what place could he be, if not the place where a crisis brewed, an explosion or a revolution took place? Deprived of rest, without conclusion, "cosmopolitan"—in the sense of a permanent shattering . . .

8 Might Not Universality Be . . . Our Own Foreignness?

Beyond the ordeal of the Revolution, the Enlightenment's moral universalism discovered its masterly discourse in Kant's reasoned longing for universal peace. In contrapuntal fashion, the Romantic inversion, the emergence of German nationalism and most particularly Herder's notion of *Volksgeist*, but especially the Hegelian Negativity—which at the same time restored and systematized, unleashed and bound the power of the Other, against and within the consciousness of the Same—might be thought of as stages on the way to the "Copernican revolution" that the discovery of the Freudian unconscious amounted to. My point here will not be to follow that philosophical journey and trace Freud's indebtedness to the course that preceded him. Hence, from the tremendous Hegelian continent that gave the impetus to and completed the *thought* of the Other, I shall retain only what pertains to the intrinsic foreignness in culture, which Hegel brilliantly expanded starting from Diderot.[1] Nevertheless, so as better to point out the political and ethical impact of the Freudian breakthrough, or rather to outline an area where that impact might be thought out by others, by those who are foreign to the present book, inasmuch as the following pages are meant to be prospective, fragmentary, "subjective," more than demonstrative or didactic—I shall draw a tentative line going from Kant

to Herder and Freud. With Freud indeed, foreignness, an uncanny one, creeps into the tranquility of reason itself, and, without being restricted to madness, beauty, or faith anymore than to
ethnicity or race, irrigates our very speaking-being, estranged by
other logics, including the heterogeneity of biology . . . Henceforth, we know that we are foreigners to ourselves, and it is with
the help of that sole support that we can attempt to live with
others.

Kant the Universalist Pacifist

While cosmopolitism is exalted or brought down according to
the course of revolutionary events, it fell to Immanuel Kant to
formulate the internationalist spirit of the Enlightenment in political, legal, and philosophical terms.

Since it is in the "nature of man" to seek the well-being that
he himself created through reason, a man—through the philosopher—finds himself confronted with his "unsocial sociability."[2] By means of that phrase, so singularly apt and compact,
Kant conjures up at the same time our tendency to create societies
and the constant resistance we put up against them by threatening to split away: reasonable man wishes for concord, nature
favors discord. The result is that "the greatest problem for the
human race, to the solution of which Nature drives man, is the
achievement of a universal civic society which administers law
among men" (p. 16). To unbridled freedom and distress, men
oppose a state of constraint: they impose a discipline on unsocia-
bility, which reminds one of the origin of art (p. 17). On the
legal and political level, such a universal law could only be achieved
"by a lawful external relation among states" (p. 18). And Kant,
like the fiery cosmopolitans of the French Revolution, but with
the logical precision of a cool argumentation, would in his turn
advocate "a league of nations, [in which] even the smallest state
could expect security and justice, not from its own power and its
own decrees, but only from this great league of nations *(Foedus*

Amphictyonum), from a united power acting according to decisions reached under the laws of their united will" (p. 19).

Kant knew that the idea seemed preposterous—"fantastical," he said, thinking of how it was laughed at by the Abbé de Saint-Pierre and by Rousseau. Nevertheless, it seemed imperative to him "as the necessary outcome of destitution" and an exigency henceforth as pressing as that which forced savage men to give up their brutish freedom for the sake of a security based on the constraint of the first laws. Even though that may be a natural trend, it is nonetheless necessary "to find [. . .] a united power to give it effect. Thus it is forced to institute a cosmopolitan condition to insure the external safety of each state" (p. 23). This does not mean eliminating dangers, without which mankind might slumber, but it would firmly set aside the risk of destruction. Kant is aware of the *time* necessary for citizens to reach maturity in interior matters as for nations to reach concord in exterior ones: this would be a cosmic time, he asserted, in a comparison involving "the path of the sun and its host of satellites." He insisted, just the same, on the ineluctable need for men to "prepare the way for a distant international government for which there is no precedent in world history": "This gives hope finally that [. . .] a universal cosmopolitan condition, which Nature has as her ultimate purpose, will come into being as the womb wherein all the original capacities of the human race can develop" (p. 23).

Echoing Montesquieu and Rousseau, and also resonating with Clootz—who, as we have seen, took up again in his visionary rhetoric the idea of a universal Republic, even providing "constitutional foundations" for the "human species"—Kant's text inscribed, at the outset of a political ethics and a legal reality that are still to be carried out, the cosmopolitan concept of a mankind finding its full accomplishment without foreigners but respecting the right of those that are different. The notion of *separation* combined with *union* was to clarify such a practical cosmopolitanism that nature foresees and men carry out. Having doubtlessly learned from the clashes between nationalisms and cosmopolitan-isms during the French Revolution, Kant elaborated upon that doctrine ten years later in *Perpetual Peace* (1795). In what manner? After having distinguished between *jus civitatis* (the civil code of a people) and *jus gentium* (international law), he defined *jus cosmopoliticum* (cosmopolitan law): "Peoples, as states, like individuals, may be judged to influence one another merely by their coexistence in the state of nature." In order to avoid the state of war that particular states are led to establish for the purpose of imposing their own interests, Kant advocated the "idea of federation, which should gradually spread to all states and thus lead to perpetual peace."[3] Such a "State of various nations" *(civitas gentium)*, such a universal Republic would include all the peoples of the World. In that spirit, the idea that was outlined by the cosmopolitans of the French Revolution concerning the integration of foreigners was taken up in similar terms: "Hospitality means the right of a stranger not to be treated as an enemy when he arrives in the land of another." Whence would such generosity follow? Quite simply . . . because the Earth is round: naturally therefore, inevitably.[4]

Far removed from that ideal, however, European states considered newly discovered countries as being "lands without owners," and they have intensified their injustices toward foreigners. In order to proceed out of that dramatic situation toward the state of nations that he proposed, Kant could only call upon "free practical reason," which will accomplish no more than a design inherent in Nature itself.[5]

This is where the acknowledgment of *difference* is inscribed at the very heart of the universal republic. First, the *coexistence* of states will guarantee their vitality and their democracy better than "amalgamation of states under one superior power," which might degenerate into one universal monarchy—a potential source of anarchy. Second, Nature, whom free practical reason respects and fulfills, "employs two means to separate peoples and to prevent them from mixing: differences of language and of religion" (p. 113). Thus *separation* and *union* would guarantee universal peace at the core of this cosmopolitanism, understood as coexistence of the differences that are imposed by the technique of international relations on the one hand and political morality on the other. In short, since politics can only be moral, the fulfillment of man and of the designs of Providence demand that it be "cosmopolitical."

This reasoned hymn to cosmopolitanism, which runs through Kant's thought as a debt to Enlightenment and the French Revolution, appears indeed, today still, like an idealistic utopia, but also as an inescapable necessity in our contemporary universe, which unifies production and trade among nations at the same time as it perpetuates among them a state of war both material and spiritual.

Once more, the ethical decision alone appears able to transcend the narrow needs of national politics. Could cosmopolitanism as moral imperative be the secular form of that bond bringing together families, languages, and states that religion claimed to be? Something beyond religion: the belief that individuals are fulfilled if and only if the entire species achieves the practice of rights for everyone, everywhere? . . .

The Patriotic Nation Between "Common Sense" and "Volksgeist"

It is nevertheless against a background of national conscience and patriotism or nationalism that the contemporary position of foreigners stands out and can be understood. Now, modern nationalism, which also has ancient roots, does not show up before the second half of the eighteenth century, and it is also during the French Revolution that it will be most firmly expressed.[6] Cosmopolitan and rationalistic, the French Enlightenment laid down at the same time the idea of the *nation* that the lengthy work of humanists had prepared since the Renaissance (particularly through the awakening of national languages and literatures) and to which absolute monarchy had given a centralized political structure. One can trace, throughout the seventeenth century, the progressive shift of a political thought advocating royal authority toward one concerned with the sovereignty of the people and of the nation. Even though a "national feeling" did not yet exist, one can detect in the England of that time the formation of public opinion tied to its geographic particularities and ethical values (*Rule Britannia* was composed in 1740), even if the word "patriotism" still retained ironic overtones in those days. Henry St. John, Viscount Bolingbroke introduced into political theory the notion of "particular law," which, while being of universal, divine inspiration, must nevertheless aim at the happiness of the various national communities. His works, *Letters on the Spirit of Patriotisme* (1736) and *The Idea of the Patriot King* (1738) endow the word with a new meaning and are quickly disseminated in France. The emphasis placed by Voltaire or Montesquieu on the specific passions and character of peoples; the distinction made by Turgot between "State" and "nation," the latter being based on a common language; the expansion of the French language through the publication of translations; the more and more confident expression of the "third estate" in a literature of manners rooted in feelings, landscape, and the social individual (from *Manon Lescaut* to *La Nouvelle Heloïse*)—all these can be numbered among the harbingers of the *national idea*. It is Rousseau (1712–1778) who expressed it best, until a cultural, social, and political community displayed itself in the very act of the Revolution: the *sovereign people* beheading the royal sovereignty.

An essential vein of the Enlightenment, along the same lines as and sometimes contradictory with respect to its universalism, this patriotic and nationalistic Rousseauism still underlies contemporary nationalism. It is, however, only one of its components. Nostalgia for the Geneva hearth, which identifies the individual with his geographic and familial origin; the concern for preserving the person even within its closest kinship; the emphasis on free will, which alone must create a national community—such are some of the features of Rousseau's patriotism, which combine sentimentalism and rationalism, passionate withdrawal and demand for justice and freedom, romantic latencies and political lucidity based on the contract of citizens conscious of their equality and their right to happiness. Beyond its sensitive tones, there is a political rationalism that underlies the national idea with Rousseau, allowing patriotic pride to rest on the "common sense" inspired by the Cartesian "free will" and *cogito ergo sum* as foundation of the national contract. Let us first listen to the heart: "Going through Geneva, I went to see no one, but I nearly fainted on the bridges. I have never seen the walls of that happy city, I have never entered it without experiencing a certain weakness of the heart that came from an excess of emotion"[7] Nevertheless, if the self is to merge into the national community,[8] the latter can be tolerable only if it is subservient to the happiness of its members.[9]

Such a contractual concept, wholly political and founded rationally, thus naturally, on everyone's right to freedom, is already appreciably removed from the first signs of national feeling in France, which the presence of the monarchy readily rooted in inheritance and soil. Rousseau's nationalism can be appreciated by contrasting it with Vincent Voiture's very "personalist" version, for instance, concerning Cardinal Richelieu's feats.[10]

National pride, which ignores neither boasting nor spirited jingoism, also discovered during the French Revolution a predominant terrorist feature, about which one may well ask whether it was a violent distortion of Rousseau's nationalism or its intrinsic consequence. The fact remains that patriotism in *Emile* or *The Social Contract* is subordinate to the universality of human rights. Thus, while signing "the Geneva Citizen" to his preface to the *Letter to D'Alembert* (1758), Rousseau noted: "Justice and truth, such are the primary duties of man. Mankind and fatherland, such are his first affections. Every time particular attentions cause him to change that order, he is guilty."[11] This would lead

Rousseau, following upon the Abbé de Saint-Pierre's *Projet de paix perpétuelle* (1713), to consider a confederation of peoples in order to prevent war—an idea that Kant would take up again and expand upon.[12]

Another current came to merge with that rational nationalism, which had been legalistic and respectful of the individual, and gave modern nationalism its definitive hue. Even though it grew out of the later German illuministic movements, this second nationalism was nevertheless not rooted in the *legal* and *political* idea of a sovereign nation whose laws guarantee the exercise of freedom and justice but in the more *feudal* and *spiritualistic* idea of physical kinship and linguistic identity.

The melancholy English sentimentalism was not foreign to its appearance—Richardson's *Clarissa* (1748), Edward Young's *The Complaint, or Night Thoughts* (1742–1745), or James Macpherson's *Fragments of Ancient Poetry* (1760), which rationalized the spirit of Gaelic legends, belong to this current. But it was in Germany that the mystical idea of the nation acquired its full scope.

It can be said that in central and eastern Europe the dissolution of Napoleon's Empire did not lead to the formation of a despotic state sufficiently powerful and well-ordered to further the development of a political will. It might also be suggested that Luther's Protestantism inverted into a pragmatic mystique concerned with individual accomplishment what in France produced a common sense of what social stakes were entailed and in England a democratic public opinion eager for political sovereignty. Undoubtedly numerous elements have, through Klopstock, Moser, and especially Herder, ended in the advent of the notion of national community, *Gemeinschaft:* not a political one, but organic, evolutionary, at the same time vital and metaphysical—the expression of a nearly irrational and indiscernible spirit that is summed up by the word *Gemeinsinn.*[13] A supreme value, such a national spirit, *Volksgeist,* is not, with Herder, biological, "scientific," or even political, but essentially moral. It is only after 1806 that this *cultural* concept of "nation" became *political* and became invested in the national-political struggle. As if, as a first step, the French Enlightenment had aroused in the mind of the Protestant Johann Gottfried von Herder (1744–1803) a burst of national feeling anchored in language and mindful of each nation's differential values at the core of universalistic humanism. And as if, as a second step, the repercussion of revolutionary wars had modified that *national religion* into *nationalist* and even more so *reactional politics,* seeking, in opposition to universalist abstraction, a romantic withdrawal into the mystique of the past, into the people's character, or into the individual and national genius —all irreducible, rebel, unthinkable, and restorative. Within this familial and irrational pouch there was room both for national withdrawal (in times of defeat and difficulties, as a structure insuring an archaic integrity, an indispensible guarantee for the family) and national pride (during periods of aggression, as the spearhead of a policy of economic and military expansion).

Henceforth the supreme good no longer was the individual according to Rousseau but the nation was a whole. And even if, with Herder, that nationalist supremacy was checked by a Christian ethics that caused him to be ironical about the feeling of superiority some peoples might have concerning themselves, the path was thus open to irrationalism. The very worship of the national language was heavily weighed down with ambiguities.

Nationalism as Intimacy: From Herder to the Romanticists

A translation, that of the Bible, is what founded the modern notion of German culture *(Bildung).* Indeed, when Luther (1483–1546) translated the Holy Writ into spoken German ("The mother in the house and the common man speak thus," is what he said to justify his work), he not only set himself against Roman authority by "unlatinizing" German. More ambitiously yet, he endeavored to found a national culture that, through a twofold motion of *faithfulness* to models and *expansion* of the national register as it was first given in language, persevered up until its Romantic apogee. The Romantic enthusiasm for the national genius *(Volksgeist)* between 1800 and 1830 should not allow one to forget that this cultural nationalism, from the very beginning, rested upon the need to display one's *own* while modifying it through a confrontation with the sacred or classical canon: national features are thus based upon a broadened *translatability*, which merges with the idea of *Bildung*, understood, to begin with, as a process of formation of a national language.[14]

In contradistinction to the rationalist cosmopolitanism of the Enlightenment, already perceived as hollow, one nevertheless finds in Herder the first and most explicit expression of such an anchoring of culture in the genius of the language. While remaining deeply faithful to a Christian universalism (was not Augustine's *City of God* the first cosmopolitan history of mankind?) this Protestant minister was the true founder of the worship of the national spirit so dear to Romanticists.

As early as his *Fragments on the New German Literature* (1767) Herder extolled the originality of the German language, at the same time demanding its improvement through a continuing competition with ancient and modern languages, something he contrasted with mere obedience to classical models. Following *On the Origin of Languages* (1772), *Another Philosophy of History* developed a violent patriotic polemic both against "enlightened" and cosmopolitan despotism and against the "abstract" rationalism of the Enlightenment. Every nation—whose originality, according to Herder, rests in language and literature before affecting mores, government, and religion—is conceived according to the model of the stages of existence, while being integrated into the chain of civilization where it seeks to be the equal of others. In that spirit, his *Voices of Nations in Songs* brought back into favor the medieval past and the prestige of the German people's poetry.

Meanwhile, having linked his history of mankind to biology,

Herder finally formulated his famous *Ideas on the Philosophy of History of Mankind* (1784–1791), closer to enlightened humanism than to the Lutheranism of 1774. Here Herder reveals himself to be less concerned with differences in climate or customs, even though he does blame local bad weather for what he considers the shortcomings of the blacks or the Chinese. On the other hand, he pays utmost attention to God's "peoples" (Herder does not accept the idea of "human races"), who remain brothers in their organisms but become radically differentiated on the basis of their languages and civilizations.

While it is true that he built up the cult of a "primeval national language" that owes it to itself to remain "unsullied" by any translation, since it is, as for Klopstock, "a kind of wellspring of the most original concept of people," Herder is only indirectly responsible for its appropriation by nationalist politicians. Recently still, he has been viewed as a regionalist. He was, in spite of all, a translator: he translated Spanish "romances," was interested in English literature and Greek and Roman antiquity, and often maintained a concern for balance between "one's own" and the "foreign": "I observe foreign customs in order to conform my own to the genius of my fatherland, like much ripe fruit under an alien sun"; in a centrifugal motion the translated work must be revealed "as it is," but also as it is "for us."[15] This *Volksgeist*, rooted in a language that is seen as a constant process of alteration and surpassing of itself, nevertheless becomes a conservative, reactional concept when it is extracted from the *Bildung*'s tempo and exalted of its original purity or consigned to the ineffable. Intrinsically, however, such an assimilation of language to *Bildung* and, conversely, this emphasis on national *speech* as the lowest denominator of identity—all this removed Christian or humanistic cosmopolitanism from its spiritual, natural, or contractual lack of precision; furthermore, it allows us to consider what is "foreign" under the logical, familiar aspect of language and culture.

Starting from there, it would seem essential to effect a taming of foreignness on the basis of a specific logic, which would find its major developments in the philological and literary interest for national languages and literatures. One discovers such an attitude in the Romanticists' particularism, in love as they were with national peculiarities, as well as in Goethe's universalism and his advocacy of a *Weltliteratur*.

The localization of foreignness thus recognized and even positivized in national language and culture will be repeated within the Freudian unconscious, concerning which Freud specified that it followed the logic of each national language. One can even detect in Heidegger's philosophic philologism, which unfolds the concepts of Greek thought from the resonances of its vocabulary, something like an echo of that philology of the national genius inspired by Herder.

On the other hand, the generations following Herder's have extrapolated the literary autarky—which was indeed advocated by the master, who nevertheless subordinated it to the totality of human culture—to make of it an argumant extolling the "cosmopolitanism of German literary taste." The latter was then understood as a *superiority* expressing the result of the cultural absolute and thus being placed *above* other peoples, languages, and cultures—justifying the demand for a German cultural hegemony. Such a nationalist perversion of the cosmopolitan idea, vitiated and dominated by a national "superiority" that one has taken care to valorize beforehand is, as is well know, at the basis of Nazi ideology.[16]

Rooting the specific in human universality's (the gift of speech) diversified manifestations (national languages) went hand in hand, with Romanticists, with the concept of an *invisible foundation* of universal, visible nature. One imagined that such a *Grund*, specific to nature itself as well as to the human soul, was engaged less in intellectual research than in an emotional, instinctual, and intimate quest—the *Gemüt*. The Romantic leaning toward the supernatural, parapsychology, madness, dreams, the obscure forces of the *fatum*, and even animal psychology is related to the desire to grasp the strange, and by domesticating it, turn it into an integral component of the human. *Einfühlung*—an identifying harmony—with the strange and the different then became essential as the distinctive feature of the worthy, cultivated man: "The perfect man must be capable of living equally in various places and among diverse peoples," Novalis noted.[17]

The strangeness of the Romantic hero thus assumed substance and shape and presented itself as the fertilizing soil out of which a heterogeneous notion of the *unconscious* sprang froth—simultaneously as man's deep link with nature's dark substratum (with Carus and Schubert), as underlying the will to representation (with Schopenhauer), or as intelligent dynamism of Hegelian inspiration operating blindly beneath the surface of the apparent universe (with Hartmann).

One cannot hope to understand Freud's contribution, in the specific field of psychiatry, outside of its humanistic and Romantic filiation. With the Freudian notion of the unconscious the involution of the strange in the psyche loses its pathological aspect and integrates within the assumed unity of human beings an *otherness* that is both biological *and* symbolic and becomes an integral part of the *same*. Henceforth the foreigner is neither a race nor a nation. The foreigner is neither glorified as a secret *Volksgeist* nor banished as disruptive of rationalist urbanity. Uncanny, foreignness is within us: we are our own foreigners, we are divided. Even though it shows a Romanticist filiation, such an intimist restoring of the foreigner's good name undoubtedly bears the biblical tones of a foreign God or of a Foreigner apt to reveal God.[18] Freud's personal life, a Jew wandering from Galicia to Vienna and London, with stopovers in Paris, Rome, and New York (to mention only a few of the key stages of his encounters with political and cultural foreignness), conditions his concern to face the other's discontent as ill-ease in the continuous presence of the "other scene" within us. My discontent in living with the other—my strangeness, his strangeness—rests on the perturbed logic that governs this strange bundle of drive and language, of nature and symbol, constituted by the unconscious, always already shaped by the other. It is through unraveling transference—the major dynamics of otherness, of love/hatred for the other, of the foreign component of our psyche—that, on the basis of the other, I become reconciled with my own otherness-foreignness, that I play on it and live by it. Psychoanalysis is then experienced as a journey into the strangeness of the other and of oneself, toward an ethics of respect for the irreconcilable. How could one tolerate a foreigner if one did not know one was a stranger to oneself? And to think that it has taken such a long time for that small truth, which transverses or even runs against religious uniformist tendencies, to enlighten the people of our time! Will it allow them to put up with one another as irreducible, because they are desiring, desirable, mortal, and death-bearing?

Freud: "Heimlich/Unheimlich"—the Uncanny Strangeness

Explicitly given limited scope, as it was at first connected with esthetic problems and emphasized texts by E. T. A. Hoffmann, Freud's *Das Unheimliche* (1919) surreptitiously goes beyond that framework and the psychological phenomenon of "uncanny strangeness" as well, in order to acknowledge itself as an investigation into *anguish* generally speaking and, in a fashion that is even more universal, into the *dynamics of the unconscious*. Indeed, Freud wanted to demonstrate at the outset, on the basis of a semantic study of the German adjective *heimlich* and its antonym *unheimlich* that a negative meaning close to that of the antonym is already tied to the positive term *heimlich*, "friendlily comfortable," which would also signify "concealed, kept from sight," "deceitful and malicious," "behind someone's back." Thus, in the very word *heimlich*, the familiar and intimate are reversed into their opposites, brought together with the contrary meaning of "uncanny strangeness" harbored in *unheimlich*. Such an immanence of the strange within the familiar is considered as an etymological proof of the psychoanalytic hypothesis according to which "the uncanny is that class of the frightening which leads back to what is known of old and long familiar,"[19] which, as far as Freud was concerned, was confirmed by Schelling who said that "everything is *unheimlich* that ought to have remained secret and hidden but has come to light" (p. 225).

Consequently therefore, that which *is* strangely uncanny would be that which *was* (the past tense is important) familiar and, under certain conditions (which ones?), emerges. A first step was taken that removed the uncanny strangeness from the outside, where fright had anchored it, to locate it inside, not inside the familiar considered as one's own and proper, but the familiar potentially tainted with strangeness and referred (beyond its imaginative origin) to an improper past. The other is my ("own and proper") unconscious.

What "familiar"? What "past"? In order to answer such questions, Freud's thought played a strange trick on the esthetic and psychological notion of "uncanny strangeness," which had been initially posited, and rediscovered the analytical notions of *anxiety, double, repetition,* and *unconscious*. The uncanny strangeness that is aroused in Nathaniel (in Hoffmann's tale, *The Sandman*) by the paternal figure and its substitutes, as well as references to the eyes, is related to the castration anxiety experienced by the child, which was repressed but surfaced again on the occasion of a state of love.

The Other Is My (Own and Proper) Unconscious

Furthermore, Freud noted that the archaic, narcissistic self, not yet demarcated by the outside world, projects out of itself what it experiences as dangerous or unpleasant in itself, making of it an alien *double*, uncanny and demoniacal. In this instance the strange appears as a defense put up by a distraught self: it protects itself by substituting for the image of a benevolent double that used to be enough to shelter it the image of a malevolent double into which it expels the share of destruction it cannot contain.

The repetition that often accompanies the feeling of uncanny strangeness relates it to the "compulsion to repeat" that is peculiar to the unconscious and emanating out of "drive impulses"— a compulsion "proceeding from the drive impulses and probably inherent in the very nature of the drives—a compulsion powerful enough to overrule the pleasure principle" (p. 238).

The reader is henceforth ready to accept the feeling of uncanny strangeness as an instance of anxiety in which "the frightening element can be shown to be something repressed which *recurs*" (p. 241). To the extent, however, that psychic situations evidencing an absolute repression are rare, such a return of the repressed in the guise of anxiety, and more specifically of uncanny strangeness, appears as a paroxystic metaphor of the psychic functioning itself. The latter is indeed elaborated by repression and one's necessarily going through it, with the result that the builder of the *other* and, in the final analysis, of the *strange* is indeed repression itself and its perviousness. "We can understand why linguistic usage has extended *das Heimliche* into its opposite, *das Unheimliche;* for this uncanny is in reality nothing new or alien, but something which is familiar and old-established in the mind and which has become alienated from it only through the process of repression" (p. 241).

Let us say that the psychic apparatus represses representative processes and contents that are no longer necessary for pleasure, self-preservation, and the adaptive growth of the speaking subject and the living organism. Under certain conditions, however, the repressed "that ought to have remained secret" shows up again and produces a feeling of uncanny strangeness.

While saying that he would henceforth tackle "one or two more examples of the uncanny," Freud in his text actually continues, by means of a subtle, secret endeavor, to reveal the circumstances that are favorable to going through repression and generating the uncanny strangeness. The confrontation with *death* and its representation is initially imperative, for our unconscious refuses the fatality of death: "Our unconscious has as little use now as it ever had for the idea of its own mortality." The fear of death dictates an ambivalent attitude: we imagine ourselves surviving (religions promise immortality), but death just the same remains the survivor's enemy, and it accompanies him in his new existence. Apparitions and ghosts represent that ambiguity and fill with uncanny strangeness our confrontations with the image of death.

The fantasy of being buried alive induces the feeling of uncanny strangeness, accompanied by "a certain lasciviousness— the phantasy, I mean, of intra-uterine existence" (p. 244). We are confronted with a second source of the strange: "It often happens that neurotic men declare that they feel there is something uncanny about the female genital organs. This *unheimlish* place, however, is the entrance to the former *Heim* of all human beings, to the place where each one of us lived once upon a time and in the beginning." "There is a joking saying that 'Love is homesickness' " (p. 245).

The *death* and the *feminine,* the end and the beginning that engross and compose us only to frighten us when they break through, one must add "the living person [. . .] when we ascribe evil intentions to him [. . .] that are going to be carried out with the help of special powers" (p. 243). Such malevolent *powers* would amount to a weaving together of the symbolic and the organic—perhaps *drive* itself, on the border of the psyche and biology, overriding the breaking imposed by organic homeostasis. A disturbing symptom of this may be found in epilepsy and madness, and their presence in our fellow beings worries us the more as we dimly sense them in ourselves.

A Semiology of Uncanny Strangeness

Are death, the feminine, and drives always a pretext for the uncanny strangeness? After having broadened the scope of his meditation, which might have led to seeing in uncanniness the description of the working of the unconscious, which is itself dependant on repression, Freud marked its required limits by stressing a few particularities of the semiology within which it emerges. Magical practices, animism, or, in more down-to-earth fashion, "intellectual uncertainty" and "disconcerted" logic (according to E. Jentsch) are all propitious to uncanniness. Now, what brings together these symbolic processes, quite different for all that, lies in a weakening of the value of signs as such and of their specific logic. The symbol ceases to be a symbol and "takes over the full functions of the thing it symbolizes" (p. 244). In other words, the sign is not experienced as arbitrary but assumes a real importance. As a consequence, the material reality that the sign was commonly supposed to point to crumbles away to the benefit of imagination, which is no more than "the over-accentuation of psychical reality in comparison with material reality" (p. 244). We are here confronted with "the omnipotence of thought," which, in order to constitute itself invalidates the arbitrariness of signs and the autonomy of reality as well and places them both under the sway of fantasies expressing infantile desires or fears.

Obsessional neuroses, but also and differently psychoses, have the distinctive feature of "reifying" signs—of slipping from the domain of "speaking" to the domain of "doing." Such a particularity *also* evinces the fragility of repression and, without actually explaining it, allows the return of the repressed to be inscribed in the reification under the guise of the uncanny affect. While, in another semiological device, one might think that the return of the repressed would assume the shape of the somatic symptom or of the acting out, here the breakdown of the arbitrary signifier and its tendency to become reified as psychic contents that take the place of material reality would favor the experience of uncanniness. Conversely, our fleeting or more or less threatening encounter with uncanny strangeness would be a clue to our psychotic latencies and the fragility of our repression —at the same time as it is an indication of the weakness of language as a symbolic barrier that, in the final analysis, structures the repressed.

Strange indeed is the encounter with the other—whom we perceive by means of sight, hearing, smell, but do not "frame" within our consciousness. The other leaves us separate, incoherent; even more so, he can make us feel that we are not in touch with our own feelings, that we reject them or, on the contrary, that we refuse to judge them—we feel "stupid," we have "been had."

Also strange is the experience of the abyss separating me from the other who shocks me—I do not even perceive him, perhaps he crushes me because I negate him. Confronting the foreigner whom I reject and with whom at the same time I identify, I lose my boundaries, I no longer have a container, the memory of experiences when I had been abandoned overwhelm me, I lose my composure. I feel "lost," "indistinct," "hazy." The uncanny strangeness allows for many variations: they all repeat the difficulty I have in situating myself with respect to the other and keep going over the course of identification-projection that lies at the foundation of my reaching autonomy.

At this stage of the journey, one understands that Freud took pains to separate the uncanniness provoked by esthetic experience from that which is sustained in reality; he most particularly stressed those works in which the uncanny effect is abolished because of the very fact that the entire world of the narrative is fictitious. Such are fairy tales, in which the generalized artifice spares us any possible comparison between sign, imagination, and material reality. As a consequence, artifice neutralizes uncanniness and makes all returns of the repressed plausible, acceptable, and pleasurable. As if absolute enchantment—absolute sublimation—just as, on the other hand, absolute rationality—absolute repression—were our only defenses against uncanny strangeness . . . Unless, depriving us of the dangers as well as the pleasures of strangeness, they be the instruments of their liquidation.

Subjects, Artists, and . . . a King

Linked to anguish, as we have seen, the uncanny strangeness does not, however, merge with it. Initially it is a shock, something unusual, astonishment; and even if anguish comes close, uncanniness maintains that share of unease that leads the self, beyond anguish, toward depersonalization. "The sense of strangeness belongs in the same category as depersonalization," Freud noted, and many analysts have stressed the frequency of the *Unheimliche* affect in phobia, especially when the contours of the self are overtaxed by the clash with something "too good" or "too bad." In short, if anguish revolves around an *object*, uncanniness, on the other hand, is a *destructuration of the self* that may either remain as a psychotic *symptom* or fit in as an *opening* toward the new, as an attempt to tally with the incongruous. While it surely manifests the return of a familiar repressed, the *Unheimliche* requires just the same the impetus of a new encounter with an unexpected outside element: arousing images of death, automatons, doubles, or the female sex (the list is probably not complete, as Freud's text leaves such an impression of a rather distant reserve—because it is passionate), uncanniness occurs when the boundaries between *imagination* and *reality* are erased. This observation reinforces the concept—which arises out of Freud's text—of the *Unheimliche* as a crumbling of conscious defenses, resulting from the conflicts the self experiences with an other—the "strange"—with whom it maintains a conflictual bond, at the same time "a need for identification and a fear of it" (Maurice Bouvet). The clash with the other, the identification of the self with that good or bad other that transgresses the fragile boundaries of the uncertain self, would thus be at the source of an uncanny strangeness whose excessive features, as represented in literature, cannot hide its permanent presence in "normal" psychical dynamics.

A child confides in his analyst that the finest day in his life is that of his birth: "Because that day it was me—I like being me, I don't like being an other." Now he feels other when he has poor grades—when he is bad, alien to the parents' and teachers' desire. Likewise, the unnatural, "foreign" languages, such as writing or mathematics, arouse an uncanny feeling in the child.[20]

This is where we leave the extraordinary realm of literary uncanniness to find its immanence (a necessary hence commonplace one) in psychism as the experience of otherness. It is possible, as Yvon Brès said, that Freud's recourse to esthetic works in order to set up the notion of uncanny strangeness was an admission that psychoanalysis could not possibly deal with it. Man would be facing a kind of "existential apriorism," in the presence of which Freudian thought merges with Heidegger's phenomenology.[21] Without going so far as to assume such a link, let us note, however, that Freud picks up the phrase again in *The Future of an Illusion* (1927): civilization humanizes nature by endowing it with beings that look like us—it is such an animistic process that enables us "to breathe freely [and] feel at home in the uncanny [so that we] can deal by psychical means with our [previously] senseless anxiety."[22] Here uncanny strangeness is no longer an artistic or pathological product but a psychic law allowing us to confront the unknown and work it out in the process of *Kulturarbeit,* the task of civilization. Freud, who "must himself plead guilty to a special obtuseness in the matter" of the uncanny,[23] thus opens up two other prospects when confronting the strange, which is related to anguish. On the one hand, the sense of strangeness is a mainspring for identification with the other, by working out its depersonalizing impact by means of astonishment. On the other hand, analysis can throw light on such an affect but, far from insisting on breaking it down, it should make way for esthetics (some might add philosophy), with

which to saturate its phantasmal progression and insure its ca-
thartic eternal return, for instance with readers of disturbing
tales.

The violent, catastrophic aspect the encounter with the *foreigner* may assume is to be included in the generalizing consequences that seem to stem out of Freud's observations on the
activating of the uncanny. As test of our astonishment, source of
depersonalization, we cannot suppress the symptom that the foreigner provokes; but we simply must come back to it, clear it up,
give it the resources our own essential depersonalizations pro-
vide, and only thus soothe it.

And yet, the uncanny strangeness can also be evacuated: "No,
that does not bother me; I laugh or take action—I go away, I
shut my eyes, I strike, I command . . ." Such an elimination of
the strange could lead to an elimination of the psyche, leaving, at
the cost of mental impoverishment, the way open to acting out,
including paranoia and murder. From another point of view,
there is no uncanny strangeness for the person enjoying an
acknowledged power and a resplendent image. Uncanniness, for
that person, is changed into management and authorized expenditure: strangeness is for the "subjects," the sovereign ignores it,
knowing how to have it administered. An anecdote related by
Saint-Simon provides a good illustration of that situation.[24] The
Sun-King (French psychoanalysts strangely avoid questioning
major political and artistic figures of national history, even though
the latter is so weighed down with discourse and psychological
enigmas as well) erases the uncanny and his fear in order to
display the whole of his being exclusively within the law and the
pleasure of Versailles' pomp. Disturbed innerness is the courtiers'
lot; they were the compost of the psychic subtlety that the
brilliant writer of memoirs has handed down to us, often remark-
ably anticipating Freud's speculations.

Finally, some might change the weird into irony. One imagines Saint-Simon, a shrewd smile on his lips, as far removed
from regal censorship as he was from the courtiers' embarrass-

ment: the humorist goes right through uncanny strangeness and —starting from a self-confidence that is his own or is based on his belonging to an untouchable universe that is not at all threatened by the war between same and others, ghosts and doubles— seeing in it nothing more than smoke, imaginary structures, signs. To worry or to smile, such is the choice when we are assailed by the strange; our decision depends on how familiar we are with our own ghosts.

The Strange Within Us

The uncanny would thus be the royal way (but in the sense of the court, not of the king) by means of which Freud introduced the fascinated rejection of the other at the heart of that "our self," so poised and dense, which precisely no longer exists ever since Freud and shows itself to be a strange land of borders and othernesses ceaselessly constructed and deconstructed. Strangely enough, there is no mention of *foreigners* in the *Unheimliche*.

Actually, a foreigner seldom arouses the terrifying anguish provoked by death, the female sex, or the "baleful" unbridled drive. Are we nevertheless so sure that the "political" feelings of xenophobia do not include, often unconsciously, that agony of frightened joyfulness that has been called *unheimlich*, that in English is *uncanny*, and the Greeks quite simply call *xenos*, "foreign"? In the fascinated rejection that the foreigner arouses in us, there is a share of uncanny strangeness in the sense of the depersonalization that Freud discovered in it, and which takes up again our infantile desires and fears of the other—the other of death, the other of woman, the other of uncontrollable drive. The foreigner is within us. And when we flee from or struggle against the foreigner, we are fighting our unconscious—that "improper" facet of our impossible "own and proper." Delicately, analytically, Freud does not speak of foreigners: he teaches us how to detect foreignness in ourselves. That is perhaps the only way not to hound it outside of us. After Stoic cosmopolitanism, after religious universalist integration, Freud brings us the courage to call ourselves disintegrated in order not to integrate foreigners and even less so to hunt them down, but rather to welcome them to that uncanny strangeness, which is as much theirs as it is ours.

In fact, such a Freudian distraction or discretion concerning the "problem of foreigners"—which appears only as an eclipse or, if one prefers, as a symptom, through the recall of the Greek word *xenoi*[25]—might be interpreted as an invitation (a utopic or very modern one?) not to reify the foreigner, not to petrify him as such, not to petrify *us* as such. But to analyze it by analyzing us. To discover our disturbing otherness, for that indeed is what bursts in to confront that "demon," that threat, that apprehension generated by the projective apparition of the other at the heart of what we persist in maintaining as a proper, solid "us." By recognizing *our* uncanny strangeness we shall neither suffer from it nor enjoy it from the outside. The foreigner is within me, hence we are all foreigners. If I am a foreigner, there are no foreigners. Therefore Freud does not talk about them. The ethics of psychoanalysis implies a politics: it would involve a cosmopolitanism of a new sort that, cutting across governments, economies, and markets, might work for a mankind whose solidarity is founded on the consciousness of its unconscious—desiring, destructive, fearful, empty, impossible. Here we are far removed from a call to brotherhood, about which one has already ironically pointed out its debt to paternal and divine authority—"In order to have brothers there must be a father," as Louis-François Veuillot did not fail to say when he sharply addressed humanists. On the basis of an erotic, death-bearing unconscious, the uncanny strangeness—a projection as well as a first working out of death drive—which adumbrates the work of the "second" Freud, the one of *Beyond the Pleasure Principle*, sets the difference within us in its most bewildering shape and presents it as the ultimate condition of our being *with* others.

9 In Practice . . .

Should nationality be obtained automatically or, on the contrary, should it be chosen by means of a responsible, deliberate act? Is *jus solis* sufficient to erase *jus sanguinis* (when children of immigrants born on French soil are involved), or is it necessary to have an expression of desire from the parties concerned? May foreigners obtain political rights? Subsequent to the right to join labor unions and professional associations, should the very right to vote be granted them within local communities and, eventually, on the national level?

Questions do keep piling up; and the Committee of Wise Men [as it was dubbed by the media] who pondered over the "Nationality Code" has drawn up reasonable suggestions. Having noted that "France has, in both relative and absolute terms, the largest foreign population in its modern history," and that "it is not in the interest of any country to allow excessively large foreign minorities to develop on its soil, minorities that would call attention to themselves through insisting on their difference or through being excluded from social and national life," the Committee on Nationality chaired by Marceau Long advocated "granting French nationality to those foreigners who have settled in France on a long-term basis" and improving the "modalities of acquiring [French nationality] as a result of a conscious choice, which would be advantageous to the individual's integration." It posited "integration as a necessity."[1] Those suggestions will most obviously be discussed, questioned, at least partly adopted, and are necessarily evolutive in nature.

In the kaleidoscope that France is becoming—kaleidoscope first of the Mediterranean and progressively of the third world—the differences between natives and immigrants will never be as clear-cut as before. The homogenizing power of French civilization, which has been able to take in and unify over the course of centuries various influences and ethnic groups, has been tried and tested. Now France today is in the process of welcoming newcomers who do not give up their particularities. The situation is quite different from the one that presided over the beginnings of the United States of America, which offered a new religious and economic faith to uprooted people who all found themselves in the same boat. In France, at the end of the twentieth century, each is fated to remain the same *and* the other—without forgetting his original culture but putting it in perspective to the extent of having it not only exist side by side but also alternate with others' culture. A new homogeneity is not very likely, perhaps hardly desirable. We are called upon, through the pressures of the economy, the media, and history to live together in a single country, France, itself in the process of being integrated into Europe. We already have so many difficulties—but also so many advantages—coexisting in this new multinational (and not supranational) country that Europe has become—even though it is made up of nations whose cultures have been close, religions similar, and economies interdependent for centuries! Consequently one can assess the difficulty presented, in the bosom of the same political entity (even though it might be in the process of being integrated with others), by the cohabitation of people whose considerable ethnic, religious, and economic diversity clashes with the present tradition and mentality of those welcoming them. Are we headed for a jigsaw-puzzle nation made up of various particularities, whose predominant numbers remain French for the time being—but for how long?

A changed attitude of mind is necessary in order to favor the best harmony in such a versatility. What might be involved, in the final analysis, is extending to the notion of *foreigner* the right of respecting our own foreignness and, in short, of the "privacy" that insures freedom in democracies. The access of foreigners to political rights will follow on the heels of that evolution and, necessarily, with adequate legal guarantees. One might imagine, for instance, a "double nationality" statute that would give those "foreigners" who want it a number of rights—but also the political duties specific to natives, with a reciprocity clause giving the latter rights and duties in the countries of origin of those same foreigners. Such a rule, easily applicable within the European Economic Community, could be tempered and adjusted for other countries.

Nevertheless, the fundamental question that slows down such arrangements, which lawyers and politicians are presently working out under the changing constraints of national economic needs, belongs to a more psychological or even metaphysical realm. In the absence of a new community bond—a saving religion that would integrate the bulk of wanderers and different people within a new consensus, other than "more money and goods for everyone"—we are, for the first time in history, confronted with the following situation: we must live with different people while relying on our personal moral codes, without the assistance of a set that would include our particularities while transcending them. A paradoxical community is emerging, made up of foreigners who are reconciled with themselves to the extent that they recognize themselves as foreigners. The multinational society would thus be the consequence of an extreme individualism, but conscious of its discontents and limits, knowing only indomitable people ready-to-help-themselves in their weakness, a weakness whose other name is our radical strangeness.

Notes

2. The Greeks Among Barbarians, Suppliants, and Metics

1. For an analysis of this play, see A. F. Garvie, *Aeschylus' Suppliants, Play and Trilogy* (Cambridge: Cambridge University Press, 1969). [For quotations from the play I have used the translation by Seth G. Bernardete in *The Complete Greek Tragedies*, vol. I, *Aeschylus* (Chicago: University of Chicago Press, 1959)—LSR.]

2. See G. Dumézil, *La Religion romaine archaïque* (Paris: Payot, 1974), who reminds one that the Roman vestals, "at the time when the *rex* ruled [. . .] must, by some mystical means, contribute to his safety," thus recalling the Welsh tradition "according to which the legendary king Math could live, when not engaged in warring expeditions, only if he kept his feet in the bosom of a virgin" (p. 577). Along the same lines, see Dumézil's *Tarpeia* (Paris: Payot, 1947), pp. 100–109, and *Mithra et Varuna. Essai sur deux représentations indo-européennes de la souveraineté* (Paris: Presses Universitaires de France, 1940).

3. See Marcel Détienne, *L'Ecriture d'Orphée* (Paris: Gallimard, 1989).

4. *Ibid.*

5. According to Iamblichus, as quoted by Détienne.

6. Marie-Françoise Baslez, *L'Etranger dans la Grèce antique* (Paris: Les Belles Lettres, 1984), p. 82. I am indebted to this study for much of what follows.

7. Aristotle, *Politics*, 1276 b.

8. Aristotle, *The Constitution of Athens*, 26:451/o. In similar fashion, beginning with Clisthenes, citizens are identified according to the deme to which they belong, "this to prevent them from being called by the name of their father, thus exposing the new citizens" (*ibid.*, 21:508/7). "The present state of government is as follows. They take part in

government who are born of parents who both have citizenship rights" (*ibid.*, 42).

9. Euripides, *Ion*, 590–592, quoted by M.-F. Baslez, p. 94. [I have used Ronald Frederick Willets' translation, in *The Complete Greek Tragedies*, vol. 4, *Euripides* (Chicago: University of Chicago Press, 1959)—LSR.]

10. M.-F. Baslez, p. 184.

11. Strabo, 14:646, in M.-F. Baslez, p. 185.

12. See Helen Bacon, *Barbarians in Greek Tragedy* (New Haven: Yale University Press, 1961).

13. It will be noted that, in keeping with the ironic spirit of the play, the barbarians are the Greeks, not the Trojans: the word loses its ethnic meaning to emphasize its ethical value.

14. *The Apology of Socrates*, quoted by M.-F. Baslez, p. 199.

15. See M.-F. Baslez, p. 146.

16. See M.-F. Baslez, p. 111.

17. The acknowledgment of the civic qualities that entitled him to be a proxenus.

18. See M.-F. Baslez, p. 181.

19. Quoted by M.-F. Baslez, p. 261.

20. J. von Arnim, *Stoicorum Veterum Fragmenta* (Leipzig, 1921–1924), 3:329.

21. Cicero, *De Finibus Bonorum et Malorum*, 5:23, 65.

22. Terence, *The Self-Tormentor*, Act 1, scene 1.

23. Cicero, *De Officiis*, 1:9, 30.

24. Seneca, *Letters to Lucilius*, 92, 30.

25. See E. Bréhier, *Histoire de la philosophie* (Paris: Presses Universitaires de France, 1981), 1:330–331.

26. Von Arnim, 2:351–360.

27. Marcus Aurelius, *Meditations*, 4:29.

28. *Ibid.*

29. Quoted by Plutarch, *De Fraterno Amore*, 482 b.

30. Cicero, *De Officiis*, 1:23, 79; 25:88–89.

31. A. J. Voelke, *Les Rapports avec autrui dans la philosophie grecque d'Aristote à Panétius* (Paris: Vrin, 1966).

32. Cicero, *De Finibus Bonorum et Malorum*, 5:23, 67.

33. See below, pp. 191–195, for the positions of Fougeret de Monbron.

34. M.-F. Baslez, p. 325.

3. The Chosen People and the Choice of Foreignness

1. Genesis 17:7. [Unless otherwise indicated, I have used the text of the Jerusalem Bible—LSR]

2. I Samuel 15:2–3. One should remember that Amalek attacked the people of Israel on its rear guard at the time of the flight from Egypt; his descendants, Agag and Haman, were also noted for their hostility toward Israel, going so far as to consider issuing a decree of total annihilation.

3. Nehemiah 10:31.

4. The word *mamzer* is translated by "half-breed" [in French, *métèque*, a word also having a colloquial, derogatory connotation—LSR]; it originally referred to the (Jewish) son of an illicit (adulterous) union.

5. Deuteronomy 23:3–9.

6. Commentary on Numbers 14:10.

7. See A. Cohen, *Le Talmud* (Paris: Payot, 1970), p. 108.

8. Commentary on Genesis 49:2.

9. Leviticus 18:5.

10. II Samuel 7:19. [This follows the King James' version, which is closer to the French translation quoted by JK—LSR]

11. Likewise, Isaiah 26:2 and Psalms 118–20; 33:1; 125:4; etc.

12. Genesis 9:6.

13. Leviticus 19:18.

14. Avot 3:18.

15. See Leviticus 19:34, according to Torat Conahim, *Kedoshim*, 19.

16. Exodus 22:21.

17. Baba Mezia 58b.

18. Leviticus 19:33–34.

19. Deuteronomy 10:19. The quotations and commentaries in this paragraph are from the translation of Elie Munk, *La Voix de la Thora: Commentaire du Pentateuque* (Paris: Fondation S. & D. Levy, 1972).

20. Genesis 12:1.

21. Thanks are due Betty Rojtman, professor at the Hebrew University of Jerusalem, for her valuable suggestions and her commentaries on this chapter.

22. Job 31:13–15 and 32.

23. There is also the word *nochri*, which denotes the foreigner or "other" (in the sense of English "alien") and refers to the apostate (Exodus Rabbah 19:4).

24. Yebamoth 47b.

25. A. Cohen, *Le Talmud*, pp. 110–111.

26. Sanhedrin 94a; "Aramean" is the generic term used to refer to non-Jews.

27. B. Rojtman, personal letter.

28. Judges 17:6; 18:1; 21:25.

29. Baba Batra 91a.

30. Deuteronomy 23:3–9.

31. *The Book of Ruth*, a new translation with a commentary anthologized from talmudic, midrashic, and rabbinic sources, by Rabbi Meir Zlotavitz and Rabbi Nosson Scherman (New York: Mesorah Publications, 1976), p. xlvi.

32. Rabbi Meir in the Midrash, Ruth Rabba 1:4.

33. According to Zohar Chadash, in *The Book of Ruth*, p. xlix.

34. *The Book of Ruth*, p. 88.

35. It was forbidden to retrace one's steps to glean forgotten ears, for the latter were meant for the poor (Leviticus 19:9 and 13:22); likewise, it was forbidden to reap the corner of the field set aside for the poor.

36. *The Book of Ruth*, p. 95.

37. *Ibid.*, p. 96. [I have maintained the word "perfect," a literal rendering of *parfaite*, the one used in the French translation even though the Jerusalem Bible reads "rich" and the King James' version reads "full," for the meanings are close enough; otherwise, the argument would make little sense—LSR.]

38. Baba Batra 91b; see *The Book of Ruth*, p. 131.

39. Ruth Rabba 8:1; *The Book of Ruth*, p. 134.

4. Paul and Augustine: The Therapeutics of Exile and Pilgrimage

1. I Corinthians 9:20.

2. See J.-R. Armogathe, *Paul ou l'impossible unité* (Paris: Fayard-Mame, 1980), p. 24.

3. See M.-F. Baslez, "Les Voyages de saint Paul," in *L'Histoire* (September 1980), no. 26, pp, 38–47.

4. *Ibid.*, p. 42.

5. *Ibid.*, p. 47.

6. Ephesians 2:11–13 and 2:19–20.

7. II Corinthians 5:17; Galatians 6:15; Ephesians 4:24; Colossians 3:10.

8. Christine Mohrmann, *Etudes sur le latin des chrétiens*, Rome: Edizioni di Storia e di Letteratura, 1977), 4:206 ff.

9. Armogathe, p. 115.

10. I Corinthians 15:45.

11. Colossians, 3:9–11.

12. John 17:5.

13. "If the world hates you, / remember that it hated me before you. / If you belonged to the world, / the world would love you as its own; / but because you do not belong to the world, / because my choice withdrew you from the world, / therefore the world hates you" (John 15:18–19). Concerning the Johannine Jesus understood as a "stranger," see W. Meeks, "Man from Heaven," *JBL* (1972), 91:44–72, and M. de Jonge, *Jesus Stranger from Heaven* (Missoula: Missoula Scholars Press, 1977).

14. John 14:2.

15. *Enarr.*, in *Psalm* 64, 1 and 2.

16. *Ibid.*, 64, 2–3.

17. *Ibid.*, 136, 12.

18. *Ibid.*, 64, 2. Cf. Peter Brown, *La Vie de saint Augustin* (Paris: Seuil, 1971), p. 383: "Normal human society must give way to a group of individuals where each one remains conscious of being different from any other, to a *civitas . . . peregrina* for resident foreigners." (*De Civitas Dei*, 81, 1: "*etiam ista peregrina.*")

19. *De Discip. Christ.*, 3, 3.

20. *Epist.*, 243, 4.

21. *Epist.*, 192, 1–2.

22. In *Acta Apostolorum Homeliae*, 45, 4.

23. See Denys Gorce, *Les Voyages, l'hospitalité et la part des lettres dans le monde chrétien des IVe et Ve siècles* (Paris, 1925).

24. See Jean Gaudemet, "L'Etranger au Bas-Empire," in *L'Etranger* (Bruxelles: Société Jean Bodin, 1958), p. 211.

25. See above, the peregrine city according to Augustine.

26. Gaudemet, p. 215.

27. Cf. the *Notitia Dignitatum*.

28. "*Aubain*, that is to say foreigner or one born in another kingdom [. . .] Sometimes *aubain* also refers to a man or woman who is not born on a land but goes there to settle, pays homage to the lord of that land, and obtains the right of bourgeoisie." Jean de Ferrière, *Dictionnaire de droit et de pratique* (Paris: Brunet, 1740). See also *L'Usage d'Orléans selon les établissements de Saint Louis* (Paris: P. Viollet, 1881), 1:100 and 2:169–170.

29. "The essential element of the *aubain*'s foreignness thus appears to lie less in the land boundaries of the political unit in which he inserts

himself than in the de facto and de jure power of the lord who rules it."
Marguerite Boulet-Sautel, "L'Aubain dans la France coutumière du
Moyen Age," in L'Etranger, 2:70.

30. "Bastards, strays, aubains, manumitted persons cannot marry
anyone not of their condition, without the king's permission, unless
they pay a fine of 60 sols parisis." Historic excerpt from the Cour des
Comptes pertaining to the customs of the vermandois (Picardy) region.

31. Boulet-Sautel, p. 81.

32. Boulet-Sautel, p. 86.

33. See the Ancien Coutumier Champenois.

34. See L'Usage d'Qrléans selon les établissements de Saint Louis,
2:31.

35. See Henri Regnault, La Condition juridique du bâtard au Moyen
Age (Pont-Audemer, 1922), pp. 131–134.

5. By What Right Are You a Foreigner?

1. Until the law of July 17, 1978, the Nationality Code (article 81)
required the civil servants must have had the French nationality for five
years. The law of December 8, 1983, repealed that article and eliminated
all incapacities affecting persons having acquired French nationality.

2. See John Glossen in L'Etranger (Brussels: Société Jean Bodin,
1958), p. 56.

3. Danièle Lochak, Etranger: de quel droit? (Paris: Presses Universitaires de France, 1985), p. 215. Page references hereafter given parenthetically in text.

6. The Renaissance, "so Shapeless and Diverse in Composition" . . .

1. Dante, The Divine Comedy, "Paradise," Canto 17 (55–69 and
106–123), H. R. Huse, trans, (New York: Rinehart, 1954).

2. Dante, On Monarchy, "Even more so, the universality of men,
which is a kind of whole with respect to a given number of parts, is also
a given part with respect to a certain whole. It is indeed a whole from
the viewpoint of particular kingdoms and peoples [. . .]; but it is only a
part with respect to the universal whole [. . .], and therefore it also
adequately corresponds to that same universal whole or to its prince,
who is God and monarch and conforms itself to it absolutely in accordance with a single principle, that is, a sole princedom. It follows that the
monarchy is necessary to the world for it to appreciate its well-being."

3. Dante, "Paradise" 19:40–99.

4. Concerning Dante's political and religious thought, see Jacques Goudet, *Dante et la politique* (Paris: Aubier, 1969).

5. Machiavelli, *The Prince*, "The Harvard Classics" (New York: P. F. Collier, 1910), p. 86.

6. "He ought not to quit good courses if he can help it, but should know how to follow evil courses if he must" (*ibid.*, p. 58).

7. "Whoever becomes master of a city accustomed to live in freedom and does not destroy it, may reckon on being destroyed by it [. . .]. And do what you will, and take what care you may, unless the inhabitants be scattered and dispersed, this name [liberty], and the old order of things, will never cease to be remembered but will at once be turned against you whenever misfortune overtakes you" (*ibid.*, p. 18).

8. See Erasmus' *Epicureus* and *Convivium religiosum*.

9. See V.-L. Saulnier, *Rabelais dans son enquête. Etude sur le Quart et le Cinquième Livre* (Paris: Société d'Editions de l'Enseignement Supérieur, 1982).

10. Michel Mollat, *Les Explorateurs du XIIIe au XVIe siècle. Premiers Regards sur des mondes nouveaux* (Paris: Lattès, 1984).

11. Michel de Certeau, commenting on Léry's writing on the Tupinambas, which he sees as the basis of Lévi-Strauss' ethnology and even his anthropology, notes that these early texts are more like "legends" that "symbolize the changes brought about in a culture through its encounter with the other." On this account, the texts come under the heading of "interpretation of dreams." In other respects, "this work is in fact a *hermeneutics of the other*. It carries over to the New World the Christian exegetic system that, born of a necessary relation with Jewish otherness, was in turn applied to the biblical tradition, Greek and Latin antiquity, and still many other foreign totalities. Once more, it produces meaning out of the relation to the other. Ethnology is about to become an aspect of exegesis." "Ethnographie. L'oralité ou l'espace de l'Autre: Léry," in *L'Ecriture de l'histoire* (Paris: Gallimard, 1975), pp. 217–231.

12. *The Complete Essays of Montaigne*, Donald M. Frame, trans. (Stanford: Stanford University Press, 1958), p. 297. "My conceptions and my judgment move only by groping, staggering, stumbling, and blundering; and when I have gone ahead as far as I can, still I am not at all satisfied: I can still see country beyond, but with a dim and clouded vision, so that I cannot clearly distinguish it" (p. 107).

13. "In this universe of things I ignorantly and negligently let

myself be guided by the general law of the world" (Montaigne, p. 821). "We are Christians by the same title that we are Perigordians or Germans" (Montaigne, p. 325).

14. "The surest sign of wisdom is constant cheerfulness; her state is like that of things above the moon, ever serene" (Montaigne, p. 119).

15. Montaigne, pp. 487, 488.

16. Montaigne, p. 111. "In this school of dealing with men I have often noticed this flaw, that instead of gaining knowledge of others we strive only to give knowledge of ourselves, and take more pains to peddle our wares than to get new ones" (Montaigne, p. 113).

17. "I know very well that I feel no fruit or enjoyment from it except by the vanity of a fanciful opinion" (Montaigne, p. 475).

18. The French colony in Brazil, founded by Villegaignon in 1555, had been described before Montaigne, particularly by Jean de Léry who noted the presence of serene, nearly good cannibals whom he compared to the Stoics of the Roman republic! See *Histoire d'un voyage fait en la terre du Brésil, autrement dite Amérique* (La Rochelle, 1578), p. 242. At the time when Charles IX, who was still a child, met the cannibals in Rouen, the latter were surprised to see tall, armed men obeying a child. Michel de L'Hospital, who has been compared to Montaigne, noted: "Divine justice as well as natural law is no different with the savages of America from what it is among Christians in Europe" (*Oeuvres*, 9:60–61).

19. An integral part of Montaigne's philosophical demonstration, the essay "On Cannibals" foreshadows the part the foreigner was to play in eighteenth-century literature: Voltaire's *Ingénu* and Montesquieu's *Persian*.

20. "My French is corrupted, both in pronunciation and in other respects, by the barbarism of my home soil" (Montaigne, p. 484).

21. "Let attention be paid not to the matter, but to the shape I give it" (Montaigne, p. 296).

22. "As for me, then, I love life and cultivate it just as God has been pleased to grant it to us. [. . .] I accept with all my heart and with gratitude what nature has done for me, and I am pleased with myself and proud of myself that I do" (Montaigne, pp. 854, 955). "I speak to my paper as I speak to the first man I meet. That this is true, here is proof" (Montaigne, p. 599).

23. Montaigne, "To the Reader," p. 2.

24. See Geoffroy Atkinson, *Les Nouveaux Horizons de la Renaissance* (Geneva: Droz, 1935), p. 9.

25. The work by the Franciscan cosmographer André Thévet re-

corded a number of details on men and nature on the other side of the earth, without any preexisting unifying rationale harmonizing the whole. Mosaic-like and polymorphic (see *Les Singularités de la France antarctique. Le Brésil des cannibales au XVIe siècle*, choix de textes, introduction et notes de Frank Lestringant [Paris: Maspéro, 1983]), such contradictory "singularities" present a being who is savage, cannibalistic, or horsewoman, both cruel and virtuous, debauched and hospitable, ghastly on account of cannibalism and yet close to our own food rituals, brutally condemned and symmetrically showered with praise a few pages later. As if that realistic dispersion—which does not yet come to a head in the enlightened stereotype of the "good savage," nor in the universalist anthropology to which Léry comes closer—corresponded, with Thévet, to the image of that heterogeneous, wandering self that European man discovered in himself through Montaigne's pen.

26. Marc Lescarbot, *Histoire de la Nouvelle-France*, p. 7, as quoted by Atkinson, *Les Nouveaux Horizons*, p. 47.

27. "Our nation has experienced a change of taste in its readings and instead of novels, which fell out of favor with La Calprenede, travel relations have become popular and are held in high esteem both at court and among the people." Letter from Jean Chapelain to Carrel de Sainte-Garde, 1663, quoted by Atkinson, p. 30.

28. William J. Bouwsma locates him "on the outer fringe of Catholicism," in *Concordia Mundi. The Career and Thought of Guillaume Postel* (Cambridge: Harvard University Press, 1957), p. 28. On Postel, see also Pierre Mesnard, *L'Essor de la philosophie politique au XVIe siècle* (Paris: Vrin, 1951), pp. 431–453.

29. Guillaume Postel, *Les Très Merveilleuses Victoires des femmes du Nouveau Monde et comme elles doibvent à tout le monde par raison commander, et mesme a ceulx qui auront la monarchie du Monde vieil* (Paris, 1953), p. 20.

30. See Hans Kohn, *The Idea of Nationalism* (New York: Macmillan, 1951), p. 194.

7. *On Foreigners and the Enlightenment*

With Julia Kristeva's approval I have made a few very minor changes and small additions to the original text in order to clarify references that might have proven obscure or confusing to the American reader [LSR].

1. See Louis Althusser, *Montesquieu, la politique et l'histoire* (Paris: Presses Universitaires de France, 1959), who emphasizes in Montes-

quieu the contradictory pundit of the completely social and its dynamics; Robert Aron, *Dix-huits Leçons sur la société industrielle*, the chapter on Marx and Montesquieu (Paris: Gallimard, 1962), who sees in him "in one sense the last of the classical philosophers and in another the first sociologist." Also useful is Georges Benrekassa's *Montesquieu, la liberté et l'histoire* (Paris: Le Livre de Poche, 1987), which takes both theses into consideration and throws light on the various levels of Montesquieu's thought, its root in the historical and philosophical reality of the eighteenth century, and its value for modern times.

2. Charles Louis de Secondat, baron de la Brède et de Montesquieu, *Mes Pensées*, in *Œuvres complètes*, Roger Caillois, ed., Bibliothèque de la Pléiade (Paris: Gallimard, 1985), 1:1003 [all quotations from Montesquieu translated by LSR].

3. Montesquieu, p. 976.

4. "The Ancients must have had stronger feelings for their homeland than we have, for they were always buried with it. Was their city captured? They were enslaved or killed. We merely change rulers" (*ibid.*, p. 1353).

5. Montesquieu, p. 981.

6. Montesquieu, *Considérations sur la richesse d'Espagne*, *Œuvres Complètes*, 2:10.

7. Montesquieu, *Réflexions sur la monarchie universelle*, in *Œuvres complètes*, 2:34. And also: "At present Europe handles the entire trade and shipping of the universe; now, as one nation assumes a greater or lesser share in that shipping or trade, its power must increase or diminish. But as the nature of things is to change continuously, and be dependent on a thousand fortunes, especially on the wisdom of each government, it so happens that a nation that seems victorious outside bankrupts itself inside, while those that are neutral increase their strength, or those that were defeated recover it. And decadence begins especially during times of greatest success, which can be obtained or maintained only through violent means" (*ibid.*, p. 20).

8. Montesquieu, *Analyse du traité des devoirs*, 1725, *Œuvres complètes* 1:110 (emphasis mine). See below the section on the rights of man and citizen.

9. Montesquieu, *L'Esprit des lois*, *Œuvres complètes*, 2:235: "Each one feels inferior: hardly does anyone feel equal."

10. Denis Diderot, *Rameau's Nephew and Other Works*, Jacques Barzun and Ralph H. Bowen, trans. (Garden City, N.Y.: Doubleday, 1956). "I know what I say and know it as well as you know what you say" (p. 14). He uses the second-person pronoun to refer to himself, he

watches over and passes judgment upon himself: "You went, biting your fingernails: it's your tongue you should have bitten off first. You thought of that too late and here you are, in the gutter, penniless, and nowhere to go" (p. 19).

11. "And then contempt for oneself—that's unbearable" (p. 21).

12. "Can't you lick boots like the rest? Haven't you learned to lie, swear, forswear, promise, perform, or cheat like anyone else?" (p. 21).

13. "This was that they could not get along without me. I am the irreplaceable man" (p. 54).

14. Diderot, p. 55.

15. Diderot, p. 20.

16. Diderot, p. 68.

17. Diderot, p. 52. See Marian Hobson, "Pantomime, spasme et parataxe," in *Revue de Métaphysique et de Morale* (April–June 1984), no. 2 pp. 197–213.

18. Hobson speaks of the Nephew's behavior as *symptom* and as *sign*.

19. Diderot, pp. 11 and 87.

20. Diderot, p. 19.

21. See Jean Starobinski, "Diogène dans *Le Neveu de Rameau*," in *Stanford French Review*, Fall 1984, pp. 147–165. For Diderot, projecting himself as Diogenes meant "reconciling under the same auspices a tendency for physiological stripping with a taste for moral preaching" (p. 155).

22. Mikhail M. Bakhtin, *Problems of Dostoyevsky's Poetics* (Ann Arbor: University of Michigan Press, 1973).

23. The natural spasm would be the action/reaction link or natural tone, the unnatural spasm causing diseases: "All nervous disorders may strictly speaking be boiled down to paralysis and spasm, or to convulsion, which is a very rapid alternative to natural spasm or paralysis." Samuel Tissot, "Traité des nerfs et de leurs maladies," *Œuvres* (Paris: 1855), p. 10.

24. Franciscus Hemsterhuis, *Lettre sur l'homme et ses rapports avec le commentaire inédit de Diderot*, Georges May, ed. Yale Romanic Studies (New Haven: Yale University Press, 1964), p. 325, quoted by Hobson, p. 202.

25. Diderot, "D'Alembert's Dream," in *Rameau's Nephew and Other Works*, p. 117.

26. Diderot, p. 11.

27. Diderot, p. 85.

28. Voltaire, *Dictionnaire philosophique*.

29. Diderot, p. 86.

30. Diderot, p. 32.

31. The word "cosmopolite" goes back to the sixteenth century. The *Dictionnaire* of Darmsteter, Hatzfeld, and Thomas traces it to a work by Guillaume Postel, traveler and learned man, reader to the king and professor of Eastern languages under Francis I. The *Dictionnaire de l'Académie* records the word only in 1762. Lenglet du Fresnoy's *Histoire de la philosophie hermétique* (1762) credits the alchemist A. Sethon for introducing the term and notes the existence of a *Traité du Cosmopolite*, published in Prague in 1604. The word's fame dates from the eighteenth century: Trévoux, then Fougeret de Monbron (1750), before reaching the *Académie*. The true wise man is a "cosmopolite," says Dortidius (Diderot) in Charles Palissot's play, *Les Philosophes* (Act 3, scene 4). See Paul Hazard, "Cosmopolite," in *Mélanges offerts à Fernand Baldensperger* (Paris: Champion, 1930), 1:354–364. The stoic phrase, "citizen of the world," is also used. Joachim du Bellay gives it a pejorative connotation (*Siège de Calais*, Act 4, scene 2), while La Fontaine claims to be a "wise citizen of the wide universe" and Saint-Simon applies it to the Prince de Vaudemont (*Mémoires*, Bibliothèque de la Pléiade [Paris: Gallimard, 1948], 2:847). See Ferdinand Brunot, *Histoire de la langue française des origines à nos jours* (Paris: Armand Colin, 1966–1979), 6(1):118–121.

32. Diderot, *Satire I*, in *Œuvres complètes* (Paris: Garnier, 1975), 4:305 [translated by LSR].

33. See Fougeret de Monbron, *Le Cosmopolite ou le citoyen du monde* followed by *La Capitale des Gaules ou la Nouvelle Babylone*, Introduction and notes by Raymond Trousson (Bordeaux: Ducros, 1970), p. 15. [All quotations from Fougeret's works translated by LSR.]

34. Fougeret, p. 35.

35. As Fougeret wanted to board an English ship the French ambassador pointed out to him that "we were then at war with England. I answered [. . .] that I was an inhabitant of the world, and that I maintained a strict neutrality with respect to the warring powers" (p. 122).

36. Fougeret, p. 45.

37. Fougeret, p. 69.

38. "The most reasonable thing one can say in order to offend no one is that everything is equally ridiculous in this world, and the perfection of things resides only in the opinion one has of them" (p. 52). And still more fiercely: "The greatest profit I have derived from

my voyages or my journeys is that I learned to hate with reason what I hated by instinct [. . .] I thoroughly convinced myself that rectitude and humanity are everywhere but terms of social convention that contain basically nothing real or true. Everyone lives only for himself, loves only himself [. . .] I would, to speak the truth, be just a little more of a rascal" (p. 59). "Of all living creatures I am the one I love the most, without holding myself in any greater esteem [. . .] On the contrary I most sincerely admit that I am worth precisely nothing— and the only difference there is between others and myself is that I am bold enough to take off the mask, and they are afraid to do the same" (p. 60). "But I would like to make it known that I am an isolated being among the living; the universe to me is a continuous spectacle where I enjoy my entertainment free" (pp. 61–62).

39. Oliver Goldsmith, *The Citizen of the World*, 1762.

40. Laurence Sterne, *A Sentimental Journey Through France and Italy*, 1768.

41. Jean-Jacques Rousseau, *Emile*, in *Œuvres complètes*, Bibliothèque de la Pléiade (Paris: Gallimard, 1969), 4:248–249 [translated by LSR].

42. Montesquieu, *Mes Pensées*, p. 1286.

43. Montesquieu, p. 981.

44. G. W. F. Hegel, *The Phenomenology of Mind*, J. B. Baillie, trans. (New York: Harper and Row, 1967), p. 514.

45. Hegel, p. 514.

46. Hegel, p. 516. Diderot's text, which was then unknown in France, had just been translated into German by Goethe. Page references to Hegel hereafter given parenthetically in text.

47. While noting the accuracy of Hegel's reading, Hans-Robert Jauss places more stress on the differences between Hegel and Diderot, the Nephew's dialogism contrasting with philosophical dialectics. See his "*Le Neveu de Rameau*, dialogique et dialectique (ou Diderot lecteur de Socrate et Hegel lecteur de Diderot)," in *Revue de Métaphysique et de Morale* (April–June 1985), no. 2, pp. 145–181.

48. See Gabriel Compayré's preface to *La Déclaration des droits de l'homme et du citoyen* (Paris: Alcan, 1902). The *national legislative sovereignty*, the idea of which comes from Rousseau, is actually a tradition that needed to be brought up to date, but which one finds stated by Aristotle, by Thomas Aquinas, by a number of theologians who thought the councils should have precedence over the pope, by Philippe Pot (*Discours des Etats généraux*, 1484), by François Holman (*Francogallia*, 1573), by English jurists, by Spinoza. After the Revolu-

tion it found its apex with Kant, with whom it was linked to cosmopolitanism. See below, chapter 8 on universality.

49. Edmund Burke, *Reflections of the Revolution in France*, 1790.

50. Hannah Arendt, "Imperialism," in *The Origins of Totalitarianism* (New York: Harcourt, Brace, Jovanovich, 1979), p. 295.

51. Arendt, p. 296.

52. Arendt, p. 296.

53. Arendt, pp. 299–300.

54. Arendt, p. 300.

55. Albert Mathiez, *La Révolution et les étrangers* (Paris: La Renaissance du Livre, 1928), p. 31.

56. A broader-based organization brought together some of those national clubs; this was the Club of Foreign Patriots, which on August 10, 1792, became the Club of the Allobroges.

57. Mathiez, p. 72.

58. An instance of the climate of uncertainty that incited such excesses without necessarily justifying them is provided by the newspaper *Le Cosmopolite*. Founded in December 1791 by Proly, the paper was pacifist; it opposed the Girondins' warlike policy, defended the Franco-Austrian alliance, published statements by Robespierre against the war . . . It appears that it was, in large part, distributed free and was suspected of serving the emperor's purposes. The paper disappeared after the war it could not prevent was declared (Mathiez, p. 31). Proly abandoned his former bonds and became a Hébertist—was it in order to prove his patriotism?

59. This applied to any foreigner "unable to prove to the Committee either that he is established in France, or that he practices a profession, or that he has acquired real estate, or that he has a sense of civic responsibility as vouched for by five citizens having resided in the commune for one year" (quoted by Mathiez, p. 125).

60. See Louis Jacob, *Hébert, le Père Duchesne, chef des sans-culottes* (Paris: Gallimard, 1960), p. 333.

61. "They debate," Robespierre stated, "[. . .] in our administrations, in our sectional assemblies, they infiltrate our clubs, they even have been seated in the sanctuary of our national representation [. . .] They lurk around us, they discover our secrets, they flatter our passions, they try to inspire us even in our opinions, they turn our resolves against us. Are you weak? They praise your prudence. Are you prudent? They accuse you of weakness; they call your courage rashness, your justice cruelty. Treat them with consideration, they conspire in public; threaten them, they conspire in the dark and under the cloak of

patriotism. Yesterday they murdered the defenders of freedom, today they join in the funeral ceremonies [. . .] Foreigners did for a while appear as arbitrators of public peace. Money would circulate or disappear as they saw fit. When they wanted it, the people had bread to eat, when they wanted otherwise, the people were deprived of it [. . .] Their main object is to set us to fight against one another." And Barere added the following: "When we are at war with a part of Europe, no foreigner may aspire to the honor of representing the French people" (see Mathiez, p. 172).

62. Jacob, p. 347.

63. "There will come a time, I hope, when all the peoples of the earth, after having done away with their tyrants, will make up but one sole family of brothers. Perhaps some day we shall see Turks, Russians, Frenchmen, Englishmen, even Germans brought together in the same Senate and forming a great Convention of all the nations of Europe. It is a beautiful dream that can nevertheless come true . . ." (Jacob, p. 304).

64. See Mathiez, p. 182.

65. Anacharsis Clootz published *L'Orateur du genre humain ou Dépêche du Prussien Clootz au Prussien Herzberg* (Paris, 1791), and also *La République universelle* (Paris: 1792), in which it was established "that the people was the sovereign of the world, and furthermore that he was God, that France was the cradle and rallying point of the god-people, that only fools fear a Supreme Being," and so forth, as well as *Les Bases constitutionnelles de la République du genre humain* (Paris, 1793).

66. See Mathiez, pp. 169–170.

67. "I do not believe as the prophet Anacharsis Clootz does, *Le Père Duchesne* said, that we should do as Don Quixote did and undertake universal war in order to convert to freedom those who are not yet worthy of it. It is up to time and reason to effect such a miracle" (Jacob, p. 304).

68. One of the most fervent was that of Georges Avenel who, many years later, wrote Clootz' first biography, a visionary one at that, which still fascinates historians. See Avenel, *Anacharsis Clootz, L'Orateur du genre humain, Paris! France! Univers!* (1865; reissued, Paris: Champ Libre, 1976).

69. See Jean Lessay, *L'Américain de la Convention, Thomas Paine, professeur de révolutions* (Paris: Perrin, 1987), pp. 236 and 242.

70. Eric Foner, *Tom Paine and Revolutionary America* (New York: Oxford University Press, 1976), p. 261. [Reference added—LSR.]

8. Might Not Universality Be . . . Our Own Foreignness?

1. See above, "The Nephew with Hegal: Culture as Strangeness."

2. Immanuel Kant, "Idea for a Universal History from a Cosmopolitan Point of View," in *On History* (New York: Bobbs Merrill, 1963), p. 15. Page references hereafter given parenthetically in text.

3. Kant, "Perpetual Peace," *On History* p. 100.

4. "It is only a right of temporary sojourn, a right to associate, which all men have. They have it by virtue of their common possession of the surface of the earth, where, as a globe, they cannot infinitely disperse and hence must finally tolerate the presence of each other. Originally, no one had more right than another to a particular part of the earth" (Kant, p. 103).

5. "I do not mean that [nature] imposes a duty on us to do it, for this can be done only by free practical reason; rather I mean that [nature] herself does it, whether we will or not" (Kant, p. 111).

6. Hans Kohn, *The Idea of Nationalism* (New York: Macmillan, 1951).

7. Jean-Jacques Rousseau, *Les Confession*, "Bibliothèque de la Pléiade" (Paris: Gallimard, 1959), 1:144. [All translations of Rousseau texts by LSR.]

8. Thus: "The civilian is only a fractional unit attached to the denominator and whose value resides in its relation to the whole, which is the social Body [. . .] Good social institutions are best able to change the nature of man—taking away his absolute existence in order to give him a relative one and shifting the *self* to the common unit. As a result, each individual no longer believes himself to be one but a part of the unit and is perceptible only in the whole" (Rousseau, *Emile*, 4:249).

9. "The police is good, but liberty is better" (Rousseau, "Considerations sur le gouvernement de la Pologne," *ibid.*, 3:983). "Public liberty is the most precious good. And every man, in the name of the fatherland, is entitled to tear it away from the hands of the usurper: avenging such a capital crime is the right of each individual. Teach these truths to all men, let them reach down to the lowest order of citizens." Rousseau, *Correspondance générale*, Dufour-Plan, ed. (Paris: A. Colin, 1934), 20:346.

10. "But when, two hundred years from now, those who come after us read our history and see that, as long as he presided over our government, France did not have a single neighbor over whom it did not win fortresses and battles: if they have a few drops of French blood

in their veins, some love for the glory of their country, will they be able to read such things without feeling an attachment for him?" Voiture, *Œuvres* (Paris: Charpentier, 1855), 1:272, quoted by Hans Kohn, pp. 202–203.

11. Rousseau, *Lettres à D'Alembert* (Paris: Garnier-Flammarion, 1967), p. 43.

12. Rousseau, *Extrait* (1756–1760) and *Jugement sur le "Projet de paix perpétuelle"* (1782).

13. See Kohn, p. 429.

14. See Antoine Berman, *L'Epreuve de l'étranger. Culture et traduction dans l'Allemagne romantique* (Paris: Gallimard, 1984). One might compare that formation of the national concept through encounters with foreigners with what A. W. Schlegel (quoted by Berman, p. 62) observed in France: "Other nations have adopted in poetry a wholly conventional phraseology and it is consequently purely and simply impossible to translate something poetically into their language, as into French for instance [. . .] It is as if they wanted every foreigner, in their country, to behave and dress according to their customs; it follows that, properly speaking, they never know any foreigner."

15. See Berman, p. 70. Beginning with his translation of the Song of Songs and including his collection of *Volklieder* and his famous biblical exegesis *On the Spirit of Hebraic Poetry*, Herder's impulse is continuously to assimilate the foreign tongue while nevertheless maintaining its particular character in order to make of it a gift to a German language in the process of expansion and reformulation. The peoples of Central Europe have drawn on his thought in order to further the development of Slavic languages and cultures. One might note, however, that this juxtaposition of German *Bildung* with foreign elements —particularly with Hebrew—reaches a critical point with late Romanticism. And it was Herder himself who suddenly hardened his political interpretation, initially a fruitful one, changing the other into an object of assimilation, or even of murderous rejection, to the benefit of German "originality."

16. Herder on his part and through his own contradictions had nevertheless issued this warning: "How the dickens did the Germans, who were ordinarily praised for showing a manly modesty, and who were known for their cool equity in appreciating the merits of foreigners, come to be so unjustly and crudely scornful of other nations, and precisely of those they have imitated, from which they have borrowed?" Quoted by Max Rouche in his introduction to Herder's *Idées* (Paris: Aubier, 1962), p. 33. And again: "Those who study their own customs

and languages must do so when they are distinct; *for everything in Europe tends toward the progressive dying out of national characteristics*. But in doing so, the historian of mankind should be careful not to choose a given people exclusively as a favorite of his, thus diminishing the importance of lineages to which circumstances denied good fortune and fame" (p. 309).

17. As quoted in Henri E. Ellenberger, *A la découverte de l'inconscient* (Paris: Simep-Editions, 1974), p. 170.

18. See above, "The Chosen People and the Choice of Foreignness."

19. Sigmund Freud, *The Uncanny*, in *The Standard Edition of the Complete Psychological Works of Sigmund Freud*, 17:220. Hereafter page numbers given parenthetically in text refer to this volume (17) of the *Standard Edition (SE)*. [There are, as usual, discrepancies between the French and English translations of Freud. Here it is especially bothersome as *Das Unheimliche* comes out in French as *l'inquiétante étrangeté*, a phrase that matches Kristeva's vocabulary very neatly but is at a linguistic remove from our "uncanny." While following Strachey's translation, thus letting "the uncanny" stand in all the quotations from Freud's text, I have tried to bridge the gap between French and English words by occasionally rendering the French phrase, *inquiétante étrangeté*, in Kristeva's text, as "uncanny strangeness"—LSR]

20. See Paul Denis, "L'Inquiétante Etrangeté chez l'enfant," *Revue de Psychanalyse* (1981), no. 3, p. 503.

21. See Yvon Brès, "Modestie des philosophes: modestie des psychanalystes," *Psychanalyse à l'Université* (October 1986), 11(14):585–586. Beyond the frequency of the word *Unheimliche* in German, which removes a bit of spice from the encounter, Brès notes a certain thematic convergence in its use between Freud and Heidegger. With the latter, anguish, which resides in the being-in-the world, is uncanniness ("In der Angst ist einem 'unheimlich' "—*Sein und Zeit*, section 40): "But this distressing aspect, this strangeness, signifies at the same time the not-being-at-home." Later, *What Is Metaphysics* (1929) clarifies existential anguish as experienced when facing the impossibilty of any determination, and it is again described as *Unheimlichkeit*.

22. Freud, *The Future of an Illusion*, SE, 21:17.

23. Freud, *The Uncanny*, SE, 17:220.

24. "Five or six days later I was at the King's supper [. . .]. As sweets were being served, I noticed something or other, rather large, seemingly black, in the air over the table, which I was unable either to make out or point to, so rapidly did this large thing fall at the end of the table [. . .] The noise it made when falling and the weight of the

thing nearly caused it to give way and caused the dishes to jump, but without upsetting any [. . .] The King, after the impact, half turned his head and, without being disturbed in any way, I believe, he said, those are my fringes. It was indeed a bundle, larger than the hat of a priest . . . It had been thrown from far behind me [. . .] and a small bit that had come loose in the air had fallen on top of the King's wig; Livry, who was seated to his left, saw it and removed it. He came near the end of the table and saw that they were indeed fringes twisted into a bundle [. . .] Livry, wanting to remove the bundle, found a note attached to it; he took it and left the bundle [. . .]. It contained, in a misshapen, extended writing, like that of a woman, these very words: Take your fringes back, Bontemps; they are more trouble than pleasure. I kiss the King's hands. It was rolled but not sealed. The King again wanted to take it from D'Aquin's hands who stepped back, sniffed it, rubbed it, turned it every which way, and showed it to the King without letting him touch it. The King asked him to read it aloud, even though he himself read it at the same time. That, said the King, is rather insolent! —but in an even, somewhat statesmanlike tone of voice. After that he asked that the bundle be removed [. . .] Afterwards the King no longer mentioned it and no one dared speak about it, not aloud at any rate; and the remainder of the supper was served as if nothing had happened." Saint-Simon, *Mémoires*, "Bibliothèque de la Pléiade" (Paris: Gallimard, 1983), pp. 632–633. Christian David accompanies this excerpt with a keen commentary in "Irréductible étrangeté," *Revue de Psychanalyse* (1981), no. 3 pp. 463–471.

25. Freud, *The Uncanny, SE*, 17:221.

9. In Practice . . .

1. See *Etre français aujourd'hui et demain* (Paris: 10/18, 1988), 2:235–236.

Index